A NEW
COMPACT HISTORY
OF MEXICO

A NEW COMPACT HISTORY OF MEXICO

Pablo Escalante-Gonzalbo
Bernardo García-Martínez
Luis Jáuregui
Josefina Zoraida Vázquez
Elisa Speckman-Guerra
Javier Garciadiego
Luis Aboites-Aguilar

EL COLEGIO DE MÉXICO

972
N9647n

    Nueva historia mínima de México. Inglés.
       A New Compact History of Mexico / Pablo Escalante-
Gonzalbo ... [et al.] ; translation: Elaine Jones, Fionn Petch,
Susan Beth Kapilian. -- 1st ed. -- México, D.F. : El Colegio de
México, 2013

       335 p. ; 21 cm
       Incluye glosario, índice onomástico y toponímico

       ISBN 978-607-462-502-8
       Título original: Nueva historia mínima de México

    1. México -- Historia. I. Escalante, Pablo, 1963-, coautor. II.
Jones, Elaine, tr. III. Petch, Fionn, tr. IV. Kapilian, Susan Beth, tr.
V. t.

Translation: Elaine Jones, Fionn Petch, CM Idiomas, S.C. (first version – chapters and glossary) and Susan Beth Kapilian (final full version and proofreading)

First edition, 2013

© El Colegio de México, A.C.
   Camino al Ajusco 20
   Pedregal de Santa Teresa
   10740 México, D.F.
   www.colmex.mx

ISBN 978-607-462-502-8

Printed in Mexico

TABLE OF CONTENTS

PRESENTATION

In 1973, El Colegio de México published the first version of *Historia mínima de México* (followed in 1974 by the English translation *A Compact History of Mexico*, with a foreword by Robert A. Potash and translated by Marjory Mattingly Urquidi). The purpose of this book in Spanish was to provide Mexicans living at that time with basic historical knowledge of their country. Five authors participated in that first version—Daniel Cosío Villegas (director of the project), Ignacio Bernal, Alejandra Moreno Toscano, Luis González, and Eduardo Blanquel—, expressing what then was considered to be the most concise, accurate vision of Mexico's past. Subsequent editions included an additional essay (by Lorenzo Meyer) covering the ensuing years; however, the work remained essentially the same until the arrival of the twenty-first century. Over three decades since its original publication, *Historia mínima de México* reached a print run of over a million copies and was translated into fourteen different languages, as well as Braille.

Historical knowledge is renewed and enriched every day thanks to research and analysis. In the past three and a half decades, unknown facets of Mexico's past have been discovered, while others that had been ambiguous have been clarified. Inaccuracies have been corrected and greater depth of insight has been gained through new interpretations and ways for comprehending and elucidating both phenomena and events of the past. This has been reflected in all of El Colegio de México's publications on history, and should also be an essential feature of a general interest work for dissemination such as this one. Similarly, one could argue that the minimum amount of historical knowledge needed by any Mexican today is greater than before because educational levels in Mexico have increased and, most importantly, Mexicans' degree of social and political responsibility and commitment.

In 2004, El Colegio de México felt that the time had come to prepare a *Nueva historia mínima de México*, the English version of which we present to our readers here. While preserving the aim of synthesis and simplicity that served as a basic guideline for the earlier *Historia mínima de México*, this new work constitutes a completely novel and original manuscript: it contains texts expressly prepared for this edition by another seven authors. It also provides a fresh approach due to its historical periodization, proposals, explanations, wider coverage of its topics and, above all, thanks to its more modern vision grounded on the best foundations possible in view of the more complete, refined knowledge at our disposal in the early years of the twenty-first century. Naturally, these seven authors have made efforts to ensure that their chapters are both enjoyable and enlightening for any reader, at least as much, if not more, than those of the previous version.

El Colegio de México intends to see to it that future versions of this work contain, as it deems necessary, the findings of research and other studies that are carried out. With *A New Compact History of Mexico*, our institution's aim is to offer English-speaking readers a dynamic text that reflects our knowledge of this country's past, which is being enhanced and refined with each passing day.

ANCIENT MEXICO

PABLO ESCALANTE-GONZALBO

Mexico is really many Mexicos. This is so not only because of its dramatic social differences, but because of its ethnic roots, cultural traditions, and ecosystems, which vary enormously from one region to another. The oldest division, and one of the most significant for historical purposes, existed between an agricultural civilization that spread throughout the southern half of the territory and peoples devoted to shifting agriculture and hunter-gatherers who lived in the arid North. The tendency to consider the great ceremonial center of Tenochtitlan as the reference point for Mexican nationality, and familiarity with names such as Moctezuma and Nezahualcóyotl, should not lead us to forget that other forebears lived in primitive settlements in the mountains of Chihuahua, close to wolves and bears, or walked naked over the harsh lands of Baja California, keeping a close watch on the shore.

Thanks to their demographic and political importance, southern peoples such as the Nahua, Zapotec or Maya were able to survive and integrate into the new order that arose because of the Spanish Conquest. They managed to incorporate their customs, imagery, and memory into the warp and woof of the nation's history in various ways. Other groups —such as the hunters of Coahuila or the peoples of Jalisco and Zacatecas who refused to accept Spanish domination— were exterminated along with their stories and ideas. Some, like the Tarahumara and the Seri, have survived on the edges of ravines, on the fringes of deserted beaches, on the margin of history.

The brevity of this text forces us to concentrate on the central metropolitan histories of powerful groups: of the Olmecs of San Lorenzo, of Teotihuacán, of Tula, histories that belong to Mesoamerican civilization and about which we have a great deal of information. The fragmentary and dispersed nature of the data available on the peoples of the North makes it difficult to include them in this overview.

If we draw a line on a map of Mexico from west to east linking archaeological sites such as Huatabampo in Sonora, El Zape in Durango, Chalchihuites in Zacatecas, Villa de Reyes in San Luis Potosí, and San Antonio Nogalar in Tamaulipas, the result will be an arc, high at its ends and descending in the region of the Bolsones: it represents the northern frontier of Mesoamerica at the pinnacle of its expansion, around the year 900 CE. That boundary, as well as the construction of the Mesoamerican civilization itself, was the result of a long historical process that began with the domestication of corn and other plants, and included the development of intensive farming methods, the division of society into classes, the establishment of exchange networks extending for hundreds of miles, and the construction of ceremonial complexes, like the temples placed on top of pyramids and the ball courts.

THE HUNTER-GATHERERS

The Americas began to be populated around the year 40000 BCE. *Homo erectus* had learned to make fire half a million years before, but *Homo sapiens sapiens* had barely come into being and the subspecies *neanderthalensis* had not yet completely died out. So it is important to observe that humans as we know them today began their history practically at the same time in the Americas as in the rest of the world.

The passage to the Americas was made possible by a drop in sea levels characteristic of the geological era known as the Pleistocene, or Ice Age. During the last glaciation of that era, known as the Wisconsin Glaciation (ca. 100000 to 8000 BCE), there were periods of thousands of years during which northeast Asia and northwest America were joined, and that is where young *Homo sapiens sapiens* crossed over in successive waves.

The oldest indicators of human presence in what is now Mexico date from 35000 BCE. Between then and the year 5000 BCE, when domestication of corn and beans began, there were only bands of hunter-gatherers and fishermen. These bands were quite versatile, easily breaking up into their component parts. During months of scarcity, each family inhabited a different place, built its enclosure of branches or installed itself in a cave from which to take advantage of resources available nearby. Once the season of abundance arrived, generally in the summer, families congregated in places where bands were formed to hunt and gather. Several bands could join together and form "macrobands" to exchange women, organize great hunting forays or defend their territory. A single band could consist of several dozen people, and a macroband could unite several hundred.

This part of Mexican history, prior to the development of agriculture, is known as the Lithic Stage, and most of it took place during the cold Ice Age when the Americas still had horses, antelope, mammoths, and other species that became extinct due to climatic changes brought on by the Holocene.

One of the first personal stories recovered from the Mexican past occurred around the year 7000 BCE, shortly before the extinction of American megafauna. Bands of hunter-gatherers living in the Valley of Mexico used to herd mammoths down to the swampy shore of Lake Texcoco. When these giant animals bogged down in the mud, the hunters wounded them with lances until they fell exhausted or died. One day some 9 000 years ago, a woman—about 25 years old and 1.5 m (four feet 11 inches) tall—took part in a day's hunt, when she unfortunately stumbled and fell. She died and until recently remained buried face down in the mud. She is known among archaeologists as the "Tepexpan man."

The years around 7000 BCE are of special importance. The harsh climatic changes that caused the disappearance of a variety of species on this planet also prompted a diversification of economic activities. The technology of projectile points became specialized for hunting small and medium-sized animals such as pumas, peccaries, deer, rabbits, and raccoons. There is also enough archaeological evidence to state that between 7000 and 5000 BCE, bands intensified their gathering activities: they undoubtedly pulled weeds to clear the ground around beneficial plants, systematically harvesting fruits and seeds and doing some irrigating. The result of this intervention in natural plant cycles was the domestication of chili peppers, avocados, and squash (*Cucurbita mixta*). Subsequently, none of these plants could reproduce without assistance. Millstones for grinding grains—similar to a *metate* without feet—also appeared at this time.

But domesticating a few plants is not the same as being an agricultural people. Centuries of experimentation and adaptation separate the two and constituted what we call the Proto-Neolithic Period (5000 to 2500 BCE). Domesticated maize developed during this time as a result of hundreds of years of selecting primitive ears of the wild corn species *Zea mexicana* (*teosinte*). It mutated to produce small ears and finally ears about eight inches long, characteristic of the fully domesticated maize (*Zea mays*) of today. The *guaje* (bottle gourd), the common bean, and white and black zapotes were also domesticated during this period.

Toward the end of the Proto-Neolithic Period, the gatherers had become farmers. They could no longer abandon their crops;

thus, permanent villages arose. It was in these primitive settlements that characteristic Mesoamerican tools and procedures evolved: the *metate* and its club-like pestle for grinding corn appeared; pumpkin (*Cucurbita pepo*) was domesticated, and its seeds were used to prepare the daily *pipián* (a sauce made of ground pumpkin seeds, spices, and chili peppers) of all the peoples of Mesoamerica; dogs were domesticated; and there were also signs of the beginning of human sacrifice and worship of the dead. The families that lived in these villages formed more cohesive, lasting social units than their gatherer forebears. These were societies without social stratification, and they recognized no other difference among themselves than belonging to one family or another which, technically, are defined as tribes.

THE DAWN OF CIVILIZATION

The history of Mesoamerica is generally considered to have begun around 2500 BCE, when sedentary life became widespread and pottery came into existence. This date marks the start of the first Mesoamerican period, known as the Pre-Classic, and in particular its first stage, the Early Preclassic (2500 to 1200 BCE). This period is also known as Village Formative, because 90% of settlements in all regions were villages containing an average of ten to twelve dwellings and a total of 50 to 60 individuals. Households in the Early Preclassic consisted of several rooms grouped around a patio, a pattern that continued up to the time of the Spanish Conquest and even beyond. The patio was usually the work area, while the rooms around it served as dormitories and storerooms, and at least one of them could include the kitchen and an altar.

During this period, some villages grew to more than 200 dwellings sheltering more than a thousand people. Signs of long-distance exchanges and public rituals have been found in settlements of this kind. San José Mogote in the Oaxaca Valley is one such village that stands out in this region: among the artifacts archaeologists found at this site are pieces of pottery, seashells, shark teeth, as well as drums made of tortoise shell and trumpets of sea snail shell, all from the Gulf Coast. During those same years, a raised platform covered with stucco and equipped with an altar was constructed in the center of the village.

These villages were home to the first Mesoamerican chiefdoms: hierarchical societies that conferred higher rank on some members, such as the chief and his children, and perhaps on some exceptional warriors, thus promoting the use of artifacts and distinctive costumes to display rank. Religious and military authority was concentrated in the chiefs. They administered the community's surpluses and supervised its growing commerce. These chieftainships appear to have played an important role in promoting the high level of development that was to characterize the Mid-Preclassic Period, but in most Mesoamerican regions they lasted for only a short time. Distinctions of rank very soon gave way to class divisions, the work of government became specialized, and the nobility monopolized it.

Around the year 1200 BCE, a variety of waterworks—canals, terraces, and probably *chinampas* (human-made small agricultural plots anchored in the bottom of a lake)—began to appear in Mesoamerica. An improvement in agricultural productivity and an increase in population seem to be a direct consequence of these projects. From 1200 BCE to approximately 500 BCE, the Mid-Preclassic was characterized by the emergence of full-time specialized labor and social stratification, the construction of urban ceremonial centers, and the development of an array of symbolic images we usually identify as Olmec. It was precisely at this time that the first kingdoms or lordships arose in several areas of Mesoamerica.

The exchange of prestige and worship items taking place among the larger settlements of the various regions of Mesoamerica seems to have fostered a degree of agreement among ruling groups regarding religious and political concepts, and also favored the dissemination and acceptance of certain artistic and stylistic conventions and preferences. We now know that Olmec-like features appeared more or less simultaneously in the Balsas Basin, in the Valley of Mexico, on the Gulf Coast, and in other regions. This contradicts earlier ideas about the Olmec spreading throughout Mesoamerica from the Gulf of Mexico (San Lorenzo or La Venta, Tabasco) as the result of military or trade expansion.

Among the characteristics we usually identify as Olmec are the use of large "tables" of stone or masonry (in some cases used as thrones and in others, perhaps, as altars); the preference for jadeite and other green stones for offerings; the very frequent representation of the jaguar, associated in different ways with the human figure: felines that dance or fight with humans, feline skins used as capes, and anthropomorphic felines. Olmec-style human faces are characterized by narrow slanted eyes and very prominent thick lips, which sometimes open to reveal fierce fangs; there may be an incision in the upper central part of the head from which an ear of corn emerges. The "flaming eyebrow," two bands crossed in an "X," and a drop of rain with a dot and a line are also among the symbols usually called Olmec.

Most of the large, complex urban ceremonial centers, the greatest concentration of sculpture, and the largest pieces have been found on the alluvial plains of the Gulf of Mexico. An enormous earthen platform was built at San Lorenzo around 1200 BCE that protected a major complex of ceremonial plazas and elite living quarters from river flooding. Thrones, steles, colossal heads, and other sculptures were placed in various positions on this artificial meseta. The hugest sculptures were the thrones, previously thought to be altars. Sovereigns who presided over ceremonies and quite probably attended to matters of state sat on these thrones. The carved images on these gigantic seats proclaimed the ruler's special lineage and indicated his connection to the supernatural, especially to the interior of the mountain, a prime symbol of fertility. Some images also suggest identification of the ruler with the axis of the cosmos and the corn god. The gigantic heads were normally made of recycled thrones, most probably the throne used during the sovereign's lifetime, converted into his own colossal portrait. Placed directly on the ground, the heads of sovereigns would appear to be emerging from it, like trees or corn plants.

For 300 years, until 900 BCE, San Lorenzo was the political center of its region. It was then abruptly abandoned after the mutilation and burial of several of its sculptures. Between 900 BCE and 500 BCE, several sites flourished in the vicinity, but none had the grandeur of La Venta, which we can consider to be the true successor to San Lorenzo. At La Venta the first great Mesoamerican "pyramid" was built, a gigantic undulating cone of tamped earth surrounded by plazas and small platforms.

For the people of La Venta, the trip to the basalt fields of Los Tuxtlas was even longer than for the people of San Lorenzo. However, as their predecessors had done, they constantly travelled in search of stone, which they transported on rafts along the rivers and the coast, dragging the rock on rolling tree trunks where there was no body of water. These stones permitted the survival of the excellent sculptural tradition of San Lorenzo, enriching it with new creations such as tombs constructed with basalt columns. Small sculptures of semi-precious stones, such as jadeite, also became more varied during the flowering of La Venta, as attested by discoveries on the site and in places like Cerro de las Mesas and Río Pesquero.

It is tempting to suppose that the prosperous, partially urbanized villages of the Gulf of Mexico, inhabited by sculptors, priests, warriors, and rulers, constituted a kind of metropolis from which other Mesoamerican Olmec influences were derived. But, as we have said, the data does not support the hypothesis of expansion from the Gulf, but rather the idea that Olmec features had been adopted simultaneously by rising Mesoamerican nobilities who were in close contact among themselves as a result of trading.

We may continue to label the inhabitants of the Gulf alluvial plain in the Mid-Preclassic Period as "Olmec." This is an arbitrary name we have given to a group of peoples belonging to the Mixe-Zoque linguistic family. But the series of forms and symbols used in that region is not exactly an ethnic manifestation, something properly "Olmec," but part of a supra-regional phenomenon.

Among Olmec-type sites located beyond the Gulf Coast, Teopantecuanitlán in Guerrero and Chalcatzingo in Morelos stand out owing to the size and opulence of their ceremonial areas. Each of these sites has original features; for example, T-shaped steles in the former and unique representations of rain and caves in the latter. In both cases, however, Olmec artifacts, symbols, and stylistic conventions are clearly identifiable. They were also present in Tlapacoya and Tlatilco (in the Valley of Mexico), and in many other Mesoamerican sites.

THE ROOTS OF REGIONAL DIVERSITY

While uniformity is the characteristic feature of the Mid-Preclassic, regional diversity dominates the Late Preclassic (500 BCE to 200 CE). Around 500 BCE, evidence of Olmec culture is no longer found in Mesoamerica, and instead we encounter signs of several regional cultures that sprang up at that time with remarkable vigor. They included new architectural styles tending toward monumentality, as well as changes in sculpture, ritual ceramics, and the symbolic order. The motivations for this shift in the history of Mesoamerican civilization are not clear; what we can be sure of is that the regions had achieved demographic stability and economic wealth they had not enjoyed centuries before. This maturity produced very large population concentrations and allowed for the consolidation of nobilities that monopolized the functions of command. These functions came to be of a specifically political nature, ceasing to be grounded only on principles of representation and the leadership of kinship societies, and rather were based on rationale such as the efficacy of government action to win wars, organize commerce, and urbanize space.

The rise of Monte Albán is one of the events marking the beginning of the Late Preclassic. The larger villages in the three branches of the Oaxaca Valley, which had grown steadily, stopped their individual development around the year 500 BCE and participated in the joint project of creating a city. Monte Albán was a rocky, uninhabited mountain without water, but with the advantage of being situated in the center of the valley. From its summit one could see the three branches of the valley and surrounding mountain ranges. The fact that Monte Albán had been organized, from its inception, as a system of large neighborhoods or boroughs seems to strengthen the hypothesis that its foundation was the result of a broad alliance among all the settlements in the valley.

The rocky promontory was adapted to the needs of a growing population which, before the end of the Late Preclassic, had exceeded 15 000. The first public structure of the budding city was what we know today as the Gallery of the Dancers, which owes its name to the figures sculpted into the flat stones covering it that seem to move or writhe in contorted poses. Nude and with their viscera exposed, these figures might represent captive warriors and doubtless the complete series portrayed a long list of subdued groups.

This public exaltation of military victory had already appeared at San José Mogote when Monte Albán was established.

In the village of Dainzú, a small center dependent on Monte Albán located on a tributary of the Tlacolula River, reliefs of human sacrifices were also depicted—in this case decapitated—in association with the ball game. Around the year 200 BCE, a building was raised at Monte Albán in the shape of an arrowhead which, like its predecessor, is covered with stone slabs alluding to military conquest. On these slabs, however, instead of the mutilated captive, the emblem glyph for each settlement is used, associated with a head placed face down.

The foregoing and other evidence from the Classic Period appear to indicate that Monte Albán's political consolidation, urban growth, and regional dominance were achieved through intensive military activity. Among the fruits of that activity must have been large remittances of tribute capable of making the city both wealthy and prosperous.

Funerary art, generally recognized as one of the notable Zapotec features of Classic culture, was already present in these first centuries of Monte Albán's history: tombs made with large slabs of stone placed in rows and richly decorated with stucco and paint, as well as ceramic effigy vases known as urns, usually placed around the supine corpses of the dead.

Urbanization and demographic concentration processes similar to those of Oaxaca are evident in the Valley of Mexico, and are even more marked if we take into account that two cities arose on the shores of the Lake of Mexico in the Late Preclassic. This is an exciting page in our history about which little is known. We are sure that Cuicuilco was much more than a pyramid with a circular base: there was a gigantic necropolis, which today is covered by a modern housing development, and numerous mounds can still be seen from the busy streets that cross the area. Judging by the dimensions of that religious center, we may guess that the city was very large. A layer of lava almost 15 m (50 feet) thick at some points complicates research and will never allow us a complete understanding of that settlement.

Just as Cuicuilco was a magnet for the rural population in the southern part of the valley, Teotihuacán attracted peoples from the north and east. Some estimates indicate that between 200 BCE and 100 BCE, Teotihuacán held close to 40 000 inhabitants. Yet there is an important difference between the two concentrations: Cuicuilco contained a complex of religious monuments unlike any other settlement in Mesoamerica at the time. Teotihuacán was home to many people drawn there by the obsidian industry, but still lacked a ceremonial system comparable to that of Cuicuilco; it was more like an amalgamation of villages than a city.

Cuicuilco began to lose population after an eruption of the Xitle Volcano in 50 BCE, but was not totally abandoned until a hundred years later, when new eruptions covered it entirely with lava. Two of the distinguishing features of the Cuicuilco culture disappeared from the valley with the extinction of the city: the circular-based ceremonial platform and the bottle-shaped tombs, characterized by a cylindrical shaft that provided access to the inner chamber. Curiously, both features appeared in Western Mexico (Jalisco, Michoacán, Nayarit, Colima) around the year 200 BCE and became typical of that region during the following thousand years. No link has been shown to exist between the two cultures; nevertheless, the possibility cannot be ruled out.

In other regions of Mesoamerica, the works and events of the Late Preclassic showed some connection to the ancient Olmec. Such was the case of the Mezcala culture, where we observe the continuity of a very characteristic practice of the Olmec period: small anthropomorphic figures carved in stone. The abstraction of the Mezcala figures seems related to the least naturalistic tendencies of Olmec art. In addition to these vestiges, there are very clear signs of a sequel to the Olmec presence that shifted from the Gulf to the Maya region.

Between the years 500 and 400 BCE, La Venta was abruptly abandoned, but some minor sites in the region, like Tres Za-

potes and Cerro de las Mesas, remained inhabited and continued the tradition of sculpting steles and altars out of great blocks
of stone. They also preserved some of the features of Olmec
iconography. What is particularly interesting is the strong re-
semblance between the sculptures of these post-Olmec sites
and those created in areas in the South, in the Upper Grijalva
Basin and on the coasts of Chiapas and Guatemala. Such similarities have made it possible to identify a cultural phenomenon
known as the Izapa Complex. The northernmost point of that
complex seems to be La Mojarra in Veracruz, and the points
farthest south are Izapa, in Mexico, and Abaj Takalik and El
Baúl in Guatemala. Crucial links are Chiapa de Corzo and La
Libertad, both on the upper reaches of the Grijalva River. This
long curving swath, which descends from the Gulf alluvial plain
and crosses the Isthmus of Tehuantepec, coincides with the location of the Mixe-Zoque linguistic family in the Late Preclassic. Coast-to-coast communication via that route was not new;
it had existed for centuries. What seems to have occurred is that
the descendants of the Gulf Olmecs strengthened the relationship with their own ethnic roots once the Olmec era's world of
commercial and political ties had collapsed.

During this period of crisis and re-accommodation, one of
the most transcendental inventions for Mesoamerica's intellectual
history occurred at Izapa Complex sites: the "long count," a system for creating a calendar that makes it possible to date any
event with precision based on a fixed date equivalent to what is
used in the West, i.e., the birth of Christ. The reference date for
the Mesoamerican Long Count was August 13, 3114 BCE, but
we have no evidence that it refers to any particular event. The
oldest known calendar inscriptions come from the Mixe-Zoque
area: Chiapa de Corzo, 36 BCE; Tres Zapotes, 31 BCE; El Baúl,
36 CE; Abaj Takalik, 126 CE; La Mojarra, 143 CE and 156 CE;
and San Andrés Tuxtla, 162 CE. This data indicates that the system we think of as Mayan *par excellence* was actually invented by

the Mixe-Zoque during a period of regional crisis and restructuring. Nor is the combination of altar and stele an invention attributable to the Maya. As we have seen, it was in use in the Olmec era in Guerrero, in Morelos, and along the Gulf Coast, and moved to the Maya region via the Izapa Complex cultural corridor.

In the Mid-Preclassic, there were already some Mayan agricultural settlements in the jungle, such as Seibal and Altar de Sacrificios, on a tributary of the Usumacinta River called Pasión, as well as in Tikal, Uaxactún, Nakbé, and El Mirador in the Guatemalan Petén, not far from the border with Campeche. Some of these villages were the cradle of powerful chieftainships, and in the Late Preclassic developed compact, elevated ceremonial areas characterized by groups of several mounds, each crowned by two or three pyramidal platforms. These groups' architecture and ornamentation are very similar to those that were to be seen in the Classic Period, but some components are still absent: royal portraits and epigraphs accompanied by dates.

The Petén groups achieved some expansion southward and towards the Grijalva River, whether peaceful or warlike we do not know. As a result of that expansion, they came into contact with the Izapa tradition. Kaminaljuyú and other sites on the Guatemalan Altiplano may have been areas that fostered assimilation of the two tendencies, the Mixe-Zoque and the Mayan. In the year 292 CE, the long count appears associated with Mayan inscriptions and architecture in the emerging city of Tikal in the jungle, which would become one of the most prosperous in the region.

THE AGE OF EMPIRE

Between the years 100 BCE and 200 CE, a period some authors distinguish from the Preclassic and call Protoclassic, several important events took place in the Valley of Mexico. One was the

abandonment of Cuicuilco and Teotihuacán's rise as the unques-
tioned political and religious center of the region.

The Pyramids of the Sun and the Moon were built during
the first two hundred years of our era, as was the Temple of
Quetzalcóatl. The so-called Avenue of the Dead was laid out,
and the urban phase of Teotihuacán's history began. If any pre-
Hispanic settlement can properly be called a city, it was Teotihuacán. Construction and paving covered the greater part of its
surface, without leaving space for orchards or gardens, in an area
of 20 km^2 (about eight square miles).

During the Classic Period (200 to 650 CE), most of the
people of Teotihuacán occupied multifamily dwellings made of
masonry, and very few people lived in adobe huts, indicating
generalized prosperity. Groups of housing structures were constructed on large sloping aprons and their walls were window-
less, with one or two porticos allowing access. The majority of
these compounds rose on top of square foundations measuring
60 m by 60 m (about 200 feet by 200 feet), although some were
longer and others were L-shaped. All of their sides were parallel,
but the corners did not always coincide; so the intent was not to
create a precisely square grid. Each compound was equivalent
to a block or square; the streets of Teotihuacán were long, shad-
ed corridors passing between sloping aprons and high walls,
and it was impossible to see what went on in the dwellings from
the street.

Several patios within each residential compound provided
passage to the rooms and allowed light to enter. A central patio
and some larger rooms enabled all residents to congregate for
religious and administrative activities of common interest. On
average, some 20 families probably lived in each compound;
they were all active in the same craft or trade and, furthermore,
were related to one another. From genetic analyses of skeletons
we know that the males in each compound had closer connections to each other than the women, which suggests a pattern

of patrilocal residence: the women went to live in their husbands' compounds.

It has been observed that several residential compounds tended to group together to form neighborhoods or boroughs; the inner streets were usually narrower than those surrounding them. Several neighborhoods together formed a district. Each district seems to have had its own ceremonial center, equipped with three temples which converged in a small square. That must also have been the meeting point for representatives of families and neighborhoods for administrative purposes.

A major part of the population concentrated in Teotihuacán's urban area, perhaps half, were artisans devoted to trades such as the production of cores or finished artifacts of obsidian, pottery, bone and shell or cloth and cordage, among other items. The abundance and good quality of agricultural land in the valley of Teotihuacán and the limited number of villagers living there lead one to believe that many of the city's residents also carried out agricultural activities on a part- or full-time basis.

People often imagine that all pre-Hispanic societies were tyrannies in which an immensely wealthy group forced communities of producers into exhausting labor under iron-fisted political control. They were not democracies by any means, but their internal structure was far more complex than this preconception suggests. There is enough archaeological data in Teotihuacán for us to understand at least four basic ideas related to social stratification: 1] Society was founded on the basis of collective groups, like clans, which took on the form of urban neighborhoods. 2] These clans were internally differentiated; some families were more prosperous than others. The residential compounds where the leaders lived tended to be more spacious and richer than others in the same neighborhood. The remains of the highest ranking individuals in each neighborhood received special burial treatment. 3] Neighborhoods of artisans, agriculturists, and other workers enjoyed such substantial urban infrastructure (streets, market access, drainage, solid and durable dwellings) that we cannot consider them an impoverished mass. In other words, popular urban dwellings in general were not of a quality substantially different from that of the rulers. 4] Nevertheless, there are buildings whose rich mural decoration and spaciousness show them to be the dwellings of a noble class. The compounds located east of the Pyramid of the Moon and north of the Pyramid of the Sun appear to have belonged to the families of political and military leaders. There are also clusters of dwellings that seem to have been home to monks devoted entirely to religious tasks.

We know almost nothing about the kings of Teotihuacán except that it seems they had Quetzalcóatl as their supreme protective deity, just as the lords of the Olmec period identified themselves with the corn god. The power of the sovereigns of the great city in the Valley of Mexico must have emanated at least in part from their successful management of public works. The immense pyramids and the great city were proof of their effective governance. The organization of crafts and the promotion of trade assured by the arrival of raw materials and the export of products to other regions undoubtedly must have been valued by groups of specialists who depended on that commerce.

The recognition of all the neighborhoods, districts, artisans, nobles, and peasants as members of the same political unit probably occurred under the protective image of a common deity, Tláloc, God of Water, and his consort, Chalchiuhtlicue. It is likely that the pyramids which centuries later the Mexica, who were occasional visitors to the site, called "of the Sun" and "of the Moon" were really dedicated to Tláloc and Chalchiuhtlicue. The Pyramid of the Sun was a great symbolic "hill of water" because the people of Teotihuacán dug a peripheral ditch and small central canal, so that it would appear that water was springing from the natural cave located at the apex of the pyramid, and then flowed around it. In the plaza of the Pyramid of the Moon there was only a massive, almost geometric, sculpture of Chalchiuhtlicue, the goddess identified by her jade skirt.

Beyond the city and its immediate agricultural surroundings, Teotihuacán influenced all the regions of Mesoamerica in one way or another. First, the Teotihuacán state was the great organizer of production in the Valley of Mexico and undoubtedly also in the Toluca Valley. In view of available evidence, it is most likely that there were two major ethnic components in this area: the Nahua, who comprised the majority of Teotihuacán's urban population, and several groups of the Otomí family. Among the latter, there were groups primarily engaged in intensive agriculture in the Lerma River Basin (who were the forefathers of the Matlatzinca), and others devoted mainly to exploiting the forests, hunting deer, and cultivating and processing agave (to obtain pulque, rope, and textile fibers) and, to a lesser extent, to agriculture (these were the ancestors of the Otomí and the Mazahua). The Otumba and Pachuca obsidian deposits, as well as lime deposits in the Tula-Tepeji area, were among the strategic resources apparently directly controlled by Teotihuacán.

Less influential areas that also merit attention are basins in Morelos where the people from Teotihuacán obtained cotton, probably cacao, and other warm-climate agricultural products, and the Puebla-Tlaxcala Valley that supplied the clay required to make "thin orange" pottery, one of the finest craft products of Ancient Mexico. Teotihuacán must have had continuous trade with these two regions, and perhaps collected tribute from both, but we cannot be sure that it directly controlled what was produced there.

Teotihuacán's power extended into a third area of influence that involved settlements hundreds of kilometers away from the Valley of Mexico. The search for cinnabar deposits led its inhabitants to the Río Verde in San Luis Potosí, while their interest in a variety of semi-precious stones like serpentine and jadeite took them to the Balsas River Basin. We cannot say that Teotihuacán forcibly appropriated raw materials for itself without compensation. It is much more likely that it imposed asymmetrical trade conditions on the locals.

The presence of people from Teotihuacán on the coast of the Gulf of Mexico was also due to their search for certain raw materials, probably the feathers of tropical birds, cacao, and cinnabar and kaolin (a fine white clay) deposits in the area of Los Tuxtlas. They founded a colony at Matacapan near Lake Catemaco. This not only assured access to raw materials, but also supervision of an important port of exchange where trade routes met coming from northern Veracruz, the Yucatán Peninsula, the Guatemalan coast via the Isthmus of Tehuantepec, and the Mixteca region via the Teotitlán-Tuxtepec route. Among the most convincing evidence of Teotihuacán presence in Matacapan is the use of multifamily housing compounds following the model of the metropolis.

Teotihuacán's relations with the Maya and Zapotec peoples have been the subject of much debate. We are sure there was some association, that it lasted several centuries, and that it was quite close. Many Teotihuacán artifacts reached Oaxaca and the Maya region, and numerous Teotihuacán forms were imitated by the artisans of the south. But what was the nature of these relations?

The first explicit evidence of a strong Teotihuacán influence on the Maya area was found 50 years ago. Since then, archaeological projects and advances in deciphering epigraphs (engraved inscriptions) have confirmed that influence and made it possible to define its major features. There are very clear signs of Teotihuacán influence in architecture and pottery, as well as in the representation of military paraphernalia and some symbols, in several Maya cities of the Petén. Tikal is definitely the place where Teotihuacán characteristics appear with the greatest clarity. In addition to Teotihuacán-type vessels like the typical tripod vase with a cover, within this jungle metropolis there are several structures that use slope and panel (*talud y tablero*) construction, interpreted in the Teotihuacán fashion, and recently a stone standard was found almost identical to the one we know as a "ball game marker" found in Teotihuacán's La Ventilla complex.

One of the vases found at Tikal depicts obviously armed warriors in Teotihuacán dress coming before a Maya personage who receives them with burning incense. A mural at nearby Uaxactún also represents a Teotihuacán warrior being revered by a Maya noble. The epigraphs that make it possible to understand the event to which these scenes allude have only been deciphered very recently. We now know that on January 31, 378 CE, a foreigner by the name of Siyaj Kak came to Tikal. The presence of this same person was recorded eight days before at the village of El Perú, located on the banks of one of the tributaries of the Usumacinta River, a natural entry to the Petén for someone traveling from the Valley of Mexico. The king of Tikal, Chak Tok Ichaak, died on the same day as the foreigner's arrival. In other words, in all probability, the king was killed by the foreigners.

Mention is also made of the arrival of Siyaj Kak in inscriptions at Uaxactún, Bejucal, and Río Azul. In no case is it said that Siyaj established himself as ruler; the inscriptions indicate that this personage installed new monarchs. At Tikal, the ruler installed by Siyaj was from Teotihuacán and was known as *Búho-Lanzadardos* (Spearthrower Owl). After power was usurped, the newcomers removed from public areas the steles commemorating the rulers that preceded the Teotihuacán incursion. They were all destroyed or taken away from the city. It was a matter of establishing a new dynasty, and from then on, for several generations, the legitimacy of the kings of Tikal would be linked to their Teotihuacán origins. The son of Spearthrower Owl, Yax Nuun

Ayiin I, is represented on a stele in non-Maya costume and posture, and Teotihuacán-type vessels were buried in his tomb. The grandson of Spearthrower Owl, Siyaj Chan Kawiil II, is portrayed in a style closer to Maya conventions, but is flanked by two images in which his father is dressed in the attire and carrying the arms of a Teotihuacán warrior. There are also indications of Teotihuacán military presence at Piedras Negras, while at Palenque it is likely that Teotihuacán imposed a new dynasty in the year 431 CE.

On the Guatemalan Altiplano, Kaminaljuyú also suffered a Teotihuacán invasion around the year 400 CE. In this case there are no inscriptions, but the archaeological remains are very eloquent. What Michael Coe has called "a miniature version of Teotihuacán" was created at Kaminaljuyú. The colonists built temples as in the Valley of Mexico, and their pottery was decorated reproducing the artistic conventions of the metropolis. They preferred to be buried with vessels brought from their city of origin. Among Teotihuacán's motives for establishing dominion at this site in the highlands, the most important one must have been to control the obsidian deposits in the area, particularly at El Chayal.

Teotihuacán's relationship with Monte Albán seems to have been discreet and symmetrical, but although in the Maya case it is clear that there was a military aspect, at Monte Albán the association was probably more diplomatic. The Zapotec potters felt less attracted by the Teotihuacán style than the artisans of Tikal; the presence of Teotihuacán forms in Monte Albán is far scarcer. There is a lintel at Monte Albán referring to a visit by Teotihuacán ambassadors, but these ambassadors are priests carrying sacks of copal to present as an offering, and not warriors. With Oaxaca, moreover, there is a reciprocity not observable with the Maya. A neighborhood in Teotihuacán was inhabited by Zapotec who maintained their customs for centuries. These Zapotec were buried in underground chambers like those at Monte Albán, and not directly beneath the floor like other residents of Teotihuacán. Furthermore, the mortal remains of the Zapotec were surrounded by effigy urns identical to those that have been found by the hundreds in the Oaxaca Valley.

The Teotihuacán presence in Western Mesoamerica has yet to be clarified. It has repeatedly been claimed that visitors from Teotihuacán came to sites in Zacatecas, such as Alta Vista, in order to control trade in turquoise and benefit from other mining activities in the region. But so far no solid proof has been offered. On the other hand, attention has always been drawn to a settlement in Michoacán, namely Tingambato, because of the startling similarity of its architecture to that of Teotihuacán, but there is no ceramic evidence of a link between the two sites. Settlements in Nayarit, Jalisco, and Colima—characterized by their ceremonial centers with circular platforms and plazas, and burial complexes with shaft tombs and ceramic recreations of realistic scenes of daily life and animals—continued to be an essential part of a regional system linked to the pueblos of the Sierra Madre Occidental (Western Sierra Madre) and the Pacific Coast rather than to Teotihuacán.

CRISIS AND CHANGE

The years between 650 and 900 CE are commonly known by two different names. If considered from the center of Mexico, with the fall of Teotihuacán and the dramatic changes that followed, this era is called Epiclassic. But viewed from a Mayan perspective, given that the Maya were just then reaching the peak of their prosperity, these years are called Late Classic. In any event, the initial date of this period coincides with the crisis that ended Teotihuacán's dominance and the end date refers to the disappearance of classic Maya culture. To be precise, 909 CE is the last date recorded on the monuments at Calakmul and Toniná.

Sometime before the year 600 CE, Teotihuacán's influence over the Maya area ceased, and between that date and the year 700 CE, evidence of Teotihuacán's presence disappeared from all of Mesoamerica: the great port of Matacapan was no longer a center of commercial exchanges; Teotihuacán pottery was no longer found in the cinnabar mining area in San Luis Potosí; trade stopped between Morelos and the Valley of Mexico; and, in short, the Teotihuacán era came to an end. This violent contraction of the Teotihuacán system seems to have been caused by the impetus of middle-sized cities seeking a more active role in exchange networks. It is as though the regions of Mesoamerica simply shook off a dominance that sought to regulate the economic life of all. During the crisis, the former capital lost over four-fifths of its population.

The disappearance of Teotihuacán influence in the Maya area seems to have been one of the causes for more rapid regional development. Maya cities became more prosperous; architecture, sculpture, and the manufacture of ritual and luxury objects took on unprecedented variety and richness. Some of the principal Maya cities such as Palenque, at the foot of the Chiapas mountains, Piedras Negras, and Yaxchilán on the Usumacinta River, Tikal in the Petén, and Calakmul in the southern Yucatán Peninsula all flourished to the greatest extent in the seventh century. And, as is true of the rest of Maya history, this era of splendor is known to us in more nuanced detail than other parts of Mesoamerican history because the Maya used a glottographic script capable of reproducing speech and a precise dating system. Maya narratives of the Classic Period are sometimes monotonous: they list births, enthronements, declarations of war, temple dedications, and deaths. Nevertheless, a complete reading of the inscriptions, which has been particularly successful in the last 20 years, makes it possible to discover shades of meaning and singularities: not all kings behaved the same way, nor did all cities tell their tales in the same way. There are hundreds of stories to be gathered from available inscriptions, and many come from this seventh-century period of great splendor.

The inscriptions of Yaxchilán introduce us, among other individuals, to an especially fortunate king, Itzamnaaj Balam II, who governed from 681 to 742 CE. He appears in the most famous carved lintels of Yaxchilán as a great warrior and protector of the city. His government thrived and his life was long; like his mother, he lived more than 90 years. Among his several wives, Kabal Xook was the most important: one of the best temples in Yaxchilán was dedicated to her, and the interior was decorated by expert sculptors brought in from other cities. Deceased seven years after the king, Kabal Xook was buried in a magnificent temple, with an impressive offering of 20 000 obsidian knives.

Another story about the epoch of prosperity is that of Pakal (Pacal) and his son Kan Balam, lords of Palenque (called Lakamhá in their time). This city's artists preferred to record their stories in stucco on walls and on stone objects, but not on steles. Kinich Janaab Pakal I, known as Pacal the Great, received his power from his mother, something uncommon in a preferentially patrilineal society. It seems that his mother, Sak Kuk, had assumed power in the absence of male siblings, the last having died in the fierce war against Calakmul. After ruling for three years in a sort of regency, she left power in the hands of her 12-year-old son. Pakal succeeded in restoring the city after an unfortunate series of military defeats and acquired enough wealth to build one of the greatest palaces in Ancient Mexico, as well as a monumental mausoleum—the so-called Temple of the Inscriptions—for his voyage to Xibalbá, the World of the Dead. Thanks to the stability achieved by Kinich Janaab Pakal I, his son Kinich Kan Balam II brought the city to its greatest height of power and equaled his father in building by constructing the celebrated complex of the Temples of the Cross, of the Foliated Cross, and of the Sun.

Contemporaries of Pacal the Great were Yuknoom Head and Yuknoom the Great, lords of Calakmul. Singularly brave, and in charge of a city more prone to war than its neighbors, Yuknoom Head zealously maintained the military prestige of the kingdom and its authority over lesser cities. When the city of Naranjo in the Guatemalan Petén tried to become independent, Calakmul's army immediately overwhelmed it, and Yuknoom personally murdered its king. The record uses the verb *kuxaj* to express what Yuknoom did to his adversary. It may be translated in two ways: he tortured him or he ate him. The heir to Yuknoom Head, Yuknoom the Great, directed the forces of his kingdom to fight against Tikal, supporting Tikal's enemies or attacking it directly.

An indication of the power of the Maya kingdoms in the seventh century may be seen in their capacity to influence Central Mexico. However, this was part of widespread expansion of the regions that had constituted the periphery of the Teotihuacán system. Groups from Central and North-Central Veracruz, headed by the flourishing city of Tajín, penetrated the Huasteca Region and the central meseta. Some artifacts found in the city of Cholula show clear influence of Gulf of Mexico decorative styles. Mixtec groups also reached Cholula and undoubtedly contributed to the dissemination of certain iconographic features, specifically on calendars, in settlements in Puebla and Morelos. The Maya, for their part, had a decisive influence on the lives of the elites of two important cities: Cacaxtla and Xochicalco. In the renowned mural painting at Cacaxtla there are figures and symbols from the Gulf and also from Teotihuacán, but the style of the paintings, the composition of scenes, and the treatment of personages is preponderantly Mayan. The artists who painted them, and undoubtedly also a segment of the local nobility, were familiar with the artistic tradition of the Usumacinta River Basin.

In the case of Xochicalco, the confluence of regional traditions is even more surprising. The organization of urban space is similar to what we see at Monte Albán. It comes close to the Maya system of ceremonial complexes and the formation of acropolises. The architectural platforms are constructed with sloping sides and horizontal panels in the Cholula manner, but with the Tajín flying cornice. The decoration of the temple to Quetzalcóatl reproduces a Teotihuacán theme, but beyond that homage, Xochicalco eschewed contact with the declining metropolis and preferred to get its obsidian from the deposits in Michoacán, in spite of their being much farther away than those in the Valley of Mexico. Oaxacan influence is evident in the calendar inscriptions of Xochicalco, although efforts to create a new system are also apparent. And once again, as at Cacaxtla, we find at Xochicalco stylistic elements that can only be explained by close contact with elite groups well informed about Maya art. The human figures carved in the temple to Quetzalcóatl undoubtedly came from the Maya artistic tradition, probably from far-off Copán.

It seems that in confronting the void left by the demise of Teotihuacán, the people who remained all quickly worked from their respective regions to reconnect the threads of an ancient exchange network. And within that network, formerly administered by a central power, nodes now formed where several initiatives came together. Without a doubt, this was an unsettled time and a period of intense military activity. Teotenango, at the source of the Lerma River, sat on a mountain that was hard to attack, while Xochicalco and Cacaxtla, dissatisfied with their hilltop defenses, surrounded themselves with trenches and walls. In the Cacaxtla murals, the struggle between water and drought is portrayed as a cruel battle. On the upper part of the Pyramid of Quetzalcóatl at Xochicalco, the individuals sculpted display an enormous shield and handful of darts.

During the eighth century, military activity intensified in the Maya area as well, where it reached levels never before seen. Disputes over areas of influence, which ultimately took the form of struggles for economic resources, caused a spiraling increase in war that only ended with the extinction of Maya culture in the form in which it had flourished in the lowlands for centuries. Some events in the Pasión River area and at Lake Petexbatún may serve to illustrate that period of bellicose frenzy. A regional conflict developed there in the decade of 760 CE that involved Dos Pilas, Aguateca, Seibal, Aguas Calientes, and Amelia. The city of Dos Pilas, which until then had been the most powerful of the region, was abandoned by the local nobility. The people who remained there built a double rampart that crossed ancient plazas and ceremonial areas. The residents of Aguateca also used ramparts to improve their defenses, and eventually took refuge on an island, which they also fortified. At the end of this crisis, by the year 830, the only relatively prosperous city in the region was Seibal. In general, it may be said that Maya cities experienced insoluble crises throughout the ninth century and, as a result, were progressively abandoned: Yaxchilán became depopulated around 808 CE and Palenque shortly thereafter; Tikal was deserted close to 870 CE. Calakmul, in decline for almost a century, was finally abandoned around the year 909 CE, as was the city of Toniná.

Most recent historiography has refuted the earlier idea of a mysterious collapse. Today we know that it was war that brought on the final catastrophe for the ancient Maya kingdoms. Nevertheless, one must remember that behind these battles there was more than uncontrolled, irrational bellicosity. Quite probably, this was the most intense expression of a struggle for survival among the dwellers of an apparently exuberant rainforest made fragile by having to bear the burden of many cities. The Maya utilized the rich land on river banks for cultivation and frequently improved it with irrigation canals. They also grew crops inland, in soil they reclaimed from the hills by the system of felling trees and burning vegetation. But riverside land was scarce and the "slash and burn" system had a downside: after two to three years, the land used had to be allowed to lie fallow for a decade or more to recover its natural vegetation and nutrients.

The nobles saw war as a way to rapidly increase their resources from the tribute they imposed on the vanquished, but the energy and time invested in these wars ended up affecting agricultural organization and productivity, especially in irrigated zones. There is solid proof that the nutrition of the Mayan peasants deteriorated progressively during the Late Classic Period as a result of decreased agricultural production and probably also because of the many demands for tribute from elites who knew no limits when it came to making their cities richer. Less cohesive and weaker societies, and noblemen persistently seeking to improve their position and their resources by means of war, brought the kingdoms to a critical point. Many cities fell, devastated or exhausted, and in others peasants turned their backs on the nobles: peasant farmers had only to disappear into the mountains for a few months for the nobility to be left without sustenance.

THE WARRIORS OF QUETZALCÓATL

Outside the Maya area, the flourishing cities of the Epi-Classic Period—Tajín, Xochicalco, and Cacaxtla—stopped developing and became partially or totally abandoned around the year 900 CE. Teotihuacán itself, which had survived for more than two centuries as a regional center, was also deserted. Thus began the period known as the Post-Classic, which would last until the Spanish Conquest.

Another phenomenon that marks the beginning of the Post-Classic is the abandonment of many northern Mesoamerican settlements and the consequent flow of immigration to the south. Many peoples who had lived for centuries in the Bajío, in the Altos de Jalisco, and in the Sierra Madre Occidental mi-

grated toward the Valleys of Puebla-Tlaxcala, Mexico, and Toluca, and toward the Tarascan Plateau. Most of them were Nahua, but apparently there were also some Pame and perhaps
some Purépecha. Colonial sources refer to all of them as Chichimeca. These people were accustomed to living on the frontier of civilization, in harsh areas inhabited by bands of hunter-
gatherers. As in military chieftainships, they were bellicose
groups who conferred the highest social status on warriors.

The permanent conflict that characterized the post-Teoti-
huacán era and the belligerence of the newly-arrived northerners combined to place war at the center of public life in the
cities of the Post-Classic Period. Warriors appeared invested
with religious attributes; battles were fought in the name of
the gods; and human sacrifices practiced after battle were seen
as necessary for the functioning of the cosmic order. The warrior's image and values came to enjoy unprecedented social
prestige. Elite military orders, especially those represented by
eagles and jaguars, became the main support of sovereigns.
The theme of opposition between the eagle and the jaguar, portrayed as struggle, copulation or juxtaposition, was very common in Post-Classic iconography: it was the preferred metaphor
of a society at war.

But not all conflicts were resolved by force of arms, nor
could societies permanently devoted to war have survived. The
Post-Classic kingdoms sought to stabilize and manage conflict
by means of diplomatic alliances and agreements. Alliances were
usually triple, although some were quadruple. They facilitated
organizing the political domination of regions, recognizing the
influence of each of the allied kingdoms over a specific area and
population, and sharing the benefits of all the tribute collected.
Among other celebrated Post-Classic alliances, we know of those
of Chichén Itzá, Uxmal, and Mayapán on the Yucatán Peninsula;
Ihuatzio, Pátzcuaro, and Tzintzuntzan in Michoacán; and Teotihuacán, Texcoco, and Tlacopan in the Valley of Mexico. Besides

these alliances among "friends," there were also temporary pacts that permitted some degree of diplomatic relations between enemy kingdoms. A particularly eloquent example of this was the presence of lords of Michoacán at Mexica coronation celebrations. After participating in banquets and entertainment for several days, the Tarascan dignitaries returned to their territory and continued their open enmity toward Mexico-Tenochtitlan and its allies.

The most important city of the early Post-Classic Period (900 to 1200 CE) was Tula in the present-day State of Hidalgo. It was here that the warlike daring of the Chichimeca blended with the tradition of some southern Nahua, heirs to Teotihuacán. At Tula, warriors were the principal actors in society: they occupied the highest level of the most important building in the city, the base of which is decorated with a parade of coyotes, jaguars, and eagles grasping bleeding hearts in their beaks. Courts for the ball game are most important at this site, and must have been the scene of a warrior rite that culminated in the beheading of prisoners of war. Tula was the first Mesoamerican city in which the macabre *tzompantli* was used, a kind of gigantic abacus on which each crosspiece was a skewer loaded with human heads, one of the contributions of the Chichimeca peoples to the final centuries of Mesoamerican history. Also used for the first time at Tula was the monumental portico, formed by several parallel colonnades, and the anthropomorphic altar which we know as the *chac-mool*, both elements originating in mountain settlements in the West.

Tula's success was more modest than that of Teotihuacán, but its political and military might was sufficient to support long-distance trade routes that extended as far as Central America in the south and at least as far as Sinaloa in the north. Some artifacts of Mesoamerican provenance found in settlements of agricultural oases in New Mexico, such as Pueblo Bonito in Chaco Canyon, seem to be from the Toltec period, although it can-

not be affirmed with certainty whether they arrived there because of Tula's commercial reach or as a result of some regional
networks. We know that the agricultural villages of the Sonoran
rivers traded with peoples of the Sierra Madre, and there are
indications of contacts between the mountain settlements of
Chihuahua and Durango and agriculturists in Arizona and New
Mexico. The most complex agricultural settlement in the extreme north of present-day Mexico was Paquimé (also called
Casas Grandes) in Chihuahua, where a giant multifamily adobe
complex was constructed. Four stories high, and provided with
heating and drainage, it was surrounded by ceremonial platforms and plazas. It is quite probable that Paquimé was an important stopover on the road for groups taking Mesoamerican
products northward. It is not likely that merchants coming
from Tula went at least as far as Paquimé, attracted by New
Mexico's turquoise that was traded in the region.

As had been the case with the people of Teotihuacán, the
Toltec had an important presence in the Maya region, although
it is much harder to define how that relationship came about.
The city of Chichén Itzá on the Yucatán Peninsula was practically re-founded around the year 900 CE, beside the ancient
city of the Classic Period. In the new Chichén, some of Tula's
principal images and structures were recreated: the L-shaped
portico of colonnades; the Temple of the Warriors, atop which
two erect feathered serpents serve as columns flanking the en-
trance to a roofed enclosure; the pillars with warriors engraved
on their surfaces; the *chac-mools*; the friezes of eagles and jaguars; and even a carved *tzompantli* that reproduces the skewer of Toltec skulls. Were the re-founders not emigrant Toltecs
but rather powerful groups of merchants with Mayan affiliation
—usually called *putunes*—who were accustomed to visiting Nahua cities and familiar with them? We can definitely say that the
new city's architecture was designed by someone who had seen
Tula. Chichén Itzá was the most prominent city on the peninsula

until 1300 CE, although it exercised that power in alliance with Uxmal and Mayapán. The latter broke the alliance and controlled the region, apparently in a tyrannical manner, until 1450. However, the prestige of Chichén Itzá and its elite reformers, identified with Kukulkan (the Yucatec name for Quetzalcóatl), would persist until the Spanish Conquest.

In addition to its physical remains, Tula left a trail of glory among the Mesoamerican peoples. Its fame surpassed that of the Nahua and was always linked to political power and the idea of civilization. Much the same happened in the case of Quetzalcóatl, the legendary lord of the Toltecs. It was said, for instance, that the first king of the Guatemalan Maya-Quiché had been confirmed in his post by Quetzalcóatl, called Kukumatz by the Quiché. The Mixtec also attributed the foundation of the dynasties that governed in the Post-Classic to Quetzalcóatl. Both the Maya and the Mixtec refer to Tula in their narratives. The Maya stated that their rulers' ancestors came from that city, whereas the Mixtec claimed that the great conquering king Eight Deer Jaguar Claw had traveled to Tula to be confirmed in his post. For their part, the majority of the sixteenth-century Nahua peoples referred to Tula as the place of origin of their ruling lineages. The same may be said of the Chalca, Texcocan, Cholulteca, Cuauhtinchantlaca, and Mexica peoples, of course, as well as others.

The deep impression left by Tula and Quetzalcóatl in the ideology of the peoples of Mesoamerica cannot be explained merely by the acts of the Toltecs of Tula, their mercantile enterprises, and military force. There is more. The word "tula" (*tollan* in its correct Nahuatl form) etymologically means "clump of rushes," a place where rushes, or *tollin*, abound. The metaphor of rushes evokes the great conglomeration of people characteristic of a big city. In the sources preserving the indigenous tradition of the colonial period, the word referred to a marvelous, mythical city inhabited by gods like Quetzalcóatl and Tezcatlipoca, and was also used as an epithet to allude to a series of real or historical cities like Cholula, Culhuacan, Tenochtitlan, and Tula itself.

What is common to all the Tulas is their prosperity, urban dimensions, high degree of civilization, and the wisdom and religiosity of their rulers. Tula was the city *par excellence*, the marvelous city, and so was each of its terrestrial replicas. It is quite probable that the prototype of all Tulas—the largest, most powerful, and most prosperous city of Ancient Mexico—was Teotihuacán. It was there that the Nahua urban tradition began, as did the cult of Quetzalcóatl. The ancient myth was reinforced in Tula de Hidalgo, and apparently some new ideas about the exercise of power originated there: the ruler of this Tula bore the name of the god Quetzalcóatl and enjoyed the prerogative of confirming the sovereigns of other cities in their posts, which he did by perforating their nasal septum with the claw of an eagle and another of a jaguar.

The familiarity of the Maya and the Mixtec with the concept of Tula and the god Quetzalcóatl reflects the impact of the Nahua tradition on the south. Its influence was felt as of the Teotihuacán period, but it seems to have had greater political and religious consequences during the Toltec era. The Maya Kukulkan could have been the lord of Chichén Itzá, just as the Tula to which the Mixtec refer in their sources may well have been Cholula (*Tollan Cholollan*). The latter had continued the Teotihuacán tradition for several centuries, had strong links with Oaxaca, and in the Post-Classic was reputed to be the principal sanctuary of the god Quetzalcóatl. The fact is that there were several Tulas and various Quetzalcóatls, and that different Mesoamerican kingdoms, at least during the Post-Classic Period, embraced that legend and those symbols as part of a strategy to legitimize their position of power, recognize a seat of power, and render homage to a noble lineage.

If the Mexica identified Tula de Hidalgo as the sacred city of Quetzalcóatl and attributed greater historical importance to it than to Cholula or Teotihuacán, it is because that was "their Tula," their metropolis. The Mexica had been part of the northern provinces of the Toltec kingdom, perhaps located in present-day Querétaro, and had come down toward the Valley of Mexico when their metropolis suffered a crisis and was abandoned, sometime before 1200 CE. Even in their days of splendor, the Mexica marauded the ancient city of the *Atlantes* (great figures of warriors sculpted in the round) and *chacmools*, digging in search of pieces they recycled as offerings at Tenochtitlan, and finding inspiration in designs of the abandoned city to create their own works of art. The Mexica considered themselves direct heirs of that Tula, locating Teotihuacán in a more remote time, at the creation of the world.

The fall of Tula, apparently in the midst of serious conflict toward the year 1200 CE, marks the beginning of the Late Post-Classic, a period that would conclude with the Spanish Conquest.

THE WATER LORDS

On the eve of the Spanish Conquest, the Valley of Mexico was experiencing remarkable urban development. There were many cities, all of them populous. The chroniclers write of crowds in the streets and canals, and express surprise at the hubbub in the marketplaces: Chalco-Atenco, Xochimilco, Coyoacán, Culhuacan, Iztapalapa, Texcoco, Tlacopan, Azcapotzalco, Mexico-Tenochtitlan, Mexico-Tlatelolco, and dozens of medium-sized towns like Coatlinchan, Mixcoac or Tacubaya. More than two million people lived in the Valley of Mexico, spread out among these population centers.

Most of these cities were ruled by families of Nahua nobility, but many of them were home to other ethnic groups, particularly the Otomí and Matlatzinca. The Nahua used the term *altépetl* (which means water-mountain or water hill) to refer to the city, with its population and its land. Each *altépetl* was headed by its *tlatoani* or king, who was assisted by an extensive bureaucracy of judges, collectors of tribute, captains, and other administrators. Although each city enjoyed considerable independence in its internal management, there were three great kingdoms that ranked above all the others; these received tribute from the rest and could call on them to participate in wars or public works. The three kingdoms were Tlacopan, Texcoco, and Mexico-Tenochtitlan; this was the most famous of the Post-Classic Triple Alliances. Tlacopan obtained only one-fifth of the tribute from the subordinate lordships, and carried little weight in the alliance, whereas Texcoco had a fairly symmetrical relationship with Tenochtitlan, except during times of war. There was no doubt that the Mexica were the military leaders of the alliance.

This Triple Alliance was a necessity. No kingdom in the Valley of Mexico could have singlehandedly administered the complex system of routes and marketplaces, tributary provinces, and networks of loyalty among noble lineages. It was not just a matter of administrative capacity, but of the need to respect traditional authority of the kingdoms over certain populations and ethnic groups. This helps us to understand why the Mexica and Texcocan peoples, who had just fought against and defeated the Tepanec of Azcapotzalco, invited Tlacopan, also a Tepanec kingdom, to join in the alliance: they needed to count on the sway that the Tepanec wielded over the peoples to the west of the valley and the Toluca area, particularly the Matlatzinca. Furthermore, the Azcapotzalco marketplace played a crucial role in the valley's economy.

The Valley of Mexico's population density and urban complexity at the beginning of the sixteenth century were sustained by a highly prosperous agriculture. In the two centuries prior to the arrival of Cortés, referred to in detail by colonial sources, only two great famines are mentioned, which were the result of prolonged droughts. The valley's high agricultural yield is explained by the extensive use of irrigation, and by a system of *chinampas*. Fields were fertilized with mud and bat droppings, and some crops were produced from seedbeds, which made it possible to cultivate only the healthiest plants in each plot.

The agricultural products of the Post-Classic Nahua were the same as those of Teotihuacán, the Toltec, and the majority of Mesoamerican peoples: corn, beans, squash (especially pumpkin, i.e., the species *Cucurbita pepo*), chili peppers, various types of tomatoes, chia (a species of sage), and amaranth, among others. Furthermore, the valley was capable of providing many other edible resources: a great variety of fishes, birds, frogs, diverse insects, snakes, rabbits, deer, and many other species. There was salt at the bottom of the lake (in the Texcoco area), and in the neighboring forests it was possible to cultivate maguey (agave) and obtain firewood. Some fruit bushes and trees, such as *tejocote* (Mexican hawthorn) and *capulín* (chokecherry), were also among the region's resources.

Each kingdom relied on its own subjects' production, plus tribute from other populations in its sphere of influence. Settlements had to pay tribute in kind to their lords, as well as being forced to take part in war and public works. The large kingdoms, such as those that formed the Triple Alliance, received tribute from distant provinces and could fill their storehouses with quetzal and macaw feathers, gold and crafted jewelry, decorated cloths, cotton, jade, cacao, and other products. These luxury goods were reserved for use by the nobility and for religious celebrations.

The population in all the Valley of Mexico's Nahua cities was divided into two social groups, the nobles or *pipiltin* (singular *pilli*) and the common people or *macehualtin* (singular *macehualli*). One was *pilli* or *macehualli* by birth, and only in exceptional cases of military valor could a *macehualli* enter the ranks of the nobility. The *macehualtin* were agriculturists, fishermen, artisans, and other workers who all paid tribute to the nobility. *Pipiltin* were engaged in tasks related to government, the administration of justice, and the organization of war and religion. They lived off the products that the *macehualtin* paid as tribute to the palace and the *tlatoani* distributed periodically. Some of the *pipiltin* received tributary benefits directly, as in the case of judges, because the profits from certain lands were linked to that office. Some even possessed a kind of feudal property they could sell and bequeath; these were officials who had distinguished themselves in war and certain nobles whom the *tlatoani* wished to reward. Both received lands, enjoying their products, and benefited from the personal services of the peasants who lived on and worked them.

Legislation reinforced class distinctions and helped consolidate the nobility's prestige and power. The nobles used dress and jewelry that were prohibited for the rest of the population. Even supposing that he might be able to buy it in the market, a *macehualli* could not use a piece of jade jewelry, and if he did, he could be sentenced to death. The nobles wore cotton cloth, not the coarse fiber used by the common people; their houses were richer, higher, and better decorated; noblemen could have many wives, but not so for the *macehualtin*. Nobles slept on comfortable beds with feather mattresses, puffed feather pillows, cotton sheets, and deerskins. The *macehualtin* lived very austerely.

This division of society into two classes was qualified by a series of exceptions and inconsistencies. Artisans were not obliged to participate in public works and only paid tribute in kind. Moreover, there were artisans of great prestige connected with the palace who lived comfortably under the lords' protection. Merchants did not pay tribute with labor either, nor were they forced to go to war like the rest of the *macehualtin*: their service to the kingdom took the delicate form of espionage in enemy cities, to which they could travel without arousing suspicion. Elite eagle, jaguar, and coyote warriors and those of the Otomí battalion lived a very special life: they entered combat with almost maniacal enthusiasm, and frequently died on the battlefield or on their adversaries' sacrificial altars. But during peacetime they enjoyed a position of privilege and social recognition that was unique: they danced, drank cacao, enjoyed the company of courtesans and, if any of these warriors reached old age, they devoted themselves to instructing youth in the schools.

Among the peasants there were those who worked land they considered their own because they were members of one of the many *calpultin* (singular *calpulli*; neighborhoods created on the basis of former clans), whose right to settle there had been recognized in the history of an *altépetl*. These workers, which early documents called *calpuleque* (singular *calpule*), paid tribute to their *tlatoani*. But there were also peasants who worked and lived on lands that had been conquered and granted as fiefs to nobles or army officers. In some documents, these workers are called *mayeque* (singular *maye*; i.e., "those who have hands"). According to colonial documents, the situation of the *mayeque* was described as worse than that of the *calpuleque*, and this was due, apparently, to the excessive tribute in kind and labor that the *mayeque* had to pay the noble who owned the land.

The extreme lower end of the social scale was also differentiated and enhanced by those living under circumstances and in conditions far more hazardous than those of the common *macehualli*. The populous Post-Classic cities sheltered vagabonds, delinquents, and scoundrels of various descriptions. In theory, all individuals were subject to and protected by the community to which they belonged, but when they became detached from their community, it was impossible for them to incorporate themselves into another; their only recourse was vagrancy. That occurred when an adolescent decided to flout paternal authority and leave home, when someone who had committed a crime fled to evade punishment, or when a community or city sentenced one of its members to exile for a serious misdeed. This was apparently the origin of the market porters or *tamemes* (from *tlamama,* he who carries), beggars, prostitutes, thieves, and highwaymen of whom the records speak. There are some quite dramatic descriptions of ragged, disheveled individuals covered with scrapes and scratches, staggering through the streets, restless or drunk, on the fringes of humanity, rummaging nightly through the marketplace in search of scraps left by traders.

The presence of these unattached individuals is disconcerting and seems all the more out of place in a rigorously organized corporate society. Among the Nahua of the Valley of Mexico, one would belong to a *calpulli* of workers, a tribe of merchants or a noble lineage. Not belonging was virtually tantamount to not existing. Noble lineages were scrupulously documented in the codices. Persistent polygamy allowed ruling families to form a court by the end of one generation, facilitating the existence of an extensive bureaucracy comprised of the sovereign's blood relatives. As regards worker communities, we know that they were the basic unit of all pre-Hispanic social organization. Debate has raged as to whether they were family-based groups, such as clans, or administrative demarcations established by the State. All in all, documentary sources indicate that the answer lies somewhere in between; there is no doubt that there were family connections in the *calpulli*, members were related and recognized common ancestors, but at the same time, once established in a city and subject to its laws, the *calpulli* functioned as an administrative unit for purposes of tax collection and participation in war, as well as religious observance. There was a limit to the involvement of the *tlatoani* in the *calpulli*, but there were also restrictions upon the autonomy of the communities, due to their commitment to obedience to a higher political power. The communities' motivation to belong to such a political order is obvious: it provided organized urban life, a marketplace, and military and even divine protection.

The *calpullis* had an active life of their own within their urban neighborhoods. Their members prayed to their own patron god, contributed teams in rotation to the maintenance of the temple, protected the less fortunate members of their own community, organized festivities, and gathered daily in the neighborhood plazas and narrow streets to rest, chat, and tell jokes. Every *calpulli* recognized a chief, which some sources call an "older brother." This chief made the required decisions with the aid of a council of elders. The meetings of this council and of family heads from each neighborhood took place in a community house.

The *tlatoani* had collectors and foremen responsible for overseeing the taxes that every *calpulli* had to pay and organizing the people of the *calpulli* for public projects. Furthermore, the *calpulli's* male children were obliged to attend a sort of school in which they received military training, the name of which in Nahuatl was *telpochcalli*, or youth house. In this *telpochcalli* the boys received training from experienced warriors, and those who distinguished themselves by their bravery could rise to the rank of captain or elite warrior, authentic heroes in the eyes of that society.

Young nobles also went to school, called *calmécac* in the old texts. There they received a stricter education clearly geared to preparing them for positions of command: military strategy, the priesthood, and government. Some of these youths would remain in the temples as priests of the realm, while others would participate in administration and government. In the *calmécac* the students' behavior was closely supervised and contact with women was prohibited. In the *telpochcalli*, on the other hand, discipline was more relaxed, and apparently boys frequently had affairs with girls of their same rank, whom they met at evening dance practice which was conducted at the *cuicacalli,* or house of song.

Membership in a larger unit, a kingdom, was affirmed by participation in the city's many religious celebrations that took place throughout the year. School-age youths performed dances and joined in ritual games and skirmishes on top of the temples in the sacred central enclosure, while the entire populace watched, participating more actively in those that took place on city streets and in plazas and neighboring sanctuaries.

The most intense rituals of all celebrated in the Nahua cities had to be those that involved the death of human beings. The Mexica stood out among all the peoples of Ancient Mexico for the frenzy with which they practiced different types of human sacrifice. At times it was considered necessary to immolate dozens of babies to satisfy Tláloc, the god of storm and rain; they were thrown into whirlpools of water or were sacrificed on altars erected in the mountains. An old woman was beheaded at one of the yearly feasts, and a warrior ran through the city holding the severed head by its hair and waving it in all directions. To worship Xipe, the god of spring, a priest would parade around draped in the skin of a sacrificial victim. Wounds, dismemberment, and death were a constant presence in Tenochtitlan and neighboring cities. The populace was given the opportunity to recover from these dramatic scenes through the catharsis of public diversion: street games, comic rituals such as the greased pole, and satirical comedies in which people could make fun of boys dressed as bumblebees that bumped into each other and fell from the cornice of a building or of actors playing the aged, the crippled or the sick.

Besides their religious significance, doubtless some of these sacrificial occasions were devoted to demonstrating the military might of the Triple Alliance's armies. The campaign against the Huasteca Region undertaken by Ahuítzotl, the most bellicose of the Mexica *tlatoani*, culminated in the sacrifice of thousands upon thousands of enemies—men, women, and children who for a period of four days and nights formed four lines

before the steps of as many temples of the Valley of Mexico, await-
ing their turn to mount the sacrificial stone. While they marched
to their death they intoned the traditional sad song of a bird.

ON THE EVE OF THE CONQUEST

By the time of the Spanish Conquest, the Triple Alliance, led by
Tenochtitlan, had managed to extend its domain as far as both
coasts, and north and south from Querétaro to Oaxaca, besides
controlling the area of Soconusco in Chiapas. The Gulf of Mexico coastal plain had been subdued. The prosperous cities of
the Totonac, with their stone-paved streets, networks of irrigation and drainage canals, orchards and gardens, fortified ceremonial centers, and abundance of corn, cacao, vanilla, fruit,
cotton, wood, and other products, periodically received the
disturbing visit of tribute collectors sent by the Mexica. They
were also obliged to protect and shelter the merchants who
traveled through the area on expeditions originating in allied
cities. The Huastec, northern neighbors of the Totonac, constantly challenged Mexica expansion: no sooner did the Mexica
return home to celebrate their military victory over the Huastec
than the latter declared themselves in disobedience and refused to pay tribute. Colonial sources attribute the conquest of
the Huasteca Region to several *tlatoani*, an unequivocal sign that
none of them had achieved it completely.

In the south, the Mexica were able to impose their conditions of tribute and trade on the Mixtec kingdoms of the mountain areas and the Oaxaca Valley, as well as on the Zapotec in
the valley. But there were several independent kingdoms on the
coast grouped around the leadership of Tututepec, as well as on
the isthmus. In what is now the State of Guerrero, the Tlapanec
paid tribute to the Triple Alliance, but there was tenacious resistance by some settlements. The lordship of Teloloapan, a rich

producer of cacao, persistently refused to accept passage through it by trade caravans protected by the Mexica and fell victim to the most atrocious war of the time: the entire population was exterminated (including even the dogs and turkeys) and the lordship was repopulated by Nahua settlers sent from the Valley of Mexico. On the other hand, the rustic chieftainships of Yopitzinco were never subdued, and their inhabitants—linguistically related to the Apaches—occasionally attacked tributary villages and even Mexica garrisons.

In the west, the Triple Alliance was met with an impenetrable barrier. The Tarascan kingdom, with its center at Lake Pátzcuaro, was ruled by another Triple Alliance consisting of Ihuatzio, Tzintzuntzan, and Pátzcuaro. That alliance's influence extended over all of Michoacán and part of the present-day states of Guerrero, Colima, Jalisco, and Guanajuato. The Purépecha people's use of copper for certain agricultural tools and some weapons has led several researchers to suggest that a qualitative change was under way in Michoacán unlike anything Mesoamerica—with its Neolithic technology—had ever seen. Nevertheless, there is no firm evidence of agricultural production substantially different from the rest of Mesoamerica or of a military advantage comparable, for example, to that which the Assyrians enjoyed with their iron swords in the Old World. The Purépecha defended their territory well; they used walls, small forts, and lookout points; they organized their military campaigns with a unified command and were able to resist armies sent against them from the central valleys of Mexico. Yet their cities, architecture, and dress, and even their writing and artistic production were notably more austere than those that characterized the Nahua as of the Teotihuacán period.

As for the Maya region, the areas of greatest demographic concentration and largest number of cities were the highlands of Chiapas and Guatemala and, above all, the Yucatán Peninsula. After the fall of Mayapán, there were no less than 17 independent lordships on the peninsula, but this fragmentation was no obstacle to the development of a rather prosperous economy that benefited from active coastal trade. The port of Tulum in Quintana Roo was a vital link between the navigable routes that united the peninsula with Central America and the Caribbean, as well as the footpaths leading to Tehuantepec and, from there, to the territories controlled by the Triple Alliance. The Maya traded with the Late Post-Classic Nahua. The Mexica lacked the power that Teotihuacán had to invade those territories. In fact, the territorial expansion of the Triple Alliance of Mexico, Texcoco, and Tlacopan seems precarious when compared to the stable, vast imperial dominion of Teotihuacán.

EPILOGUE

The Totonac saw in Cortés an acceptable ally with whom to shake off Mexica domination, and it would be a mistake to reproach them for that alliance. They had no way of knowing, for example, that smallpox, whooping cough, and typhus would eventually kill them, and that their cities would be left deserted, their corn fields and orchards converted to pastures. The Tlaxcaltec ceased their initial resistance and chose to unite with the Spaniards because it seemed to them that such an alliance would ensure the integrity of their territory. They owed no loyalty whatsoever to the Mexica. On the contrary, the Mexica were their enemies. From the time of Cortés' arrival in Yucatán until the end of the siege of Tlatelolco with the capture of Cuauhtémoc, there were many lordships which, after having been defeated in combat or coming to terms with Cortés, joined his ranks. The conquest of Tenochtitlan was a victory of the Tlaxcaltec, Texcocan, Totonac, and many other indigenous groups. It was the last war of pre-Hispanic Mexico, albeit led by a small army that was not part of that story.

With the fall of the Mexica capital, the Spaniards controlled most of the former territories subjected to the Triple Alliance. In the following three years, with a few battles and numerous pacts, the Spaniards subjected even the independent territories to the crown of Castile: Michoacán, Metztitlán, Tututepec, Tehuantepec, and several localities in the highlands of Chiapas and Guatemala. The much slower conquest of Yucatán was inconclusive for close to two hundred years. The lordship of Tayasal, a refuge in Lake Petén-Itzá, was not subjugated until 1697. The conquest and occupation of the Sierra Madre Occidental and territories north of Mesoamerica, populated by hunter-gatherers and some village agriculturists, was a goal that was not entirely achieved even during the three centuries of colonial history.

THE COLONIAL ERA TO 1760

BERNARDO GARCÍA-MARTÍNEZ

THE SECOND MAJOR PERIOD OF MEXICO'S HISTORY is the colonial era, defined as the years of Spanish rule, during which the country (as we can now call it) achieved political unity under the name of New Spain. Historians have traditionally said that the colonial era (also referred to as viceregal) began with the fall of Mexico-Tenochtitlan in 1521 and ended with the declaration of independence three centuries later.

But such chronological precision is valid only with regard to the formal existence of New Spain as a political entity, and is not applicable to other aspects of this era. In terms of economics and society, for example, or demographics and culture, it is impossible to speak of a period that commenced in 1521 and ended in 1821. Trying to set exact dates in these matters would not make sense. The market economy, for instance, changed gradually as the Spaniards expanded their activities in the areas of commerce, agriculture/livestock, and mining throughout the sixteenth century, but the subsistence economy of pre-Hispanic times persisted alongside it, and both types of economic organization continued through the years of independence without changing in any fundamental way. There were economic tremors in the early nineteenth century, but the primary cause consisted of the aggressive tax measures that Spain implemented in 1804. The population declined drastically between 1519 and 1575, followed by several years of relative stability, and then a period of growth which changed in about 1736, but not in 1821. Environmental history, which studies humans' impact on their physical surroundings, shows that the Conquest caused very substantial changes in the landscape of Mesoamerica, as happened with the introduction of livestock. But in environmental history, the end of the colonial era has no special significance; rather, it is more important to mark a chronological boundary at around 1780, when large-scale logging began to supply wood for shipbuilding, or approximately 1880, when the railroads caused very profound changes in land use.

Considering these factors, the colonial era can be delimited by different time frames, depending on the topic being addressed. The beginning dates do not vary much, because they coincide with a time during which almost the entire world experienced the enormous transformations that followed Columbus' voyages and the subsequent contacts and exchanges between Europe, Africa, Asia, and the Americas. However, the era's end dates differ widely, because the changes involved were not as momentous nor did they all happen at the same time. Nevertheless, we can agree that there were major and diverse political, social, economic, and cultural transformations as of around 1760. This is an acceptable date for the end of the stage of Mexico's history that began when the Spaniards arrived on Mesoamerican soil. We will call this the colonial era because that is the custom and for the sake of convenience, realizing that we are excluding the last 50 or 60 years of Spanish rule. Those years will be considered in a separate chapter that also addresses—despite the political rupture—the years subsequent to the process of gaining independence.

1519-1610: LAYING THE FOUNDATION

1519-1530: The invasion of the conquistadors

The beginning of the colonial era was associated with a series of very dramatic events that started with the arrival of the Spaniards and their first incursions into Mesoamerica. This action initiated the Conquest, a term we should understand not only as the outcome of a military victory, but also as a complex process of confrontation and accommodation that continued until around 1560. Viewed in this way, the Conquest lasted slightly more than 40 years (divided between an initial phase and a consolidation phase), which were followed by a period of another 50 years that it took for the results of the Conquest—i.e., New Spain—to progress beyond the formative years of its founding and become mature.

Before going into detail about early events, we must reflect on the context in which they occurred. This subject takes us to the expansion of Europe's economy and culture as a result of Portuguese maritime exploration. As of the mid-fifteenth century, Portugal's voyages led to the creation of trade enclaves at some points on the coasts of Africa, India, and Southeast Asia, as well as to Portuguese occupation of Cape Verde, the Azores, and other islands in the Atlantic. These ventures were prompted by European demand for spices and silks and, in the case of the islands, an interest in planting sugarcane. Since some were not inhabited and in others the native population was decimated, the sugar economy was built on slave labor. Thus, the first major movement of people that occurred at this time was the transport of African slaves from the coasts of Guinea and Angola. The slaves were purchased by the Portuguese—or captured by them—to work on the islands. The neighboring Castilian Spaniards copied the Portuguese by bringing slaves to the Canary Islands.

The desire of the Kings of Castile and León to participate more actively in the new trade routes motivated them to finance Christopher Columbus' voyage in search of India in 1492, which produced the results we are all well aware of. Spanish occupation of the Caribbean Islands, especially Cuba, Jamaica, Santo Domingo, and Puerto Rico, to a great extent replicated their experience on the Canary Islands: violent occupation, sugar production, collapse of the native population, and introduction of African slaves. There was, however, one difference, namely the Castilian Spaniards' interest in emigrating to those new lands and establishing permanent settlements and a formal government, including some sort of legal system, while also maintaining ongoing ties with their country of origin, importing livestock, and engaging in a variety of agricultural activities. In short, they wished to reproduce, insofar as possible, the Castilian cultural and social milieu. This is understandable because Castile experienced a high rate of demographic growth and an economy incapable of meeting the needs of a large portion of its population. Then the Portuguese were the ones to follow in the footsteps of the Castilians, repeating the process on the Brazilian coast.

These events, which occurred after the expulsion of the Muslims from the Iberian Peninsula, coincided in 1492 with the consolidation of the monarchy under the crowns of Castile and Aragón, and were soon reaffirmed by the ascension of Charles I of the House of Habsburg (also known as the House of Austria) to the throne. He is better known as Charles V, Holy Roman Emperor. Supported by this unification, the political power of its new king, and the economic advantages obtained in the Americas, Spain was on its way to becoming the dominant power in the European world.[1] This potential was realized

---

[1] The use of the name "Spain" and calling people "Spaniards" in the context of the sixteenth and seventeenth centuries is fairly inexact, because the

with the conquest of Mexico and the subsequent conquest of Peru, which resulted from the Spanish advancing beyond the islands and onto the continent itself.

At the same time, the American continent, which did not yet have that name but was defined as the New World, began to play a role in the circuit of exchanges that was gradually beginning to encompass the globe. Such exchanges involved people, animals, plants, metals, manufactured goods, and everything associated with them, from diseases to culture. Naturally, exchange activities were managed first and foremost with a view to serving European interests, and Spanish interests in particular. That explains the evolution of colonial dependence which would characterize the Americas in the centuries to come.

In general terms, that was the context in which the events associated with the beginning of the colonial era in Mexico took place. Specifically, those events originated in Cuba, where the Spaniards had already been established for almost 20 years. Wanting to expand, they organized several expeditions. In 1517, a voyage led by Francisco Hernández de Córdoba brought them to the coast of Yucatán. This trip, which was more of an exploratory journey, produced the first contact between the European and Mesoamerican worlds.

The first expedition was followed by another, and a third, by then with the goal of conquest clearly in mind. This implied that the Spaniards had to resolve a variety of legal issues among themselves in order to define and regulate the privileges or rights to which the conquistadors aspired. The third expedition, organized by Hernando Cortés (also known as Hernán Cortés), left Cuba in 1519, cut off its ties there, and ended up

---

various monarchies on the Iberian Peninsula maintained their individuality and no "Spanish kingdom" existed as such. With this clarified, we must note that from a New World perspective, and especially from that of New Spain, the reference to Spain and Spaniards is justifiable and has been common practice since the sixteenth century.

founding a town—Veracruz—and setting up a *cabildo* (town council or body of local government in the Castilian tradition). This is how Cortés justified and managed to organize this incursion into the interior on his own. The invasion, which included some military encounters, reached its climax with the Spaniards' entry into Mexico-Tenochtitlan at the end of that same year. Cortés resorted to several political maneuvers to achieve his goals, most notably an alliance with the lords of the Tlaxcalan region.

We should recall that Mesoamerica then consisted of hundreds of lordships or small states, principalities or political entities that enjoyed varying degrees of autonomy. In Nahuatl, these were called *altépetl*. Although the same concept existed in other indigenous languages, the Nahuatl word was most commonly used; later, the Spanish would translate *altépetl* as *pueblo de indios* or merely *pueblo* (native autonomous municipality). Almost all of these entities were headed by a ruler or hereditary "lord" who, in fact, acted as a minor king and was the person who represented political legitimacy (*tlatoani* in Nahuatl, a word the Spanish later translated as *cacique*). These lordships or principalities were the basic units of pre-Hispanic political organization. Many paid tribute to the Triple Alliance (the imperial structure prevailing at the time), but others—such as the Tlaxcalans—were independent.

The Spaniards' entry into Mexico-Tenochtitlan was peaceful in terms of formalities, but within a few days it became a military occupation based on the subjection and imprisonment of Moteczuma, the Mexica king (also known in English as Montezuma). This occupation lasted for seven months, from November 1519 to June 1520. The Spaniards took advantage of this period to gather information and muster resources, but above all to establish alliances with other lords or kings in a way that was consistent with existing Mesoamerican political practices. During these seven months, the political integrity of the Triple

Alliance crumbled, although at the same time a Mexica resistance movement emerged that culminated in the overthrow of Moteczuma and the expulsion of the Spaniards and their allies (an event they call the *Noche Triste* [Night of Sorrows or Sad Night], which would become quite important in popular history).

Almost immediately, a smallpox epidemic broke out in the country, an occurrence whose devastating effects were immediate. The disease first sprang up in Veracruz around May 1520, introduced by a Spanish group loyal to Cuban interests that arrived there with the idea of stopping Cortés (the Pánfilo de Narváez expedition). Smallpox was one of the components of the above-mentioned circuit of exchanges that was making its way around the world, and until that time, was unknown in Mesoamerica. As a result, the population was extremely vulnerable to the contagion: in less than a year, it had spread inland, causing the death of no less than three million people. Some estimates place this figure as high as ten million.

That was when the war for the conquest of Mexico really began: a tremendously violent and unequal battle in which the Spaniards' exclusive ownership of horses and firearms gave them the advantage. The war's most prominent episode was the siege of Mexico-Tenochtitlan which, although weakened by smallpox, held out for a long year that ended when the Spanish took the city and captured the Mexica's last king, Cuauhtémoc, on August 13, 1521 (the date that the Spaniards used as a symbol of their triumph in the Conquest and celebrated throughout the entire colonial era). But this episode was not the whole war. Battles took place in other lordships or principalities, both those within the Triple Alliance and others that were independent, until 1525 or 1526. The Spaniards won every military encounter, but not without intense fighting and great difficulties (of which we know little, since most sources limit themselves to telling about the siege of Mexico-Tenochtitlan). At the same time, many of the political entities in the central and southern parts of the country came under Spanish control through a variety of pressures and political maneuvers without violence, or at least without open warfare. The kingdom of Michoacán was the most prominent of these owing to its size and political importance.

The direct result of this process was the creation of a formal relationship of domination between the Spaniards and each of the native political entities, which numbered more than 500. Accomplishing this entailed the intense political activity which took place from 1522 to 1525 involving discussions, negotiations, and accommodations—often violent ones. To set up this relationship the Spanish used the *encomienda,* a sort of concession system which consisted of formally granting each political entity to an individual conquistador, who became its *encomendero* or overseer. On the one hand, this system meant that the lordships or principalities would continue to be about the same type of political entities they had been before, with the same powers to govern and collect tribute. On the other, it implied that the *encomendero* would receive a substantial part of that tribute. The *encomenderos* were responsible for staying on the alert militarily and for ensuring there were no reversals of the Spanish victories and alliances. Some political entities—those considered very important or special, such as Mexico-Tenochtitlan or the Tlaxcalan lordships, for example—were placed under the direct control of representatives of the Spanish Crown.

Installation of a central government representing the Castilian monarchy was being accomplished by the time the conquistadors consolidated their victories on the king's behalf. A political formality that declared and legitimized the "Kingdom of New Spain" as the successor to "Moteczuma's Empire" (i.e., the Triple Alliance) was the first step in the process. Consistent with this approach, the conquistadors decided to rebuild the defeated and partially destroyed city of Mexico (despite the problems created by the city's location on a lakebed) in order to turn it into the capital of their new conquest. Aside from these measures of enormous symbolic significance, installing a government entailed organizing a variety of positions and functions, especially for tribute collection and the administration of justice, which were of great importance to the Crown. For its part, the Crown felt it was appropriate to remove some provinces or regions from Mexico's sphere of authority. Thus, it arranged for the creation of separate governments in Pánuco (for a short time only), Guatemala (beginning in 1527), and Yucatán (from 1527 to 1549 and again as of 1565).

While all this was happening, starting in 1522 or 1523 many Spaniards began arriving and made their increasingly numerous presence felt. They were called *pobladores* (settlers) to distinguish them from the military conquistadors, with whom they were forced to get along, although their interests gradually diverged further and further. Both groups, but especially the settlers, went about establishing several population centers (which they made official by erecting a town hall in each), as well as commercial ties both domestically and with the West Indies and Spain. They also began importing European animals, plants, and goods to New Spain, and promoted the spread of livestock breeding, farming, and manufacturing. By doing so they planted the seeds of what would inevitably, over time, become well-defined culturally Hispanicized regions. This occurred, for instance, around the most important of these new towns, Puebla de los Ángeles, founded in 1531.

The arrival of friars from mendicant orders (Franciscans, Dominicans, and Augustinians) from 1524 on and the gradual establishment of their *doctrinas* (evangelization and ecclesiastical administration units) in each of the conquered lordships were no less important in this context. The friars were held in high regard and were of capital importance for the ideological justification of the Conquest, since according to Christian think-ing the Conquest was only acceptable if it advanced the conver-sion of pagans as its ultimate goal. In practice friars, also called *doctrineros* and serving as parish priests, carried out their tasks with the support of the *encomenderos* and, most importantly, the aid of the native lords. Moreover, they depended on tribute for their sustenance. From this means of operation and fortified by the zeal with which they worked, in a short period of time they were able to disseminate a variety of religious practices such as baptism, attendance at mass (which was accompanied by mu-sic, songs, and various fiestas), and the adoration of the saints. They also imposed Christian standards with regard to sexuality and marriage.

* * *

The events described above call for some commentary in order to appropriately portray those initial years of the colonial era. First, the Mesoamerican world experienced radical changes, but there were also continuities and aspects that persisted. The most noteworthy of these was the maintenance of the lordships, which remained vital to local government, the tribute system, and evangelization. Continuity was apparent among the lord-ships that entered into alliances with the conquistadors, very notably those of the Tlaxcalans (who maintained privileged sta-tus throughout the whole colonial era), but it was also evident where lords were subjected by force. In most, once they had been defeated as a result of military actions, new lords allied with the Spaniards took their place and kept local institutions functioning.

The explanation for this continuity is very simple: there were very few Spaniards and their ability to act was limited. They had achieved a dominant position, but they could not —nor did they want to—take responsibility for the infinite number of government tasks required in such a large and diverse country. So how could they meet their goals, which were to stay there, obtain wealth and other benefits, impose their values, and maintain an acceptable degree of security? Only by delegating the duties and work they themselves could not do, that is, by establishing a system of indirect rule. In Mesoamerica this was possible both owing to the former existence of the Triple Alliance (which was largely based on an equally indirect system of domination), and because it had a political, social, and economic system that was compatible with the Spaniards' goals. The key lay in the continuity of the lordships, which meant continuity in government functions, the administration of justice, maintaining order, organizing labor, and collecting tribute. These principles were put into practice thanks to Cortés' political shrewdness. It may seem paradoxical, but hundreds of lordships survived through these years of earth-shaking changes without any alteration in the lineage of their rulers, the composition of their society, their economic life, territorial boundaries, possessions, relative autonomy, and basic culture. After all, the arrangement was also advantageous to the lordships, or at least to the ruling elites who, for the time being, maintained their privileged status.

There was a great deal more conflict in relations among the Spaniards themselves. The conquistadors competed fiercely for the best positions, such as the most profitable *encomiendas* or the choicest government appointments. The good judgment of some was clouded by the greed, irresponsibility, and violence of others, and by 1525 they were embroiled in such visceral fights that the whole Conquest itself was at the point of collapse. Intervention by the Crown, which established an *audiencia* (royal tribunal or court of justice with governing powers) in 1528, and the arrival of the friars and other settlers counteracted the instability, although they also brought in other reasons for conflict. The most serious bone of contention was represented by

Nuño de Guzmán, who led an ill-fated administration as the first president of the *audiencia* and later set out to conquer Western Mesoamerica using much more violent and less political methods than Cortés had. Anxious to distance himself from New Spain, he christened his conquests as the "Kingdom of New Galicia" and gave them their own government in 1531. This political construct was formally recognized by the Crown, but never managed to become completely independent from Mexico.

1530-1560: Consolidation of the Conquest

What can be termed the consolidation of the Conquest took place from about 1530 to 1560. Compared with the previous years, it was a period of relative calm, but even so there was a great deal of ferment. We will now summarize the most important aspects of those years.

First, and in very general terms, we should note that this was a peaceful period. Peace descended as a result of the end of the almost constant wars among the native states, the conclusion of the military phase of the Conquest, and the cessation of armed clashes between the Spaniards, but also because of the wise decision to use the system of indirect rule discussed above. There were exceptions to this chronology or timeline in Yucatán, where the Conquest began later and took longer, and in New Galicia, where Guzmán's aggressive policies provoked a bloody rebellion by the Caxcan Indians known as the Mixtón War (1540-1542) in the north of what is now the State of Jalisco.

A second aspect of this consolidation period was, paradoxically, the removal of conquistadors from formal positions of power and their replacement by learned officials (or at least ones who behaved in a more civilized manner) within the highest spheres of government. This was equivalent to establishing a civilian government, which caused resentment among the conquistadors. Yet the Crown imposed its will, and beginning in 1535 insisted that it be represented by the most authoritative figure available: a *virrey* or viceroy (literally, a vice-king). Most of the viceroys would be members of the Castilian high nobility.

The consolidation of the Conquest was also manifest in the accommodation of the lordships or principalities (*altépetl*) —the basic units of pre-Hispanic political organization—to the colonial regime. It was a complex process influenced by a variety of circumstances. Of particular importance was another terrible epidemic that broke out in 1545. This time it was measles, another disease that had been completely unknown in Mesoamerica, and it caused a second and probably even more devastating drop in the Mesoamerican population.

Regardless of this tragedy, the adjustment of the lordships to the colonial regime involved profound changes that can to a certain degree be understood as the price they had to pay for their survival. There were enormous differences between native political entities reflecting their complex and varied pre-Hispanic background, but the Spaniards set out to erase these differences, partly because they could not understand them and also partially due to their desire to create certain homogeneity. They took several measures to accomplish this.

The first was to impose a corporate organization similar to that of the Castilian *cabildos* or town councils on the native political entities. There was a logic to this, given that both the lordships and town councils were recognized as political entities with legal standing, territorial boundaries, and relative autonomy. Part of this accommodation can be seen in the fact that the native lordships were redefined, as previously mentioned, using the concept of *pueblo de indios*, or merely pueblo (although the Nahuatl concept of *altépetl* was also preserved, as was its equivalents in other languages). The new town councils of the pueblos were called *cuerpos de república* (literally, "republican bodies," meaning local corporate governments) and were composed of mayors and councillors with roles fairly similar to those of their Spanish counterparts. These positions were reserved for noblemen or people of distinguished lineage (called *principales*). One additional position—that of governor—was set aside for the caciques (the former lords or their legitimate heirs, as explained above). A system of restricted elections was designed to allow the rotation of different groups or interests in power, and creation of a treasury or *caja de comunidad* was encouraged, although this only made sense over time as the use of money gradually became more common. In some cases, this sort of accommodation meant little more than putting a new name on pre-Hispanic practices, while in others it entailed a profound change, rife with conflict.

The second measure was to standardize all tribute charges. The model was for each household head in every pueblo to pay his *encomendero*, or directly to the Crown, as the case might be, one peso and half a *fanega* (about 0.8 bushels) of corn or its equivalent annually. (This was in addition to any local taxes carried over from previous times.) These tribute adjustments took a long time to implement (since, once again, the use of money had to become widespread) and, as could be expected, their effects on the commoners varied a great deal. The nobility and *principales* were usually exempt from these charges, as were their personal dependents (*mayeques*), who in some pueblos were almost as numerous as those who had to pay formal tribute (*macehuales*).

The third measure was to encourage or pressure the pueblos to bring their people together in urbanlike settlements. This was the origin of towns or villages with a central square, prominent church, and grid of streets, which exist to this day. Ordinarily, several settlements with these characteristics were formed in each pueblo, with the principal one designated the head village or seat (*cabecera*) and the others, subordinate villages (*sujetos*).

That idea was implemented very slowly in the early years, but ended up becoming one of the factors that had the greatest impact on the pueblos' adjustment to the colonial system and on their gradual transformation.

The development of evangelization was closely tied to the formation of settlements because the Christianizing friars or *doctrineros* were instrumental in all of the changes mentioned. We must remember that the pueblos constituted the friars' base of operations. They planned to establish a monastery with its respective church in each pueblo —preferably in the *cabecera*— and promoted the worship of a specific saint in each village or settlement. Furthermore, they played a role in the elections of the *cuerpos de república* and channeled a major part of the tribute they received to the expenses involved in worship. All this contributed to reinforcing a new identity for the pueblos and to highlighting the central role assigned to the Church, and to the saints in particular. With the use of this infrastructure, in addition to their ability to indoctrinate children and the natural turnover from one generation to the next, the friars managed (at times using violence) to suppress or marginalize pre-Hispanic rites and priests. But they consolidated positive aspects of their work at the same time, spreading cultural elements and conducting enormously valuable historical and linguistic studies, such as the works of Fray Toribio de Motolinía and Fray Bernardino de Sahagún. They also began construction of their monumental and beautiful monasteries, designed to shelter multitudes and to house the functions that were part of their mission of conquest and acculturation.

In another sphere, an additional aspect of the Conquest's consolidation was the strengthening of ties with the outside world, although this was somewhat limited. Spain did not allow its American possessions any freedom in this regard, and the movements of people, goods, and news were strictly controlled and subject to restrictions, quotas, and fixed trade routes.

In Spain, Seville was the only port authorized to do business with the Americas. In New Spain, this was the exclusive privilege of Veracruz. In contrast, trade in the Pacific was less encumbered, and New Spain quickly established ties with Peru, using ports such as Huatulco and Acapulco.

Despite such restrictions, many Spanish settlers immigrated, numbering around 20 000 by mid-century. They located primarily in the interior (where they founded cities like Antequera de Oaxaca and Valladolid de Michoacán), and avoided mountainous and coastal areas. Together with Mexico City and Puebla (plus Guadalajara in New Galicia and Mérida in Yucatán), those cities established themselves as centers of power and the economy. Each city set up a town hall and council and a cathedral with its own bishop (and a church council), constructed European-style buildings, and developed its own cultural traits. Mexico City remained the most important urban center, not only because of its political supremacy, but also owing to its economic and cultural importance (it opened its own university in 1553). But all of these cities extended their influence over comparable areas defined by their respective bishoprics. Years later, these areas would provide the basis for several of the *intendencias* (new formal administrative provinces) of the late colonial era and, subsequently, the states of Mexico.

Concomitantly, both biological and cultural forms of *mestizaje* (crossbreeding, miscegenation or mixture) were emerging. Although some (especially the friars) were opposed to contact between the natives and the Spaniards, and despite the fact that laws always stressed differences between them, the two peoples rapidly established close ties. Most were informal sexual relationships, but there were also recognized marriages, especially between Spaniards and prominent Indian women. By 1550, many Spanish settlers already spoke Nahuatl and other native languages fluently. Similarly, quite a few native caciques and noblemen quickly adopted Spanish ways, and some reli-

gious schools made sophisticated aspects of European culture—such as Latin rhetoric—available to the indigenous elites
(although only for a short time). Furthermore, we must note
the inclusion of a large contingent of Africans (some 15 000 by
mid-century), who were brought to New Spain as slaves. The
vast majority were men, and they immediately began intermin-
gling with native women.

The development of this *mestizaje* ran parallel to the introduction of economic activities that were new to Mesoamerica,
and whose effects were felt both within the country and abroad.
Internally, they were stimulated by livestock breeding (particularly cattle- and sheep-raising), wheat and sugar production,
raising silkworms, and silver mining, all of which led to profound environmental changes. Elsewhere, trade with Spain and
Peru involved the exchange of silver, dyes, and manufactured
goods (textiles, tools, and furniture). At the same time, a labor
market emerged (especially in urban areas), new means of
transportation were created (with the use of mules being the
most common practice), and the use of money—minted in
Mexico as of 1536—started to spread. All this planted the seeds
of a capitalist economy and inserted New Spain into worldwide
exchange networks.

The demand created by a growing Spanish population and
the opening up of new trade routes encouraged the rise of a
special kind of agricultural/livestock business endowed with
solid infrastructure, a local labor force, rigorous organization,
and a clear profit motive. The sugar mills around Cuernavaca,
whose original labor force was composed primarily of African
slaves, was the first example of this. In these companies we can
discern an embryonic form of the haciendas that would come
to play such a major role in New Spain's rural life.

The final feature that should be associated with the consolidation of the Conquest is the beginning of northward expansion. This started with a variety of incursions or exploratory

trips, some motivated by the dream of finding riches that were said to be in the imaginary "Seven Cities of Cibola" located somewhere in the center of the continent. But what really sparked the expansion was the discovery in 1548 of silver mines in Zacatecas, in New Galicia. This event attracted huge numbers of settlers of every kind to this area and its surroundings—previously occupied only by tribes of hunter-gatherers— and that, in turn, fostered road construction, opening lands to cultivation, and a significant expansion of livestock activities.

* * *

Although most of New Spain was at peace, this does not mean there were no conflicts. They existed and were very intense, but were resolved without creating much of a ruckus. While in previous years the focus had been on dealing with the encounter between the Spaniards and the Indians, between 1530 and 1560 the dominant enterprise was making New Spain into something more than a conquistador's dream.

To build a country, however, there were as many projects as the varied interests nation-building inspired. For the most part, the Spaniards identified with one or more of the three main projects. One originated directly from their experience of initial contact with the natives and centered around a system of indirect rule based on the continuation of the pre-Hispanic basic political entities or *altépetl*, as we have explained. The key players would continue to be the *encomenderos, doctrineros* or Christianizing friars, and caciques. In other words, they wanted New Spain to solidify as a closed and conservative aristocratic society in which power and decision-making were the domain of privileged dignitaries. Furthermore, or so the argument went, it was essential to reward the conquistadors, no one could better spread the faith than the Christianizing friars, and the caciques were indispensable for maintaining power.

Nevertheless, other Spaniards had a different vision and thought otherwise, especially the settlers—and the number of these kept growing. First of all, they demanded their own space and a government that represented them, since (as was logical) they were not willing to subject themselves to the authority of the *encomenderos*. Since the settlers predominated in the new cities, they favored a scenario including strong local governments (*cabildos*) with a great deal of autonomy. They also wanted access to native labor, but ran into the obstacle of this labor being monopolized by the *encomenderos,* friars, and caciques. In religious matters, they preferred bishops and secular priests. They wanted a New Spain more akin to Spain, which meant a freer and more open society and, by the same token, more direct rule oriented toward exploitation.

The Crown had its own great enterprise, which was the third proposal. It was willing to cede some ground to the above-mentioned projects, but its first priority was to establish a strong central government that would rule over both the Indians and the Spaniards. In addition, that government would have to fulfill the essential function of channeling to the Crown the largest portion possible of the resources that could be extracted from the country and its inhabitants. Controlling the Spaniards turned out to be the most difficult task, because almost all of those who crossed the Atlantic were ambitious and rebellious.

The Crown knew that although it held the authority, it lacked effective means of enforcement: it had neither an army nor a bureaucracy, so if it wanted to impose laws and install officials, limit the ambitions of the *encomenderos* and friars, or control the aggressive urban town councils, it would have to take a very political approach and be quite patient. That royal power had its limits was a fact which became clear in 1543 with the opposition that arose when the Crown tried to institute a set of restrictive measures known as the "New Laws." In Peru, local interests were so aggrieved that they started an insurrection which led to the assassination of the Peruvian viceroy. His Mexican counterpart, Antonio de Mendoza, did not fail to learn from this lesson: he realized it was better to let matters take their course, promote contradictory legislation, let others handle the confrontation, and intervene as an arbiter only as a last resort. He believed this approach to government would be the most appropriate for keeping the undisciplined Spaniards of New Spain at peace. He proved he was right in 1549, when he found a formula for giving the settlers access to some benefits of tribute. This was the so-called *repartimiento* (literally, parceling out or sharing), a system of forced (although paid) labor imposed on the male inhabitants of the pueblos. And he accomplished this without the solution being considered part of an anti-*encomendero* movement.

The Crown's project benefited from favorable circumstances, because the dynamic economy and northward expansion provided escape valves that pacified the most ambitious and discontented. This also prevented serious and recurring confrontations with the pueblos, which probably would have been inevitable if available resources had been scarcer. For example, expansion opened up space for huge livestock ranches. Even the natives saw benefits in the country's dynamism and growth, and so some took advantage of the demand for labor and their unprecedented individual freedom to move to the cities or migrate to the North. Opportunities were also seized by the Mestizos (people of mixed race), many of whom had an innate cultural flexibility that enabled them to fit in almost anywhere.

1560-1610: The end of the founding phase

Between about 1560 and 1610, the Crown managed to further its aims and strengthen its system of government. These dates cover a period of diverse and extremely complex events, many of which opened up unprecedented prospects for New Spain. Thus, to a certain extent, this period provided a clearer preview of the future than earlier years had. Nevertheless, the defining feature of those events is the fact that, taken as a whole, they contributed to concluding the process of founding New Spain.

The beginning of this stage was marked by the onset of expansion into the North, or Tierradentro (Inland), as it was then called. The major triggering event was the discovery of silver mines, which produced immediate economic benefits, although agricultural and livestock interests were also involved. The possibility that all this would benefit New Galicia to the detriment of Mexico City prompted the viceroys to draw up their own plans for occupation, and in 1562 to create a separate government for areas north of Zacatecas. The new government, the "Kingdom of New Biscay," originally covered what are now the states of Durango, Chihuahua, and Sonora, as well as most of Sinaloa. The kingdom maintained a semblance of autonomy, but in fact was an extension of New Spain and safeguarded its interests. For the same purpose, New Spain created separate governments to distinguish other areas occupied later in accordance with the viceroy's guidelines: New León and New Mexico. All these jurisdictional divisions exist with essentially the same boundaries to this day.

The political, social, and economic inclusion of the areas occupied during the preliminary phase of expansion into the North produced the immediate result of growth in the heart of New Spain. Most importantly, these lands—originally outside Mesoamerica—soon became the most dynamic and, in time, richest region in New Spain, later to be known as the Bajío. Many of the numerous settlements established in this area eventually comprised the hacienda model of an agricultural/livestock enterprise that functioned as a basic component of colonization.

Expansion was accompanied by a mania for founding new cities, both in the Bajío and in the North: Durango (1563), Santa Bárbara (1567), Jerez (1569), Celaya (1571), Zamora (1574), Aguascalientes (1575), León (1576), Saltillo (1577), San Luis Potosí (1592), Salamanca (1602), Santa Fe (1609), and others that over time lost their importance, although they still exist. As of 1591, towns were also founded in these parts of the country by indigenous groups from Tlaxcala and Michoacán.

The flow of Spaniards into the North set off a new cycle of violence which, although not very intense, was the most long-lasting of all that were experienced during the colonial era. We are referring to the Chichimeca War, as historians call a succession of skirmishes with semi-nomadic tribes of Tierradentro. These tribes acted independently and conducted isolated raids. Perhaps that war would not have occurred had it been possible to reproduce the system of rule established in the Mesoamerican regions. However, the enormous cultural inequality between the tribes and the Spanish, the absence of any stable political organization and tribute system among the tribes, and the out-sized ambitions of the new occupants and their interest in capturing natives to work as slaves (something that was shamelessly blatant in New León) hindered arriving at a viable solution. The government tried to impose itself on the region by establishing military outposts or *presidios* (garrisons), which made it possible to control expansion and peopling, but also led to a greater cycle of violence. The conflict only ended when the viceroy Marquis of Villamanrique developed a policy for peace beginning in 1585, although by then many of the tribes had been wiped out. Even so, violence was common in the North. A short time later, rebellions broke out involving the northern sedentary native peoples (as occurred with the Acaxee in 1600 and the Tepehuan in 1616).

These years were disastrous for the indigenous population in general, and not only in the North. A third great epidemic

(1576-1581), probably of typhus, constituted a final catastrophe, leaving the total population at less than two million and dealing a definitive death blow to many pueblos in the lowlands and along the coasts. The population would shrink even further during the following decades, to later recover very slowly. But the days when the Spanish world may have been suffocated by the overwhelming majority of indigenous peoples were gone. By about 1600, without considering regional differences, one out of every four or five residents of New Spain was a Spaniard or a person assimilated into Spanish culture. That proportion was higher in New Galicia, but not in Guatemala, Yucatán, and the northern provinces, where the Spanish presence was relatively less significant.

The population drop had a variety of consequences in other spheres. The most noteworthy was the gradual displacement of the *encomenderos, doctrineros,* and caciques, all of whom saw their power and income affected. As regards the *encomenderos,* the passing of a generation made it easy to remove them from their positions, after which the collection of tribute from almost all the pueblos came into government hands. The Christianizing friars (whose orders entered into a period of decline) were gradually replaced by parish priests dependent on bishops. The caciques, marginalized and impoverished, could not cope with the emergence of new power groups within their pueblos, and by the beginning of the seventeenth century they were excluded from most of the *cuerpos de república.*

Paradoxically, it was then, chiefly in the years between the end of the Conquest and the great epidemic, that the friars managed to complete their magnificent architectural projects (a carryover produced by the circumstances of the Conquest) and develop artistic expressions associated with them: paintings, *retablos* (altarpieces), sculptures, and more. The harmonious whole of these works, created in many pueblos of Central Mexico (but not in the lowlands, except for Chiapas and

Yucatán), opened the first chapter of the brilliant history of colonial art.

In this context, the central government benefited from the decline of the groups that had been dominant during the years of the Conquest and was able to definitively consolidate its position and affirm the predominance of the viceroy, the *audiencias*, and other authorities representing the Crown's efforts to assert its dominion. This happened, for instance, with its local (district-level) government officials, indistinctly named *corregidores* or *alcaldes mayores*. These officials gradually replaced the *encomenderos* as the liaison with the pueblos and took charge of collecting tribute or, in some places located next to the Spanish settlers' city councils, undermining their authority. Governmental control of the labor-sharing agreement (*repartimiento*) turned out to be a powerful weapon in the political bargaining that took place with Spanish settlers.

Several major events also supported the consolidation of the central government. Some were political, such as the discrediting of *encomenderos* that occurred after an alleged uprising involving Martín Cortés (the conquistador's son) in 1566, or the establishment five years later of the Tribunal of the Holy Inquisition, whose sway in matters of political and ideological control was no less than in matters of religious orthodoxy. The growth of the bureaucracy—as demonstrated by the increase in the number of staff working in the *audiencias* in 1568 and the creation of the *Juzgado de Indios* (General Indian Court) in 1592, as well as the *Tribunal de Cuentas* (Court of Accounts or Audit Court) in 1605—was equally important. Lastly, there were other events of an economic nature, particularly the imposition of the *alcabala* tax in 1574 (a toll or tax on the transportation of merchandise, from which pueblo and church goods were exempt) and other measures that augmented the Crown's tax revenues.

At the same time, the corps of ecclesiastical personnel not associated with the Conquest grew more robust and was controlled by the government thanks to the privileges that popes granted to the Spanish monarchs (which constituted what was called the *Real Patronato*, or Royal Patronage). In this process, cathedrals and bishops became much stronger due to the collection of the tithe, a church tax imposed on the Spanish settlers' agricultural production. The tithe increased as the number of settlers grew. The arrival of the Jesuits in 1572 was also significant. They did not intervene in the religious administration of the native population (except in the North), but rather concentrated on educating the Spaniards and creating an intellectual elite.

In the commercial arena, Spain prescribed a closed protectionist system that affected both New Spain and other Spanish possessions in the Americas. Its most notable feature was the requirement that all transatlantic trade be done exclusively by one means. Beginning in 1561, a system of *flotas* (fleets or convoys) was organized, and all trade was formally required to be effected via a single annual voyage during which the ships sailed together, escorted by an armed squadron. Their cargo was carefully accounted for and subject to several taxes. In Seville, a guild of merchants was formed, known as a *consulado* or consulate. Although trade had never been free, the imposition of the fleet constrained it even further and added to the cost. At the same time, it made smuggling more appealing.

Parallel to these developments, starting with the reign of Philip II (1556-1598), the Spaniards again pursued their dream of reaching Asia across the Pacific. They finally achieved this goal by sailing from the port of Navidad in 1564, opening up a feasible route and establishing themselves in Manila in 1571. Once the Philippines had come under the rule of New Spain, Pacific trade took on a new dimension. Dozens of Chinese junks from Canton carried spices, silks, and porcelain to Manila. The Spanish bought these goods with Mexican silver and shipped them to Acapulco using a system of galleons regulated by the Crown that made an annual voyage.

Acapulco also provided a connection to Peruvian trade, and—since the latter had come to be almost as prosperous as New Spain trade—exchanges in the Pacific grew exponentially. By the end of the sixteenth century, their value was far greater than the trade between Veracruz and Seville. But because this was in competition with European Spanish interests, the Crown took action to limit exchanges between Mexico and Peru and barred them outright in 1631. Eight years later, it again allowed this trade, but under the condition that it did not include the transport of Chinese goods.

In New Spain the development of trade discussed above was accompanied by the emergence of a powerful merchant elite. Its members organized their own consulate in Mexico City in 1592, imitating the consulate in Seville. The management of maritime connections in both oceans, the control of imports and, naturally, prices rested in their hands. They began to hoard goods and money, and their political influence and economic power grew continuously. The Crown was inclined to prohibit the production of some consumer goods (tools, wine, paper, fine textiles) on American soil, apparently to protect Spanish manufacturers. But basically, it just gave in to the interests of the insatiable merchant traders. Still not satisfied with the privileges they had acquired, the merchants supplemented their earnings by taking advantage of the additional benefits of dealing in contraband.

* * *

All of the above allows us to see that the circumstances prevailing during the Conquest were a thing of the past, and that a genuine system of colonial rule had developed in their place. The new system formulated a policy for exploiting resources on a global scale adapted to the realities, complexities, and interests of the Spaniards' world. This was a far cry from the restricted and unstable environment of the conquistadors and *encomenderos*, and also far removed from the concerns that put the natives at the center of projects and ideals involving the Americas, such as when the original plans for evangelization were laid out. The second half of the sixteenth century witnessed the overlapping of the dying world of the Conquest—anchored in the Spanish past as much as it was in the pre-Hispanic world—and the first manifestations of an essentially new order.

To a great extent, New Spain's personality was based on the continuation of many aspects of the pre-Hispanic past, but this did not mean these factors persisted in a static manner. The breakdown of some of these carryovers was already evident, for example, in the decline of the caciques. In addition, changes kept accumulating, paving the way toward a world which, by the beginning of the seventeenth century, had distanced itself significantly from its past. New Spain could look back on 90 years of experience that had essentially been a success, at least from the Spanish point of view. The problems of dealing with the pre-Hispanic world—political and economic domination, how to coexist physically with the natives, and religious conversion, among others—had not been completely resolved, but had been overcome. And those inherent in the colonial setting per se, such as disputes that the Spanish created and continued creating among themselves, had been addressed with measures that made it possible to view them as at least under control, if not surmounted. From the perspective of national history, we can discern the basic features of the combined elements that would comprise the nation that was to declare independence in 1821, especially if we keep the expansion into the North in mind.

We must emphasize the position New Spain occupied on the world scene. Its silver production (like that of Peru) spread not only throughout Spain, but also through much of Europe, since its end use was to pay the Spanish Crown's huge debts and buy goods that Spain, with its low level of industrial development, did not know how to produce. This flood of precious metal had a tremendous impact on the European economy. Furthermore, silver from New Spain also circulated in China (where Mexican coins were in common use until the nineteenth century) and through other trade routes reached as far as India and other areas of Asia. When a Japanese trade mission arrived in Mexico in 1610 with great expectations, all indications were that New Spain, or at least part of it, had managed to achieve a key position in the new network that connected the entire globe. This is surprising if we consider the isolation that had characterized Mesoamerica's evolution just a few decades before. Moreover, these interactions were not purely commercial, but also involved a substantial amount of cultural exchange, including a close relationship with Peru. But New Spain would inevitably run up against repression of its impulse for outreach just when it was about to take its place in a cosmopolitan world.

Note that Spain was undergoing major changes at about the same time. One of the Crown's primary motivations in extending its administrative apparatus was to broaden its tax base and enhance its collection capabilities. This acquired greater importance as Spain—which was poorly governed, continually at war, in debt, and impoverished—attempted to recover from the huge trauma of the defeat of its Invincible Armada at the hands of the English in 1588. Several critics and social reformers (the so-called *arbitristas*) proposed and implemented different principles of governance known as *arbitrios,* with a view to preventing or at least mitigating what all of Spain could clearly see ahead: the end of its imperial hegemony, barely made up for by the brilliance of its literary Golden Age. The balance of power was shifting in favor of the northern European countries. For Spain's possessions in the Americas, this essentially meant that they would have to submit to ever-increasing economic demands.

1610-1760: MATURITY AND AUTONOMY

1610-1650: Encountering the outside world

The three stages of development in Mexico's colonial history outlined above completed what we can call the founding phase of New Spain while also providing the first glimpses of the elements characterizing its mature phase. At the beginning of this phase, and continuing until the mid-seventeenth century, there was a period of considerable effervescence.

Indeed, the Dutch (recently freed from Spanish domination), the English, and the French were asserting their dominion over the seas. The new balance of power became evident in 1621 with the creation of the Dutch West India Company, which held Spanish ships in check in both the Atlantic and the Pacific. The capture of a fleet sailing from Veracruz by a Dutch squadron near Cuba in 1628 revealed Spain's declining strength and caused huge losses for Mexican traders. From then on, the lack of security on sea routes became a chronic problem.

Confronting this panorama, the *arbitristas*, who had come into power in 1621 in the person of the Count-Duke of Olivares—who was appointed *valido* (a position equivalent to prime minister) to King Philip IV—, promoted an ambitious program of reforms throughout the empire. In New Spain, implementation was the responsibility of a viceroy, the Marquis of Gelves, who was assigned the mission of improving tax collection, combating smuggling, and fighting against vested interests. But this viceroy lacked political tact, acted with excessive zeal, and ignored local viewpoints, which won him the enmity of New Spain's most powerful groups: the *audiencia* or court of justice, the Mexico City government, the merchant guild, and the church hierarchy, among others. Once he had a confrontation with the archbishop, his situation became untenable.

The denouement was an extraordinary event in colonial history: the viceroy was overthrown in 1624 by a coup d'état orchestrated by the *audiencia*, which took advantage of a critical moment to violently remove him from power, claiming there was a mutiny among the people. The significance of this was that it made clear that in New Spain politics was handled according to the colony's own rules and that, although it was true that a central government had been firmly established, it was far from being a monolithic and all-powerful bloc in service to Spain. The king's authority was recognized, but reality placed limits on it. The Spaniards in New Spain saw to it that their opinions and interests were respected. The moment had arrived when they could guide a more modern course for one of the great national endeavors begun during the founding period: the settlers' goal of a freer and more open society more similar to the Spanish metropolis, and one that enabled the town councils, secular clergy, farmers and ranchers, miners, and merchants to play a larger role.

The Crown had to accept what had happened or risk even greater losses. Besides, it had other priorities, and to pursue those it needed the goodwill of the local elites. One of those priorities was consolidating the so-called *Unión de Armas*, a financial scheme that required the empire's wealthiest corporations to contribute large sums of money to aid the Crown. Likewise, in 1635 the king decreed the formation of a naval force to defend the Caribbean, the *Armada de Barlovento* (Windward Fleet), which was to be financed and supported by the town councils and merchants of New Spain. The *situados*—subsidies to fund building fortifications and finance defensive armies located outside of New Spain's territories—were also increased.

As a result of these measures, much of New Spain's silver was no longer sent to Seville. Instead, it was channeled to the sustenance and defense of other Spanish possessions: the Philippines, Cuba, Santo Domingo, Jamaica, and Florida. At the end of the seventeenth century, almost half of New Spain's tax revenues were dedicated to this purpose. Spain compensated for its loss with the enormous remittances it was receiving from Peru, which was then at the height of its wealth.

New Spain had to get used to living with the problems brought on by the Spanish metropolis's weakness and to assuming the new role being assigned to it within the Spanish Empire. In concrete terms, this meant that the town councils, merchants, and other corporations were obliged to keep their treasuries available. But it was not all negative, since in exchange they negotiated quite considerable privileges, such that the events taking place in high political circles and local issues were interwoven.

The most important of these local issues, due to its political implications and because it briefly changed New Spain's economic situation, was the flooding in Mexico City over a period of five years, beginning in 1629. Providing adequate drainage to keep the basin in which the city was located free of water posed a great problem. Huge sums of money had been invested in building tunnels and canals, but they were clearly insufficient. The flooding provoked bitter political recriminations (for example, the deposed viceroy was accused of having ordered suspension of critical drainage works in his zeal to save money) and prompted extraordinary demands for *repartimiento* (forced labor system imposed upon the pueblos) to finish and enlarge those drainage works, which affected all the pueblos in Central Mexico. There was a proposal to move the city to slightly higher ground, to the shore of the former lake, but vested interests prevailed. Meanwhile, the city of Puebla took advantage of the situation and became the country's most vigorous commercial and manufacturing center, albeit only for a short time.

An indirect consequence of the flooding was that it made the *repartimiento* that had been in place since 1549 unsustainable. Needing labor for urgent drainage projects, the government had to make some adjustments in 1632. The most important entailed excluding the Spanish settlers from the benefits of the system. This was a difficult decision for the viceroy, because it deprived him of a weapon that had served him well to pressure local governments. For example, some years previously, the Puebla town council had been reluctant to contribute to the *Unión de Armas*, but changed its mind when threatened with losing its portion of the *repartimiento*. In general, the settlers were resentful at the time, but in the end came out ahead, because this opened up a labor market free from government control just when a decrease in population had made labor scarce and in great demand.

One last effort at putting politics on a sound footing was undertaken in 1640, shortly before the reformist group was removed from power in Spain. The person implementing the project was Juan de Palafox, Bishop of Puebla, who at various times held the highest positions in civilian government, including serving as viceroy. Palafox dealt with New Spain's complexity intelligently and tried to strike a balance among the interests involved, but he could not avoid confrontations that obliged him to return to Spain in 1649. His disagreement with the Jesuits about episcopal prerogatives grew into a full-blown political scandal. The repercussions of that scandal and their potentially destabilizing effects put an end to whatever remained of the Crown's zeal for reform. In defending the secular clergy and all that it entailed, Palafox had ended up championing the political and social aims of the Spaniards of New Spain: the American Spaniards, or Creoles.

The Crown's financial hardships contributed to this process. When there was a conflict between tax collection and other issues, taxes were always given priority. Thus, the Crown supported some governmental practices that ensured administrative savings and secure revenues despite their doubtful value in combating vested interests or dishonesty. The most remarkable of these was the practice of selling government positions, that is, of treating posts in civil administration or the public treasury as concessions, including, for example, notaries public, the administration of the royal mail, the mint, the collection of tribute, and the collection of the *alcabala* tax (which for a long time was granted as a concession to the Mexico City town council and later to the merchant guild). The Crown also put positions in the town councils themselves up for sale, at times offering a lifetime appointment. Such posts went to the highest bidder, and obviously the prices varied depending on the possibilities they offered for obtaining greater or lesser advantages or prestige. The practice opened the door for families in New Spain to consolidate their position in society and increase their intervention in government affairs.

This period saw the gradual ascent of Spaniards born in New Spain to positions of influence and power in a variety of administrative posts (although only rarely in the highest ones). Of course, they also became wealthy. While it is true that the status of being a Spaniard was determined by ancestry and not by place of birth, it was natural that the Spaniards born in Europe differed in their opinions and interests from the Americans or Creoles (a concept that did not exclude people with varying proportions of mixed blood). The European Spaniards enjoyed advantages for earning or purchasing the best positions, although this was not always true, and Spain's inability to exercise unlimited authority gave the American Spaniards or Creoles of those times great freedom of action.

The period was also distinguished by its cultural vitality, which grew out of the consolidation of several colleges (especially Jesuit colleges) and the university, as well as thanks to the availability of funds devoted to paying for the construction of cathedrals, parishes, and urban residences, and to commissioning paintings, sculptures, literary pieces, musical compositions, and so forth. The primarily rural expressions of art during the

Conquest were left to the past, and in their place expressions of urban art appeared. Within this movement there were outstanding and diverse examples of cultural *mestizaje*, among which the historical work of Fernando de Alva Ixtlilxóchitl (before 1625) is noteworthy. His works glorified the pre-Hispanic past, and their spirit added to the somewhat older poetic art, such as *Grandeza mexicana (Mexican Greatness)* by Bernardo de Balbuena, which sang of the beauties and values of New Spain. An additional aspect of New Spain's identity can be found in the proliferation during the seventeenth century of nuns' convents, whose orders—in contrast to those of men—were purely contemplative and secluded.

Lastly, we must not forget the advance into the North, which received new impetus in 1631 after the discovery of silver ore in Parral. Much of the expansion during this period was oriented toward Sinaloa and Sonora to found missions, establishments promoted by the Franciscans or Jesuits, whose goal was to reorganize and convert the native population in the newly occupied areas. The missions were based on the consolidation of fixed settlements and sought to reproduce an organization somewhat like that of the pueblos of Central Mexico. Some achieved their purpose, but others could not survive or had to resort to force to maintain their new converts. They also faced rebellions, such as the Tarahumara revolt in 1648. At the same time, new garrisons or military outposts and civilian settlements were also founded in the North.

* * *

New Spain entered its mature phase with several distinguishing features. To begin with, none of the individuals that the Crown had placed in the power structure possessed all the authority required to pull the necessary political strings. While the central government had been consolidated, the responsibilities and jurisdictions of both viceroys and *audiencias* or courts of justice were never completely sorted out, but rather overlapped. Similarly, there were conflicts with church authorities and the Inquisition, as well as with town councils. The fragmentation of authority had been a factor since Cortés' days, but was accentuated as a result of the complicated and contradictory legal resolutions that determined the form (or rather, partially determined the form) of government institutions. As if this were not enough, the Crown occasionally decreed a *visita* (tour of inspection), a procedure that implied sending an official directly from Spain with a fairly broad portfolio for supervision. It was never completely clear whether or not the inspectors could give orders to other authorities. Palafox, for example, was both an inspector and viceroy at the same time. To all this, we must add the vagueness of jurisdictional boundaries and terms. The result was a system of checks and balances that allowed a variety of tendencies and opinions to flourish and brought interests out into the open, recognizing supreme authority but also distancing themselves from it.

In New Spain, the Crown had not found the ideal place for installing the government that was most suitable for it. When, as the situation required, it had to impose its will in one area and cede some ground in another, things did not always turn out as the Crown wished. But neither was it a disaster. The system of checks and balances served the Crown well; there were good reasons why it peacefully kept its possessions for such a long time.

First, the system was not an accident, but rather derived from the concepts prevailing in the Hispanic world about the exercise of power, which assumed authority was established through the administration of justice rather than by executive action. Imparting justice was the king's supreme power, and his representatives and delegates—from the viceroys to local officials—participated in that function in their respective spheres.

That is why they also were commonly called judges. Laws were adapted to individual cases and gave officials broad discretionary powers in applying them. In practice, the possible (and frequent) excesses of these officials were kept in check by the *juicios de residencia* (public performance assessments), through which all of the Crown's representatives, including viceroys, were subject to public review and possibly censure at the end of their terms of office. Many received heavy fines for their faults or abuses; others managed to avoid punishment. Despite its imperfections, the system seldom descended into tyrannical episodes, and when they did occur, they were resolved relatively quickly.

Second, the system of checks and balances made the dangerous and costly option of an authoritarian regime based on armed force unnecessary, although in any event, Spain could not have provided for such an army in so vast an empire. The reasoning behind the system was no different from that which led to the system of indirect rule over the pre-Hispanic lordships.

We must bear in mind that the prevailing concept of society in the Hispanic world of that era emphasized corporate association. Individuals became important according to whether they belonged to a particular entity or group, and it was through some such entity that a person acquired a role in the political world. New Spain arrived at its period of maturity at a time when many corporations had become firmly established and had delimited their respective spheres of action: the *audiencia*, the town councils, the merchant guild, the religious orders, the pueblos, the university, and the artisans' guilds, among others. Each corporation, with its own legal status, represented and defended the interests of its constituents and, like the Crown itself, was occasionally obliged to compromise on some issues in order to get its way on others. Naturally, there were also divergent opinions within these organizations, and each was a microcosm of society as a whole. In New Spain, the main internal differences most of these corporations began to experience as of the seventeenth century were between Creoles and European-born Spaniards.

Politics favored Creoles' interests to the degree that they made their presence felt in the most influential corporations. The economic situation also favored them. In the first half of the seventeenth century, New Spain experienced years of prosperity and reaped the fruits of what had been sown, or at least the Spaniards did. Mining was growing steadily, and the successful introduction of livestock, wheat, and other species was later accompanied by the development of manufacturing activities that had originated in Europe. A large number of mills produced huge quantities of flour, and bread consumption skyrocketed throughout colonial society at the same time that dozens of sugar mills and refineries supplied an abundance of sugar. There were more than 100 *obrajes* (workshops engaged in the production of textiles, especially woolens), and they employed an average of about 50 workers each. Resting on this foundation, the largest sums of money were those involved in New Spain's dominant economic activity: trade, and especially overseas trade. Many of the pueblos were also doing quite well, because they benefited (relatively) from their participation in the new trade networks, getting good prices for their products (particularly *cochinilla*, or cochineal, an insect used to produce a red dye) and partly controlling the business of muleteering and transportation.

With this panorama in mind, consider the contrasting penury of the Crown. As it became increasingly involved in more serious economic difficulties, its interests grew narrower. The upshot was that raising money had priority over everything else. Through taxes, surcharges, and the sale of positions, the Spanish metropolis did obtain substantial revenue and insurance, but also had to forfeit part of its power—that same power

so laboriously achieved by limiting the action of *encomenderos,*
doctrineros, and caciques during the sixteenth century—in favor
of a middle-level bureaucracy dominated by merchants, town
councils and, in general, local oligarchies. Thus, government
paid a price for its consolidation: that of allowing a broad distribution of power which, from the perspective of New Spain,
took the form of a great degree of autonomy. Taking this into
account, combined with the reality of Spain's dependence on its
American possessions to maintain its weakened position on the
world scene, the balance is quite favorable for New Spain, or at
least for its privileged elites.

1650-1715: Prosperous times and their limits

As of the second quarter of the seventeenth century, New Spain
underwent a series of highly complex developments that became notably evident, although indications of some of them
were perceptible before then. This period of New Spain's history shows unmistakable signs of expansion, but also an encounter with limits.

As in earlier times, we should note that one feature of this
period was the taking root and development of a unique identity in New Spain. On the one hand, people successfully cultivated local versions of European culture, such as in literature
and polyphonic music. On the other, artistic forms and styles
were created that unmistakably had arisen in New Spain, such
as in architecture. Sor (Sister) Juana Inés de la Cruz, whose literary production was concentrated primarily between 1680 and
1695, achieved recognition as a poet of the first order in Spanish literature and, although she never left Mexico, the values
she expressed are recognized as universal to this day. Musical
production was enthusiastically promoted by church councils.
The magnificence of New Spain's architecture was fostered by

dynamic activity in urban centers, most of which had now enjoyed several decades of stability and growth. The secular clergy demanded the most privileged locations in each and every inhabited place and made its presence felt with new architectural proposals, always inspired by the Baroque, that competed in splendor with the old (and already nearly abandoned) monasteries of the mendicant friars. Clearly, religion dominated and limited the cultural panorama, but there were also rather appreciable developments in the realm of scientific knowledge, especially in mining, cosmography, and mathematics, as evidenced by the works of Fray Diego Rodríguez and Carlos de Sigüenza y Góngora, among others.

Also during this period, other cultural elements that can be defined as specific to New Spain—and, from today's viewpoint, quintessentially Mexican—took on their unique individuality or reached maturity, including cuisine, dress, furniture, language, popular music, dance, and so forth. Processes of cultural *mestizaje* were involved in all of these art forms, drawing mostly on pre-Hispanic and Spanish antecedents, but also on Asian and African ones (apparent, for example, in the widespread use of silks and ivory, in Puebla's pottery, in fireworks, in the popular taste for cinnamon, and in some musical styles). Many slaves of African origin had been assigned to domestic service, and that lent urban life a special tone. These cultural exchanges operated both ways. Thus, for example, mid-seventeenth-century Nahuatl had already made many changes in its expressive forms that differed from how the language was spoken in pre-Hispanic times. Other phenomena had an environmental component: the expansion of livestock breeding, for instance, not only had caused a cultural revolution (since the use of wool and regular consumption of meat changed the dress and diet of almost the entire indigenous population), but the animals themselves, with their detritus, contributed to permanently changing some agrosystems.

The uniqueness of New Spain's culture could also be seen in the rise of several religious cults, especially those dedicated to a variety of ways of worshipping the Virgin Mary. None of these was more impressive than devotion to the Virgin of Guadalupe, particularly beginning in 1648, when her fame began to spread throughout New Spain from the original chapel dedicated to her on the outskirts of Mexico City.

In economic matters it bears mention that on the one hand, the features of the previous period continued to spread while, on the other, a free labor market was consolidated. That market was no longer subject to tribute requirements and benefited agricultural enterprises managed by Spanish individuals or corporations like the monasteries and convents or Jesuit colleges, which had become major landowners. This process was triggered by the previously mentioned reform of the *repartimiento* in 1632 and the increasingly widespread use of money. Laborers, most of whom came from pueblos, began to offer their services in exchange for payment. Agricultural products entered into far-reaching and competitive marketing networks that were equally independent of the tributary systems established during the Conquest.

These developments were related to the final structure and proliferation of haciendas. In their definitive form, haciendas were a combination of real estate holding, agricultural/livestock enterprise, and stable population settlement. In contrast to their predecessors in earlier periods, their essential feature was no longer the use of slave labor (although some had slaves) or their association with colonization; rather, it was that they depended on free laborers and were scattered among the pueblos in the central regions of Mexico. These new haciendas, which would become one of the most characteristic elements of rural New Spain, took root because there was a large free population, usually of mixed race (Mestizo), that was seeking a place to settle, or because people from the pueblos preferred to leave them (tem-

porarily or permanently) to find work or to escape the obliga-
tion of paying tribute. Thus, these laborers established themselves as peons, i.e., as resident salaried workers on hacienda
lands, where they were offered a degree of protection. This was
possible because, at the time, labor was relatively scarce and
valuable. Similarly, hacienda owners made efforts to expand their
holdings by buying or leasing land from neighboring pueblos.
The pueblos and the haciendas established a relationship that
remained in relative equilibrium for a hundred years.

Although the haciendas tended to have a broad land base,
not all were large properties. Their value lay in their production, as well as in the land itself. Nor were all rural properties
haciendas. Landowners also constituted a heterogeneous group.
Among the most modest were middle-class settlers and some
clergymen, almost all of whom were Creoles or Mestizos (sometimes it was difficult to distinguish one from the other), but there
were also some caciques and other prominent Indians. At the
other end of the spectrum were wealthy merchants and miners
(Creoles and European-born Spaniards) who completed their
portfolios of business interests by owning five or six large haciendas; and ecclesiastical corporations—such as religious orders
(except the Franciscans), Jesuit colleges, and convents of nuns—
that had acquired many properties through purchase and, primarily, donations from the pious. These institutions also came
to possess countless urban properties, and their large accumu-
lations of capital enabled them to operate as lenders as well.
They held the mortgage on an ever-increasing number of rural
properties.

In contrast to these accounts of expansion, the pueblos in
almost all regions of New Spain entered into a period of political fragmentation beginning in the mid-seventeenth century.
The pueblos, heirs to the pre-Hispanic political entities but with
their caciques or hereditary lords in decadence, tended to divide up along the lines of their different sections or groupings

(either subordinate villages or neighborhoods). These began to stop recognizing established *cuerpos de república* and to demand the right to create their own, reproducing on a small scale the organizational features of the original entities. The government did not object to this practice, and as a result there came to be about five or six tiny pueblos where a hundred years before there would have only been one. Although with this move many villages were able to meet their immediate or circumstantial needs, such as greater security for corporate property, this process cancelled out whatever political relevance the pueblos might otherwise have maintained—yet another indication of how far into the past the conditions prevailing during the Conquest had receded.

For the pueblos it was not easy to decide how to best position themselves within a setting undergoing so much change. The second half of the seventeenth century was marked by several upheavals resulting from vices and abuses in the exercise of government, shortages, hoarding, and other problems of this kind. Most evident was the spread of a practice in which many local officials participated: the so-called *repartimiento de mercancías* (compulsory consumption of goods), which consisted of forcing the residents of the pueblos to buy goods of all kinds (and at inflated prices). On occasion this also involved the shameless exploitation of labor, such as when people were obliged to buy thread so that they would later be forced to sell cloth at extremely low prices. The practice was tolerated to some degree because it was just one more tribute payment that plagued the pueblos, and came to be accepted as the means of paying these officials, since they did not receive any salary to speak of or had purchased their position. But even abuses like this can only be tolerated by society to a certain extent, and when that limit was exceeded, many forms of protest broke out. Although they certainly were not exclusive to this period, during this time there were relatively violent regional uprisings

(Tehuantepec, 1660) and urban riots (Mexico City, 1692) that had major political repercussions. Gangs of bandits, which had previously been almost unheard of, took control of the roads.

In a different context, comparable abuses of power led to a wholesale revolt of the pueblos of New Mexico in 1680 that resulted in the expulsion of Spaniards from the province, to which they could not return until ten years later. It is true that New Mexico was an outlying region, but the event was very significant: it marked the first reverse suffered in the heretofore vigorous expansion into the North and, moreover, the beginning of several years in which the empire suffered other no less serious defeats, although for very different reasons.

The French, who were then enemies of Spain (they had just finished the Five Years' War and would soon begin another), were making aggressive incursions into North America. In 1685, a point along the Texas coast was occupied by an ill-fated French expedition whose members soon perished. Because the Spanish Crown had become extremely sensitive to anything happening on this part of the continent, its response was immediate. It involved, among other measures, advancing into Coahuila (which resulted in the founding of Monclova in 1689) and reinforcing several military outposts. But none of this could counteract an event whose enormous significance would only be understood years later: the establishment of the French colony of Louisiana. Spain compensated for this blow by occupying Baja California, an effort promoted by the Jesuits as of 1697 for the sole purpose of extending their missions, an enterprise that yielded meager results.

If the outcome of the situation in the North concerned the Crown, the increasing activity of the British, French, and Dutch was even more worrisome. They took over the Caribbean, making use of their pirates or privateers who, among other acts of aggression, brutally attacked Veracruz and Campeche in 1683 and 1685. Neither the money of the *situados* (funds earmarked for defense) nor the weak Spanish defenses could prevent the English from taking Jamaica in 1655, or—supported by this base of operations—from their occupying, five years later, an extensive area in eastern Tabasco (around the Términos Lagoon, where they remained until 1716). The British also occupied Belize, which they would never leave. Their brief occupation of Havana in 1692 caused enormous anxiety. The Spanish setbacks were barely made up for by their taking control in 1697 of a Mayan fortress in Tayasal in the heart of the Petén, which for all practical purposes had remained independent until that time.

* * *

The fact that New Spain bid the seventeenth century farewell with a pair of British settlements within its territory was of great import. This intrusion, which would have been unimaginable a hundred years earlier, reflected the decline in Spain's maritime powers and the ascent of its enemies. Furthermore, New Spain had reached maturity at the same time that it was emerging from the isolation of its founding period. Events in the outside world were directly affecting it.

But not too much. The British invasions troubled a part of the country that had remained almost unpopulated since the end of the sixteenth century and, besides, New Spain had oriented its expansion and interests toward the North, distancing itself from Central America and even Yucatán. If New Spain was involved in Caribbean issues, it was because the Crown demanded it. The temporary loss of New Mexico and the proximity of the French on northeastern shores were more traumatic. These events provoked an immediate and vigorous response. All of this, however, affected the periphery, but not the center of New Spain, and that made a great difference.

Despite its closer relationship to events in the outside world, New Spain had reached maturity as an inward-looking country surrounded by a virtually closed environment. On coasts and shores, all possibilities of maritime exchange were ruled out, with the exception of Veracruz, Campeche, and Acapulco. An additional factor that discouraged orienting life toward the oceans was a justified fear of pirates.

The significance of New Spain's eastern border—Tabasco, Yucatán, and the Guatemalan borderlands—had been remarkably overlooked. The previously mentioned British occupation of Belize and the Términos Lagoon was seen as a mishap that did not merit punitive action. Commercial ties with Guatemala (which since its founding as a separate government included Chiapas) had been important well into the seventeenth century, but were now diminishing. The Soconusco coastal region, almost uninhabited since the most recent epidemics, was the object of jurisdictional disputes that almost no one tried to resolve. Meanwhile, in Yucatán the unique features that made this province a virtually separate entity grew more prominent. It was subject to Mexico in legal and ecclesiastical matters, and its government theoretically acknowledged its subordination to the viceroy, but Yucatán's affairs were managed with complete autonomy and, if a problem arose, it was dealt with directly in Spain. The province had a tightly closed economy and had preserved archaic structures, including most notably the *encomienda*. The viceroy's government rarely indicated any interest in these matters.

The borders with foreign lands to the North (which in this era were usually called simply *Septentrión,* "the North") remained completely undefined and extended through an area that was virtually empty. But the first incursions of the Athabascan Indians from the northern part of the continent, generically called the Apache, were a major source of concern. The government spent a great deal of money organizing a variety of control methods. Among an endless series of projects for reorganizing and defending the North, one that gained favor was to establish a chain of *presidios* (garrisons or military outposts) from Texas to Sonora. This yielded very doubtful results, largely owing to the small number of poorly-trained people who had to run them. Yet despite their shortcomings, these projects contributed to shaping the experience of individuals who would soon become part of the military leadership and occupy important government positions. Familiarity with the *Septentrión* and interest in its problems and circumstances would leave a major imprint on New Spain in times to come.

But with all that and even given its increasing importance, the North was still an area almost as marginal as New Spain's coasts and eastern front. This, it bears repeating, was a nation turned inward. All the major cities, most dynamic regions, economic activity, communication routes, artistic expressions, wealth, and people were concentrated on Central Mexico's Altiplano (high plateau). This general configuration of New Spain, created during the sixteenth century and consolidated during the seventeenth, dominates Mexico's geography even today. Climatic and environmental reasons partially explain this fact, which to a great extent is also a result of the original founding of New Spain on the site of Mexico-Tenochtitlan. But an equally important reason is that the Crown deliberately built an extremely restrictive system of trade and closed borders.

These were the general outlines of the map of New Spain, a country that was already two centuries old, a hundred years of which in its mature phase. Looking at it in detail, and especially at its core, by then we could already see clear definition of the regions created by the colonial experience. Some echoed spatial arrangements inherited from the pre-Hispanic past with few variations, as was the case in the Mixteca Alta and many other mountainous areas. But others were purely colonial in origin and development, such as the Valley of Puebla. Among these, none was as conspicuous or dynamic as the Bajío, initially a product of the first advances toward the North, but which quickly became integrated into the heart of the country. In the early eighteenth century, the Bajío was the region with the most rapid population growth, the greatest urban development, the highest agricultural production, and most dynamic society, and thus would play an increasingly prominent role in the history of New Spain.

1715-1760: Approaching the final period

Dynastic change occurred in Spain when there was no heir to the throne. The Crown passed from the House of Austria (the House of Habsburg) to the House of Bourbon, which ruled France. Philip V, the new King of Spain, was a grandson of Louis XIV. The event caused great commotion in Spain, but in Mexico the normal course of affairs was hardly altered, or at least it did not change immediately or obviously. Only a few years later, in about 1715, was it possible to see that a new era was dawning. The configuration of one more stage in the history of New Spain, the last to be addressed in this chapter, was also shaped by certain developments in European politics.

The rapprochement between the Spanish and French dynasties did not eliminate the mistrust between the two nations, but did ensure their stable coexistence. In contrast, the relationship with the British was fraught with tension that led to several wars, beginning with a very long one that involved Britain in conflicts over the Spanish succession. The Treaty of Utrecht, which ended this war in 1713, sanctioned the subsistence of the House of Bourbon in Spain, but compelled it to make several trade concessions in favor of the British. From then on, the British had an *asiento* or exclusive right to take African slaves to the Americas to sell them there.

In Spain, the authorities wanted to take advantage of the situation to make some reforms to the rigid system that governed transatlantic trade. Control of maritime traffic was moved from Seville to Cádiz, and some adjustments were made to the fleet system. In addition, to better control its movements, the celebration of annual trade fairs was made to coincide with the arrival of convoys to the Americas. New Spain's trade fair was held in Jalapa beginning in 1728. But these measures were quite superficial and failed to effectively cope with a fact that became more obvious year after year: the British were taking advantage of the opportunity offered by the exclusive right to the slave trade (which in New Spain never grew beyond modest proportions) to introduce European textiles and establish contacts that enabled them to start what quickly grew into a well-organized system of contraband. These illicit activities co-opted a good share of Spain's trade with its American possessions. The excessive trade restrictions that Spain imposed had created fertile ground in New Spain for such activities.

Another war with Britain in 1739 had more direct consequences on trade matters, among which the paralysis of the fleet system until 1754 is very noteworthy. The most significant result of this event was that, without the fleets, trade was successfully conducted by independent ships called *navíos de registro* (officially registered ships), establishing a new precedent that a few decades later would provide the basis for gradually freeing up commercial traffic.

New circumstances were evident in more than commercial matters alone. Beginning in 1714 the Crown undertook a reorganization of the government agencies responsible for managing affairs in the Americas. During the next 20 years the fate of New Spain was placed in the hands of two successive viceroys (the Marquises of Valero and Casafuerte), who achieved a stable, well-coordinated government that gradually became more efficient. Other later viceroys were generally better trained than their predecessors had been. There were also significant changes in the government's manner and language, and we can say that on the whole the government became much more bureaucratic.

Establishment of the Tribunal of the Acordada in 1719 was an event of great importance. The tribunal constituted the country's first effective law enforcement body, and can be understood as the response to the alarming number of bandits who plagued the roads of New Spain. Its greatest significance, however, lies in it being the first concrete manifestation of a new philosophy of government that emphasized the effectiveness of a higher authority and the necessity of providing that authority with the means required to enforce its rule. It bears mention that in New Spain the only armed forces which had existed up to that time were the viceroy's guard and a variety of local militias, some of which were irregular, while others were organized on a more permanent basis, whose job it was to defend the coasts and the northern border (or at least appear to do so). None of these groups was composed of professional military men, nor was there any hierarchical organized structure appropriate for a modern army.

Another relevant event was the typhus epidemic or *matlazáhuatl*, which lasted from 1736 to 1739. Less deadly than the sixteenth-century epidemics, it extended over a larger geographic area due to the increased movement of people and goods. The epidemic was not so intense as to reverse the population growth trend that had persisted since the mid-seventeenth century, but had substantial economic impact and opened the door to government intervention in a variety of efforts to figure out how to best control it. This is another of the early examples of the government's changing attitude and desire to modernize.

We should mention that by about 1750, the population of New Spain was a little more than 4.5 million, half or more of whom had ties to the pueblos (that is, Indians, namely people registered as payers of tribute, and their dependents), whereas the rest were mainly Creoles or Mestizos (or Mulattoes or a variety of other racial or ethnic combinations, which it had become customary to call *castas*). Within that figure, certain specific groups were not very large. Individuals of African origin, including slaves and freedmen, numbered about 10 000, while European-born Spaniards did not exceed 20 000 at any given time. In some areas, particularly the Bajío, New Galicia, and the North, the majority were Mestizos.

With the growing presence of Mestizos and Mulattoes in rural areas, there was a substantial increase in the number of free settlers who were also small proprietors (that is, not obliged to pay tribute and not part of either a pueblo or hacienda). These people were commonly known as *rancheros,* because they originally lived in *ranchos* or small informal villages. Some found a place as tenant farmers on haciendas. In certain cases, aware of the legal advantages of formalizing their settlements, the *rancheros* incorporated them as pueblos, even though neither their social composition nor their history were similar to the traditional, real pueblos that developed out of pre-Hispanic political entities. In any event, as their presence grew in importance, it led to various changes in the rural social structure, which was becoming increasingly complex.

At this stage in the life of New Spain, exciting things were happening in the North, and not only because of the mining boom that we will discuss later. We must point out that missionary activity was at its peak, with the Jesuits primarily in Sonora and the Franciscans in Texas (which was definitively colonized from 1715 on). Aside from their religious duties and local political organization, some of the missions created their own stable and relatively populous villages, and this in turn encouraged the immigration of a variety of settlers who put down roots in their outskirts (something the missionaries were never happy about). Exchange networks became denser and more heavily used, and diverse groups of Yaqui, Ópata, Tarahumara, and others participated alongside the Mestizo population, which had very varied backgrounds and enjoyed a great deal of social mobility.

The occupation of Tamaulipas or New Santander as of 1748 was also important for the North and deserves to be addressed for two reasons. The first is that it occupied one of the wide-open spaces where expansion had not yet penetrated, filling it with small settlements. The second reason, of greater significance, is that in Tamaulipas a new model of colonization was inaugurated and implemented under the government's control—rigorously planned and organized along almost military lines: yet another example of the innovative spirit with which the authorities approached their endeavors.

Taken as a whole, population density in the North remained very low, and large landed estates took control of vast uninhabited areas. Amid all these circumstances, a cultural pattern was bound to form that, over time, has come to be understood as a typically northern lifestyle, distinct in some ways from the culture at the country's center. But a generalization like this, although valid to some extent, must not obscure the major differences that the North was gradually nurturing throughout its history. The exceptional case of the Nayar region (the mountain region where the Cora and Huichol Indians lived) provides an illustration of this. The Nayar is a relatively centrally located enclave that had remained outside Spanish control and was not conquered until 1722. One could say that, similar to 25 years earlier in the Petén, the government wanted to tie up loose ends.

But the new priorities that had been put on the table were costly and ran up against the Crown's increasingly obvious financial weakness. Luckily, New Spain continued to enjoy appreciable economic prosperity based on its trade, rich agricultural production and, most especially, a new and very conspicuous boom in mining, represented by the discovery of silver deposits not only in northern sites like Guanaceví, Cusihuiriáchic, Batopilas, Chihuahua, and Álamos, but also notably in places near the country's center, such as Guanajuato, Real del Monte, and Taxco. Enormous and ostentatious fortunes came from the incredibly rich mines in these locations and, of course, the Spanish metropolis did not fail to notice.

Always seeking new and lucrative sources of revenue, and consistent with its policy of selling public posts, the Crown took things a step farther and offered positions of greater value, for example positions on the *audiencia* (court of justice). This provided an opportunity for the Creoles to improve their station in life and their contacts. At the same time, the Crown opened the door to the acquisition of new grandiose noble titles. This created a new element of inequality in New Spain's already heterogeneous social structure (which shortly before 1700 had only three old titled families, while that number grew to 14 by 1759). The new nobles consisted principally of mine owners, most of them European-born Spaniards, or individuals who had earned position and money conducting arduous tasks in the *Septentrión*.

* * *

By the middle of the eighteenth century, New Spain was a country that had achieved a sound enough footing to include, despite its colonial status, many of the elements of identity that would later be expressed in independent Mexico. The consolidation of a national identity or, in more general terms, an "American" identity, was a basic preoccupation of Creole and Mestizo culture. Historians who once again adopted indigenist approaches that had been used in the previous century, such as José Joaquín Granados Gálvez, were soon to revive and to a large extent create the idea of a great "Toltec nation" that began with the story of a "Land of Anáhuac" and of the legitimate monarchy or "Mexican Empire." This was just one step away from defining the nationality that was taking shape in New Spain as "Mexican."

Naturally, attempts at creating an identity were restricted to a very small intellectual elite which consisted of perhaps a little over 1 000 individuals. The common people were far from being aware of these issues, particularly because few had access to even the most rudimentary education, and what schooling there was did not even begin to deal with historical subject matter. But this lack of awareness did not mean there were no common denominators, many of which we mentioned when discussing the previous period. The cult of the Virgin of Guadalupe, which was increasingly popular, was an excellent catalyst for ideology. But the strongest identities were based on regional loyalties and, in the case of the indigenous population, on the individuality of the pueblos which, despite their evolution and fragmentation, continued to be a basic and often the only point of reference in social and cultural life. Identification with corporate institutions, it should be noted, was very strong regardless of the organization involved and, as such, represented a counterbalance to any other loyalties.

In the economic sphere, both signs of integration and the lack of it were alternately apparent. Mining inputs and production traveled through networks that encompassed practically the whole country; credit operations based on bills of exchange, consignments, promissory notes, and other instruments were effected from one end of New Spain to the other; and loans or mortgages backing agricultural/livestock activities linked urban centers with all of the regions. Supplying meat to cities implied moving herds of cattle as far as from Sinaloa to Mexico City. One way or another, commerce like this contributed to shaping a comprehensive web of connections. But considering other aspects of economic life, most crops and manufactured goods had markets that rarely extended beyond their respective region, and the differences in prices and availability of goods among regions were very large. Furthermore, especially on *ranchos* and in pueblos, a subsistence economy was the general rule.

Communication networks were complete in one sense, but incomplete in another. On the one hand, a person could walk or ride throughout almost all of New Spain along paths and roads designed for horses that crisscrossed all the plains and mountains, with the exception of the jungles and totally uninhabited areas, and free transit was impeded only by the rainy season. On the other, roads able to accommodate wagons, bridges, and other necessary infrastructure for inexpensive, large-scale transport of a variety of goods were few, of poor quality, and limited to the center of the country and some places in the North. Relatively wide-ranging spatial mobility was possible, but movement was easier for people than for goods.

Considering social mobility alongside this panorama, in the mid-eighteenth century New Spain provided a picture with just as many contrasts. The precise social categories of the era of the Conquest—Spaniards and Indians—were still recognizable among some groups of people who maintained their social distance or cultural isolation. Yet barring these exceptions, such categories were no longer operational: the population had intermarried so much that it no longer made sense to mark off social boundaries in those terms, and it continued to become more mixed both racially and culturally. Legislation made it possible to preserve differences that many people benefited from reinforcing in order to secure various privileges, but that was a deceptive reflection of social reality. Rather, during this stage of colonial history there were indications of the coming emergence of social classes defined more by economic status than by any other consideration. The distance between rich and poor, with very few of the former and many of the latter, as well as their opposing interests and differing perceptions of reality, would inevitably have a major influence on New Spain's final years. Nevertheless, there would also be affinities that would unite the most privileged elites on one side and those paying tribute (i.e., Indians), peons, *rancheros*, artisans, and the lowest level of government and church workers, on the other. These socio-economic differences would become more critical as the Crown increasingly lost interest in maintaining the principle of legitimacy based on justice and concerned itself more with asserting its power and satisfying its hunger for revenue.

CONCLUSION

Spain suffered many losses by supporting France against England during the Seven Years' War (1756-1763), a European altercation that had major repercussions on the American Continent. The English took Havana in 1762, causing the definitive breakdown of the fleet system and great anxiety within the Spanish government. When the peace was signed, Spain recovered Havana and could resume its trade operations, but the experience had been traumatic. Just as had occurred after the defeat of the Invincible Armada in 1588, Spain became more and more determined to remedy the empire's weaknesses and return to it some of the glory that had been lost. Also, like nearly two centuries before, the Crown made use of what resources it could obtain from its overseas possessions. But notwithstanding these similarities, the circumstances were actually very different. First, the leading European nations had changed their concept of power and the State, abandoning many of their former patrimonial ideas to shift towards a philosophy known as "enlightened despotism" or "enlightened absolutism," that is, the idealization of an authoritarian, centralized, efficient, and rational government preoccupied with material progress, but also interested in, if not obsessed with, expanding its tax base at all costs. In addition, in 1759, the Spanish throne had been assumed by Charles III, a monarch who was extremely active. Charles and his ministers would eventually conduct a plethora of adjustments and reforms, and replace many of the individuals who were serving in government. A new generation of officials—natives of Spain, many with military training and experience with the harsh conditions of the North—would come to replace the colonial bureaucracy, which in the eyes of the zealous sons of the Enlightenment was inefficient and corrupt. And having so many positions of power in the hands of Creoles was intolerable.

Taking into account that during the seventeenth century New Spain had been able to act with a significant dose of autonomy and had managed to keep a large part of the wealth it generated on American soil, the Crown's actions and intentions were an omen of substantial changes to come, as well as a claim on that wealth. Some historians have understandably defined these years in the mid-eighteenth century as those in which the enlightened government would put an end to the era of impotence to begin one in which authority was to hold sway.

THE BOURBON REFORMS

Luis Jáuregui

In the early years of the eighteenth century, the Spanish Crown began instituting changes in the way it managed its vast possessions in the Americas. In the first half of the century, reforms were rather timid, but the Crown later implemented vigorous, innovative measures that are commonly referred to as the "Bourbon Reforms." Timid or bold, all responded to the desire of Spain's Bourbon dynasty to regain its hold on the reins of power in the Americas and especially in New Spain, its richest possession. Thus began a process of modernization that would last almost the entire century.

Bourbon modernization was the outgrowth of a way of thinking and a value system known as the Enlightenment. The main characteristics of this illustrated movement were trust in human reason, discredit of traditions, antagonism toward ignorance, defense of scientific and technological knowledge as a means of transforming the world, and the search—more through reason than through religion—for a solution to social problems. In brief, the Enlightenment followed a reformist ideal. Its application was a process of modernization implemented in the eighteenth century by practically all European monarchs, giving rise to the form of government known as "enlightened despotism" (or "enlightened absolutism").

Because it encountered opposition in a society attached to traditional values, the Enlightenment arrived in Spain through the aristocracy, government officials, and the clergy. One of these was Benito Jerónimo Feijoo, who used pleasant, direct prose —in a way that did not challenge the Catholic faith—to question common notions he considered mistaken. The writings of Father Feijoo were very popular, widely read and commented on by both laymen and religious officials. Furthermore, the Bourbon dynasty's exercise of power was a clear example of enlightened despotism. The ministers of Charles III (1759-1788) and of his son Charles IV (1788-1808) influenced the reformist spirit of both kings and spread the concepts of the Enlightenment through the so-called Economic Societies of Friends of the Country and the nascent periodical press.

In the Americas, these new ideas were applied within the framework of an enlightened form of government with an absolute monarch whose authority was never questioned. Thus, over time, modernizing changes were made to the way the viceroy (the king's alter ego in places like New Spain) and his staff governed. The most noteworthy reforms were instituted between 1760 and 1808. Commonly known as the "Bourbon Reforms," these were the imperial government's strategy to develop material interests and increase the monarchy's wealth by effecting major changes in fiscal, military, and commercial systems, and by fostering a variety of productive activities. Under these reforms, privileges were slightly reduced and the Indians' living conditions more or less improved. The imperial reforms had a great deal to do with the dissemination of culture, since distinguished Europeans infused with the ideas of the Enlightenment were sent to the New World to develop science, art, and industry. But the Spanish Americans also played a role in the adoption of new ideas because they had access to emancipatory and even revolutionary enlightened ideas, albeit in a covert way. Their greater level of culture and prosperity made it clear to the Creoles that Spanish rule was plagued with abuses and defects. So the period of the Bourbon Reforms in New Spain is important not only because of greater economic growth and contact with the Atlantic World, but also because it involved years of crisis within a society that came to realize it was different from the Mother Country.

AN OVERVIEW

In New Spain, the Bourbon Reforms began with three *visitas* (tours of inspection of office-holders and offices) ordered by King Philip V (1700-1746), which indicated the Crown was fully aware that the administrative situation in the viceroyalty was deplorable. Since the economy was experiencing healthy growth, changes of an administrative nature were made to ensure the Crown had the resources to carry out other more far-reaching reforms. These first changes consisted of the so-called "centralization of royal revenues," i.e., a transfer of tax collection duties from private hands to those of royal officials.

The occupation of Havana by the British Navy in 1762 highlighted the necessity of undertaking a second round of reforms, more aggressive than previous ones. Charles III's ascension to the throne a few years earlier was a major factor leading up to these reforms. The new monarch undoubtedly had broad experience in the art of governing; but circumstances now called for him to undertake the political and administrative reorganization of the Spanish American Empire, which for the most part was still ruled by decrees issued in the late sixteenth century. International and military issues were involved. Charles III's reforms addressed strengthening the defensive system, especially in the Caribbean and the North of New Spain, as well as centralizing power in the hands of the king's own officials. The two tasks required large amounts of tax revenue, so the Crown also launched a thoroughgoing reform of the management of New Spain's royal treasury.

In contrast to most of the viceroys in previous centuries, those who governed New Spain during Charles III's reign were extraordinary men: none was noble by birth and all reached their high positions through their own merit. Even more important, all were motivated by the desire to renew the empire in general and New Spain in particular. As if this were not enough, in the mid-1770s the Spanish Crown ordered a general inspection of all of New Spain's royal treasuries: the famous visit of José de Gálvez (1765-1771). After this distinguished man was named Minister General of the Indies in 1775, the corrective measures he found to be necessary during his tour of inspection to New Spain began to be forcefully implemented. This is when the viceroyalty's defense corps and the *Comandancia General de las Provincias Internas* (General Command for the Interior [Northern] Provinces) (1776) were formed. There was also an attempt at that time to reduce the viceroy's power, and reforms to provincial administration were begun by establishing *intendencias* (administrative units covering a region, set up to administer justice, oversee tax collection, and promote agriculture, economic growth, and defense) headed by officials known as *intendentes* (intendants), who had assistants known as *subdelegados* (subdelegates) (1786).

Despite the initial momentum of this modernization program, Gálvez's death in 1787 and the ascension to the throne of Charles IV, who had to face more adverse international circumstances than his father, prompted a change in the Bourbon reformism that distorted its initial purpose. From an economic standpoint, this change is also explained by three related aspects. In the first place, the viceroyalty experienced a slowdown of the economy in relation to the previous twenty years. Secondly, the excessive extraction of fiscal resources from the inhabitants of New Spain during the middle years of the century forced the Crown to resort in greater proportion to loans and donations, increasing even more the appropriation of the viceroyalty's wealth. Lastly, international conflict exposed the economy of New Spain to "neutral trade" (1796-1802 and 1804-1808), which was disastrous in view of its technological backwardness and lack of competitiveness.

The Bourbon Reforms also had an impact on social and cultural affairs. In these years, the population resented Spanish rule, a system that allowed only the most privileged to advance, and even they paid a high price in the form of support for the Crown. Despite the bitterness accumulated over this period, the Creoles benefited from the tremendous development of cultural institutions and the opening up to other societies of the Atlantic World. The Indians also bore the burden of Spanish domination, but were more affected by the various subsistence crises that occurred in these years, particularly in 1785-1787 and 1808-1810. Notwithstanding difficulties, by the first decade of the nineteenth century, New Spain had become the Spanish monarch's treasure chest, with an economy undergoing consolidation and an identity of its own. The pressure put on the people of New Spain by the Crown in the last years of the Bourbon era impoverished part of the population and destroyed the potential for future economic growth in the colony and in an independent Mexico. What the Spanish government and its last viceroys did not alter was the feeling that the situation could shift in favor of the people of New Spain.

This overview of the principal set of reforms undertaken by the Bourbon disciples of the Enlightenment provides a frame of reference for the final years of New Spain and the first decades of independent Mexico. It can even be said that most of the geographic divisions that would characterize the Mexican Republic were established during the era of the Bourbon Reforms. As resentment of Spanish rule developed during this period, the seeds of independent Mexico's economic decline were also sown during New Spain's prosperous years of Bourbon rule.

THE BOURBON DYNASTY'S FIRST REFORMS

The Imperial Spanish government found the situation in its richest possession in the Americas intolerable. Three incomplete and troubled tours of inspection (1710-1715, 1716, and 1729-1733) had demonstrated the need to modify the current state of affairs. For example, since 1711 the Spanish monarchy had been told that revenue from the *alcabala* (internal taxes charged for the movement of goods through *suelo alcabalatorio,* regions in which tolls were charged on merchandise) would be greater if these taxes were managed by Crown officials, rather than giving the concession for collection to some other corporation (such as merchant groups or town councils). The problem was that almost always, the viceroys decided to contract out the collection of the *alcabala* tax to an organization instead of keeping it in imperial hands.

For the *alcabala* taxes, like many other sources of royal income (the royal mint, Indian tributes, and monopolies over gunpowder, tobacco, playing cards, ore assaying rights, bulls, pulque taxes, etc.), the situation began to change in 1732 with the Crown regaining control of the most important positions at the Mexico City Royal Mint, rather than selling them to the highest bidder. The process of centralizing revenues continued throughout almost the entire century. The most important example of this process was the inclusion of the *alcabala* taxes in New Spain's fiscal apparatus, a change that took several years (1754-1776) and was temporarily suspended by Inspector Gálvez. The centralization process consisted of ceasing to "rent" the tax collection function for a fixed amount to private entities, which obliged the Crown to assume this responsibility itself and thereby have an opportunity to increase collections and reduce expenses.

Undoubtedly, the Crown had to spend large amounts of money to achieve this centralization of revenues, but it was also necessary to put the administrative structure of New Spain's treasury on a sounder footing. Fortunately, the colonial economy performed well from the end of the seventeenth century on. Specifically, judging by the taxes paid, mining activity grew at a reasonable pace until 1750; like the rest of the economy, it stagnated during the middle years of the century, but prospered in the 1770s and 1780s.

Costly though they were, by mid-century the first changes promised to allow for major increases in revenues to the colonial treasury. The blow Spain received to its supremacy over the Atlantic at the end of the Seven Year's War (1756-1763) was what accelerated the reform process. On the one hand, revenues fell. With Havana, Manila in the Philippines fell to the English, suspending for several years the arrival of the galleon from the Far East and the monies it contributed to New Spain's treasury. On the other, expenses rose considerably, owing to the costs of installing the military in the Greater Antilles, and the port of Havana in particular. With the occupation of Havana, the British had come too close to the Crown's principal source of wealth: New Spain. That is why in 1764 a plan was developed to fortify Veracruz, secure the road from there to Mexico City, and form a large contingent of veteran troops and militias. In November of that year, the first permanent army, the *Regimiento de América* (Infantry Regiment "America") led by commanding officer Juan de Villalba, landed in New Spain.

Simultaneously, a tour of inspection was planned to study the viceroyalty's administrative and judicial situation. José de Gálvez from Málaga was appointed to carry out this task.

THE GENERAL TOUR OF INSPECTION (*VISITA*) OF THE COURTS AND ROYAL TREASURIES OF NEW SPAIN

Inspector Gálvez was not only asked to diagnose problems; he was also given broad powers to reform anything that need-

ed to be changed. However, he did have two primary man-
dates: to increase the wealth of New Spain's treasury and to
prevent abuse and squandering in order to improve the management of revenues. In addressing the first assignment, the
inspector consolidated the royal monopoly on tobacco. This
meant that the Crown took full charge of planting, processing,
and selling tobacco, mostly in the form of small cigars, which
were widely consumed in New Spain, above all by women. In
terms of its value, the tobacco business was the second largest
productive activity in the viceroyalty, surpassed only by extremely lucrative mining activity. Furthermore, Gálvez legal-
ized rum. Because its production was prohibited, illegal consumption was very high, with the resulting loss of duties for
the royal treasury. By the same token, the inspector established the *Contaduría General de Propios y Arbitrios* (Accoun-
tant's Office for City Public Property and Taxes), through which
the Crown took over management of the resources of pueblos,
villages, and urban settlements. The measure centralized all
these monies in royal coffers, and although they did not really belong to the king, they would pose a major temptation
several years later in view of the urgent need to finance imperial wars.

The appointment of Carlos Francisco de Croix as viceroy
(1766-1771) facilitated the tour of inspection, because he shared
Gálvez's ideas about reform. Both men agreed on the need to
visit New Santander which, since its founding in 1748, had
been almost entirely neglected. In addition, months later the
inspector would personally visit the vast lands in northwestern
New Spain with a view to designing a strategy that would make
it possible to increase the area's population, pacify the Indians,
and exploit its mineral deposits.

Meanwhile, the colonial treasury's expenditures grew by leaps
and bounds, owing to increased charges on the *situados* (money
allocated to the defense of Spanish possessions in the Caribbean)

and in view of the need to quell the 1767 uprisings caused by the expulsion of the Jesuits.

The viceroy left the inspector to his work, and Gálvez devoted himself to reviewing royal treasuries and courts, determining which managers and judges were corrupt and removing them from office and, when necessary, closing offices, as was the case at the Acapulco treasury office, which only operated three months of the year. As part of their efforts to enhance the wealth of the royal treasury, Gálvez and Croix defended one cause that seemed contrary to the Crown's interests: reducing the price of quicksilver (or mercury, on which the Crown had a monopoly) in order to promote mining, since it was an essential ingredient for processing silver ore. As with some of Gálvez's other proposals, over time this one would prove its effectiveness in promoting economic activity and subsequently revenues to the royal treasury.

* * *

Regalism (the doctrine of royal prerogative or supremacy), understood as subordination of the Church to the king, was the hallmark of the Bourbon government. For Charles III and his ministers, the Church's privileges were incompatible with the State's interests. Therefore, they were determined to put an end to the old metaphor that the king was the father and the Church the mother of the Hispanic family, and to develop a masculine concept of politics with a single head, namely the king. In Spain, writers and politicians of the Enlightenment defended this stand, which subjected to scrutiny the entire legal structure of the Church and its participation in social life. This point of view could not have prevailed without the support of a sector within the Church, namely the Jansenist faction. This group found the churches of the Late Baroque extravagant, with excessive *sobredorado* (surface gilding), and in bad taste, and advocated the simplicity and sobriety of the neoclassical style. Jansenists in both Europe and the Americas were the ones who virulently attacked the Jesuits because they defended the power of the pope and sought to maintain their independence from the bishops' authority.

The expulsion of the Jesuits from New Spain was not the result of an ideological stand that took shape in the viceroyalty, but rather of a decree issued by the Spanish king in early 1767 which reflected the desire to eliminate that religious order's resistance to the king's power, especially since they swore absolute obedience to the pope.

The Jesuits had large and efficient agricultural estates in New Spain; they were also major urban landowners. However, their greatest influence in the viceroyalty came from their work in education, which was based on a method that turned students into disciplined thinkers. In the hands of the Jesuit order, this form of education was considered dangerous in those years of the eighteenth century, when science and philosophy were modernizing, despite the grim efforts of the Inquisition.

When the royal decree was received, Gálvez and Croix were in almost complete agreement. This made it possible to expel the Jesuits in a surprisingly rapid and orderly manner, in keeping with the monarch's instructions: "thus ... the subjects of the great king who sits on the throne of Spain must know that they were born to remain silent and obey, and not to discuss or express an opinion on the sovereign's lofty affairs." Expulsion of the Company of Jesus caused the people to rebel, or at least that was the excuse used for the uprisings which occurred. San Luis de la Paz, San Luis Potosí, Guanajuato, and Valladolid de Michoacán all fell victim to the severe repression inflicted by Inspector Gálvez (as commissioned by the viceroy), which clearly demonstrated his blind obedience to the Crown and his desire to eradicate any sign of sedition, at whatever the cost.

The treatment of the Jesuits in 1767 was one of the Crown's most obvious moves to attack ecclesiastical privileges. Another was the adoption of regulations regarding the State's power to judge and punish members of the clergy who violated civil law. The expulsion of the Jesuits was an affront to the educated segments of society, which had benefited until then from Jesuit colleges in 21 towns of New Spain, from Chihuahua to Mérida. This social group not only learned to read and write from the Jesuits, but also Latin grammar and advanced studies in philosophy and science. Moreover, the judgment of priests by civil law incensed the entire population of New Spain, especially its poorest and most ignorant members, who viewed priests as semidivine beings in a class apart from lay persons. In the end, the whole Bourbon strategy for attacking the Church only served to weaken the colonial regime.

*   *   *

The most important period of economic splendor in the history of New Spain began in the 1770s after a period of stagnation which, judging by the statistics, had begun in around 1750. The beginning of the prosperous years coincided with Viceroy Antonio María de Bucareli's term in office (1771-1779). This boom is largely explained by demographic growth: between 1742 and 1810, the number of people in New Spain rose from 3.3 million to 6.1 million, a huge increase that occurred particularly among the indigenous population. The Indians lived primarily in rural areas or in the approximately 4 682 villages whose population ranged from 2 000 to 3 000.

Although most people lived in rural areas, the number of villages, "small urban settlements," and cities grew during this period. The *intendencia* of México, where the seat of the colonial government was located, had a high proportion of urban population, as did the *intendencias* of Guanajuato and Puebla.

In contrast, Oaxaca and Guadalajara (which covered part of the current State of Jalisco) were predominantly rural, with only one or two urban settlements of importance in each *intendencia*. It was similar in the provinces of Valladolid (Michoacán) and Veracruz.

The population was composed mostly of young people under 16 years of age; life expectancy was between 55 and 58 for white people, but was lower for Indians and the *castas*.[1] It is noteworthy that viceroyal authorities were aware that people's living conditions needed to be improved. Quite apart from humanitarian considerations, the epidemics had been devastating for the very poor, impairing the viceroyal economy's capacity for growth. Viceroy Juan Vicente de Güemes Count of Revillagigedo (1789-1794) took decisive action to better hygienic conditions in the *intendencia* capital cities. The primary measures implemented were creation of cemeteries, prohibition of burials in churches, regulations covering used clothing, the establishment of quarantine hospitals, and the like. A few years later, in 1802, a smallpox vaccine reached the viceroyalty, parish churches were selected as health-care centers, and the clergy was in charge of administering it.

THE VICEROY'S POWER AND THE ORDINANCE OF INTENDANTS FOR NEW SPAIN

More as a measure of prudence than of opposition, Bucareli interrupted to a certain extent the reforms that Gálvez was attempting to implement in New Spain. He was right to do so, since when he took charge of the government the royal treasury's

---

[1] In colonial Mexico, a *casta* was one of a variety of racial combinations considered a separate group of a lower class than either pure Indians or Spaniards.

resources were still at a low level and its debts were very large, particularly as regards the *situados* (funds earmarked for defense). Five years later, he reported a substantial increase in net revenues as a result of a strict savings plan. A major aspect of this plan was first postponing, and later openly opposing, the appointment of *intendentes* in the viceroyalty under his administration.

The *intendencia* system—which had been in the process of implementation for several years in other American colonies—had been inherited from seventeenth-century France. In his tour of inspection, Gálvez had the goal, among others, of establishing *intendentes* to govern the provinces and *subdelegados* for smaller regions; these would replace the former *alcaldes mayores*. Bucareli's opposition to this administrative program was not merely a response to practical difficulties, but also had an important political backdrop, since the new scheme took away part of the viceroy's power, as had precisely been Gálvez's intention.

The Spanish Crown's viceroys played a variety of roles, including serving as judge, administrator, tax collector, and military commander-in-chief; on the local level, they had a corps of civil servants called *corregidores* or *alcaldes mayores*. These employees of the Crown did not receive a salary (or received a very small one), which obliged them to take on activities unrelated to their official jobs. One of these was the *repartimiento de mercancías*, which amounted to the *alcaldes mayores* serving as intermediaries for the merchants who belonged to the powerful Mexico City merchant guild. The former sold imported or colonial goods at high prices to the Indians in exchange for local products, which they purchased at low prices. This situation could not be tolerated by an enlightened ruler, because it made governing difficult, since the *alcaldes mayores* devoted themselves to their own business ventures instead of working to ensure public compliance with governmental measures.

Gálvez's proposal was to create a group of employees (the *intendentes*) who would carry out part of the viceroy's work at the provincial level: twelve men, each of whom would take charge of collecting taxes, administering justice, organizing militias, and managing the cities and pueblos within his jurisdiction. These tasks were called *causas:* thus, the *intendentes* would be familiar with the *causas* of the treasury, justice, war, and police (in this era, the latter was a concept that covered much more than the mere pursuit of criminals). Furthermore, Gálvez had in mind the militarization of the far North, as well as the creation of an office devoted exclusively to tax matters: the Overseer of the Royal Treasury, directly subordinate to the metropolitan Ministry of the Treasury. Both proposals sought to take duties away from the viceroy. Bucareli opposed all these changes and managed to bring them to a halt during his administration, both because the Minister General of the Indies in Spain also took a dim view of them and because the excellent flow of taxes coming from New Spain made them unnecessary. In 1776, José de Gálvez was named Minister General of the Indies. From that time until his death ten years later, all the proposals that had been an outgrowth of his tour of inspection were implemented in New Spain. Thus, the viceroyalty experienced a deluge of reforms virtually from the moment Gálvez assumed his new post. For example, in 1776, the General Command for the Interior (Northern) Provinces was created; although it never managed to completely escape from the control of the viceroy in Mexico City, this jurisdiction did foster the material, demographic, and cultural progress of the vast northern territories.

The final years of the 1770s brought profound changes. For one, New Spain was granted greater freedom to conduct its commercial trade within the Spanish American dominions, although it was limited to Peru and New Granada. Moreover, in the administrative sphere, Gálvez delivered another blow to the viceroy's power by creating the office of the Overseer of the Royal Treasury and appointing one of his former colleagues to be in charge. This measure sought to establish "technocratic rule" that would support the financial needs of the Spanish metropolitan government. It also meant taking tax collection duties and the allocation of resources out of the hands of the viceroy and his employees, such that they would continue only as judges. These financial responsibilities were instead placed in the hands of a new group of officials who oversaw the treasury and the *intendentes*. This effort failed because it was not well designed, and with time a number of gaps in the legal system came to light that precluded its implementation.

To foster a more technocratic regime, the Ordinance of Intendants was sent to New Spain, the last viceroyalty in which it was to be put into effect, at a very difficult moment for the empire. The Ordinance had just been adopted when Minister General of the Indies José de Gálvez died (1787), and was being fully applied (1788) when Charles III, the most reform-minded of the Bourbons, passed away. The regulations continued to be carried out anyway, in an attempt to create a more rational division of the viceroyalty to replace the confusion and discordance that had been the rule in the past. The ordinance stipulated that each of the 12 *intendencias* (Durango, Guadalajara, Guanajuato, Mérida, México, Oaxaca, Puebla, San Luis Potosí, Sonora/Sinaloa, Valladolid, Veracruz, and Zacatecas) would be assigned a large number of already established jurisdictions (*gobernaciones*, or provincial governments, *alcaldías mayores*, and *corregimientos*), each of which would be called a district. The implementation of the *intendencia* system was plagued with technical problems, which were in part due to the fact that the officers who designed the districts did not know their boundaries. The result was that the organization of colonial territory which was so ardently desired did not materialize. Even so, the

Bourbon *intendencias* provided the basis for the later division of Republican Mexico.

*   *   *

The 1780s were years of cultural brilliance characteristic of, among other factors, an economy that continued to grow, although inequalities existed. Viceroy Matías de Gálvez, brother of the Minister General of the Indies, founded the San Carlos Royal Academy of Fine Arts in Mexico City, and the newspaper *La Gaceta de México* was born. To improve the urban environment, this viceroy divided the city into *cuarteles* (wards) and established an *alcalde de barrio* (justice of the peace) for each. The viceroy's son, Bernardo de Gálvez (who was himself viceroy between June 1785 and November 1786) ordered the installation of street lighting, and Mexico City began to look more like Madrid.

Furthermore, the Enlightenment's interest in scientific expeditions led Viceroy Manuel Antonio Flores (1787-1789) to begin construction of the Botanical Garden in Mexico City, which was completed by his successor, Viceroy Revillagigedo. The latter launched the works for building the School of Mines (also known as the College of Mining), which was entrusted to Manuel Tolsá of Valencia. This institution was a pioneer in introducing methods of higher education, and its curriculum embraced the most modern currents of scientific thought and new experimental techniques. The building that housed it, inaugurated in 1811, remains one of the most splendid in all of Mexico City today.

THE 1790s: A CHANGE OF COURSE

The Bourbon modernization effort sought to centralize power. However, the Ordinance of Intendants for New Spain did not clearly focus on this purpose: rather, what the Crown wanted was to simplify colonial administration. The ordinance meant new officials came to replace the former *alcaldes mayores/corregidores*. The *repartimiento de mercancías* was prohibited in this process because—unlike the *alcaldes mayores*—the *subdelegados* received a salary. In some areas it was easy to eliminate the *repartimiento*; in others neither the law nor human intervention could destroy the old system, which simply changed its name to avoid punishment.

In time, the *intendentes* and *subdelegados* came to control more and more of the people of New Spain, and that is why the ordinance and related laws encountered so much resistance. That is also why the death of its principal advocate, José de Gálvez, in 1787 led the Crown to give in to the pressures being exerted on it. Thus, before the ordinance could be properly implemented, some of its regulations were declared to be infeasible and, in many cases, things reverted to their previous state, which caused the ordinance as a whole to lose coherence, as did some of its most important provisions.

Both the establishment of the *intendencias* and *subdelegaciones* and the centralization of revenue that was initiated years before were useful for tax collection, as we will discuss later. However, once set in motion, the new administrative scheme was plagued with difficulties. First, Viceroy Revillagigedo, the most enlightened of all of Charles IV's viceroys, defended the *intendencias* but opposed their taking power away from his own position. Revillagigedo's proposal was accepted, and after 1789 the *intendentes'* initiatives had to be authorized by the viceroy. Second, the territorial boundaries of New Spain's twelve *intendencias* were superimposed on those of the bishoprics and the jurisdictions for some centralized revenues. We might say that the *intendencias* "arrived late," since there was already a revenue-generating system in place in New Spain with which that of the *intendentes* came to overlap. It does not take much imagination to understand the difficulties between, for instance, the *inten-*

dentes of San Luis Potosí and Zacatecas when half of the Zacatecas *alcabala* taxes collected really belonged to San Luis Potosí.
The matter was even more complicated if we consider that both
intendentes were accountable to the Office of *Alcabalas* and Pul-
ques (in Mexico City), when according to the law they should
only have to report to the Ministry of the Treasury (in Spain) and,
after Revillagigedo's reforms in 1789, to the viceroy of New Spain.
The latter problem provoked spectacular battles between *intendentes* and the viceroyal central administration.

With all its troubles, the results of this and other components of the reform plan were outstanding. According to records, royal income quadrupled between 1765 and 1804. This is
explained by several factors: an increase in the number of taxes
(both regular and extraordinary); growth in tax rates; greater
pressure to deliver as a result of administrative changes; and economic growth. Regardless of the causes, the impact of this extraction of resources was tremendous. Indeed, estimates indicate
that the people of New Spain paid 70% more per capita in taxes than people in Spain did.

The tax burden on the people of New Spain was particularly heavy in the 1790s. This was because by then it was politically impossible for the Crown to raise more money through
regular taxes. Thus, owing to the military clashes in which the
Spanish Empire had become embroiled (the war with the French
National Convention in 1793 and the conflict with England in
1796), the Crown had to ask for loans and donations. These
differed from traditional taxes, because the king made a commitment to pay interest on these contributions.

And this was actually done until a few years before independence was achieved. The king paid interest to the most effective "tax collectors" of the viceroyalty: the Mexico City merchant guild, the recently created (1795) guilds of Veracruz and
Guadalajara, and the *Tribunal de Minería* (Mining Guild). Nevertheless, when there were many urgent demands on the trea-

sury, the king—with the help of his *intendentes*—dipped into funds that were not theirs, but which by law they held in escrow. This money was obtained from personal accounts and *arbitrios* (funds belonging to the pueblos, villages, and urban settlements), assets of Indian communities (the "savings" that those pueblos set aside for emergencies), *montepíos* (money that civil servants and military officers put aside for their widows), and so forth. This money was never reimbursed, and of course no interest was paid on it either. Some accounts disappeared during the liberal periods (1808-1814; 1820-1821), and others had to be reinitiated after 1821.

THE CONSOLIDATION OF *VALES REALES* (ROYAL BONDS) AND THE ECONOMY OF NEW SPAIN

One of the most desperate financial situations that the Crown faced was when it was forced to "stabilize" the price of the many promissory notes the king had signed (known as *vales reales* or royal bonds), which circulated almost like currency in Spain.[2] The intention of the so-called "consolidation of royal bonds" was for the Church in Spain to sell its properties and "lend" the money to the royal treasury. In New Spain, the Church did not own many properties and the wealthy Jesuit haciendas had already been transferred to the coffers of the royal treasury in

---

[2] The situation was that the king asked his subjects for loans and in exchange issued *vales reales* (papers signed by the king indicating the amount that the Crown had borrowed). These were used by people as if they were currency. At first, they were accepted at face value. However, over time and with the issuance of an ever-increasing number of such financial instruments, their value began to decline. The Crown's desire to "stabilize the price" derived from the fact that if no one accepted *vales reales* without significant discounts, the Crown would no longer be able to borrow money, at least not by using this mechanism of promissory notes.

accounts known as *temporalidades* (temporalities). What the Colonial Church did have was a great deal of money it received from both rich and poor for the celebration of masses for the redemption of their souls. The *Juzgado de Capellanías y Obras Pías* (Benefice of Chaplains and Pious Works) loaned out this money for the operation of haciendas, *ranchos,* and *obrajes* (textile workshops). This was the money that the Church had to "call in" from its debtors in order to "lend" it to the royal treasury.

The Consolidation Decree was promulgated in New Spain in late 1804, and its impact was dreadful. It reduced the availability of loanable funds and capital needed to run countless production units; savings were exhausted; and many people and institutions fell into poverty. The decree was suspended at the beginning of 1809 as a result of the *coup d'état* that deposed Viceroy José de Iturrigaray (1803-1808). Nevertheless, its effects were long-lasting because they undermined the economy's ability to recover in the short and medium terms.

Be that as it may, the tremendous amount of resources drained from New Spain during the Bourbon Era is evidence of an economy which, at the same time as it grew substantially, was bled off by the Spanish authorities. The population increase translated into greater market demand. Demographic growth also prompted more trade, which in turn benefited agricultural and livestock activities. In this period we find that agriculture was geared more toward urban settlements and was no longer focused on satisfying the demand of mining centers. Mining, for its part, experienced major growth beginning in 1772; in general terms, that growth would last until 1795. The dynamic nature of the mining sector was in keeping with the Crown's development policies: quicksilver and gunpowder were sold at special prices, and sales of implements directly related to mining were exempt from *alcabala* taxes. Another factor that accounts for the growth in mining was the relative liberalization of trade that Spanish dominions in the Americas began to enjoy in those years. Facing a downturn in benefits from mercantile activities, traders reoriented their investments toward exploiting mineral deposits.

In this context and given the relative increase in the number of mercantile transactions, it is important to note that during the period these conditions did not lead to the creation of one unified market within New Spain. Rather, there were several markets where goods were produced to meet the regional demand. Thus, for example, the Oaxaca *intendencia* produced corn that was consumed within the area, and it was not worthwhile to transport it to the Durango *intendencia*. This was not true, however, of certain products whose price justified the cost of long-distance transportation over extremely poor roads and subject to high *alcabala* taxes. Products such as silver, some textiles, and alcoholic beverages were widely distributed; but imported goods shipped in through Veracruz that made their way to Chihuahua and even farther north were still more lucrative. The demand for imported goods was met both through foreign trade liberalization, which was at its height in 1789, and through what was called "neutral trade," which Spain had to accept due to the blockade of its ports by England during the wars between the two nations. Neutral trade involved a permit granted by the Spanish Crown to nations not involved in the conflict, allowing them to enter and depart from the ports of New Spain. The main advantage of this measure was that it made it possible for essential supplies of quicksilver to reach the viceroyalty, and for the Spanish authorities in Europe to make use of the money generated from this wealthy dominion. Here is how it worked: the King of Spain asked for a loan from a financier—for example a Frenchman. The creditor would receive payment directly from the Mexico City treasury, which held the monies derived from regular taxes, loans, donations, and later—as a result of the consolidation decree—from the

Church, which called in loans made to New Spain's producers in order to lend the proceeds to the king. Actually, these resources ended up in Napoleon's coffers as a result of a pact that the Spanish monarchy had signed with him (1803) to support his war campaigns against England. Thus, a major part of New Spain's savings financed a conflict largely irrelevant to the residents of the colony.

Internally, New Spain had an increasingly dynamic market. The Bajío and Michoacán continued supplying mining districts and a growing number of manufactured goods to colonial cities. Puebla supplied flour to the West Indies, and although competition from the United States of America eliminated this business once neutral trade was established, textiles from Puebla were sold in Zacatecas, Sinaloa, Durango, Oaxaca, and Guatemala.

Population growth in the capital of the Guadalajara *intendencia* increased the city's prominence within the economy of New Spain. During this period its manufacturing centers expanded and there was a more active exchange of goods, including with Indian communities. Guadalajara's progress was to a great extent driven by the boost provided to its economy by formation of the city's merchant guild in 1795. In contrast to their counterparts in Mexico City, merchants in Guadalajara used more open trading practices from the very beginning. As a result, the largest trade fair in New Spain, which was held in San Juan de los Lagos and was provided for primarily by the Guadalajara guild members, became the supply post for the mining and urban centers of the far north. This area, especially the Northwest, experienced dramatic economic growth owing to the discovery of new silver deposits.

Elsewhere, the *intendencia* of San Luis Potosí (which covered the current states of San Luis Potosí, Coahuila, Nuevo León, Tamaulipas, and part of Texas) continued its rapid economic growth mainly as a result of a relatively large expansion of its cities, including Saltillo, Monterrey, and several settlements in

New Santander. Since the region lacked major mineral deposits, except for those in what is now the State of San Luis Potosí, its economy grew at a moderate pace because it specialized in producing goods that facilitated stronger trade linkages with the center of New Spain. The most important of these was livestock and related products, an activity for which Mexico City, the colony's central valleys, and the Bajío were already large markets by the end of the century. Something similar happened in the northern part of Oaxaca, which supplied some livestock and sugar to markets in the center of the country. This *intendencia*, especially in the Mixteca Alta area, continued to produce *cochinilla* or cochineal, an insect used to make a red dye which was exported through Veracruz. As a result, this region did not eliminate the *repartimiento de mercancías*, because it was still too lucrative a business to allow royal orders to ruin it. The valleys surrounding Oaxaca City maintained their economy by supplying the city and trading with the Isthmus of Tehuantepec, Chiapas, and Guatemala. As for the Yucatán Peninsula, the Crown treated it differently from the rest of New Spain. For instance, free trade was permitted in Yucatán beginning in 1770, thereby creating in this province a kind of right to enjoy special status, which generated an endless string of problems throughout the nineteenth century. Operating out of the port of Campeche, Yucatán became the supplier of regional products to the rest of New Spain, Cuba, and New Orleans; its population growth made it necessary to import goods from these and other regions.

NATIONALIST SENTIMENT IN NEW SPAIN

The process of modifying the structure of government, new educational methods, cultural institutions, and the almost clandestine access to European and U.S. thought, as well as prevailing economic conditions, inevitably led to changes in the minds of the people of New Spain. How could it be otherwise when throughout the entire period there had been constant conflict between Spanish colonial policy and the viceroyalty's domestic needs? Early on, before the 1790s, all kinds of public projects were undertaken: infrastructure was built and cultural institutions were founded, for example. This ended when the Crown feared that libertarian ideas from the French Revolution would reach New Spain. In the 1790s, differences between European-born and American-born Spaniards grew, as did mistrust between them. Despite the government's efforts to avoid it, words like "liberty," "progress," and "nation" were being spoken. It was a time of change in New Spain's ways of thinking. Contrary to the opinion in the Mother Country that nothing produced in the Americas was worth much, as of mid-century many writers in Spanish America had lauded the inhabitants' ability to create all kinds of works of art and intellect.

The Bourbon Reforms did a lot to develop Creole sentiment, since in many recently founded institutions (the San Carlos Academy of Fine Arts, the College of Mining, the Royal Botanical Garden) European-born Spaniards were appointed as their directors, while Creoles were given jobs as assistants. By the same token, high government positions were occupied by European-born Spaniards. As regards governance, however, there were alliances between—for example—*intendentes* and economically powerful local groups, alliances that formed when defending a position of power or economic privilege. Nevertheless, when the moment of truth—the beginning of the war for independence—arrived, the bureaucrats' loyalty to Spanish authority generally prevailed.

One important factor that explains nationalist sentiment was the advent of neutral trade, which put the people of New Spain in contact with foreigners and allowed them to acquire more self-confidence. Curiously, this self-confidence was reinforced by one of the most venal viceroys of the colonial era,

José de Iturrigaray, when he ordered the formation of provincial militias (military corps made up of residents of the provinces). This order, prompted by the desire to defend the colony in 1804 in view of the war between Spain and Britain, built awareness among the people of New Spain of their military power as a nation.

Under these conditions, the final years of Bourbon rule (1808-1809) were very difficult. Among many other events, the colony was driven to the brink of bankruptcy, and discontent was aggravated by a drought during those same years. The royal bond consolidation decree and its implementation had an economic impact, but the crisis of trust in the Spanish colonial and European governments that it created among the people of New Spain was even more damaging. The first warning (1808) was the frustrated attempt at a liberal revolution that broke out in Valladolid de Michoacán. The second (1810) marked the beginning of a long final period that had lasting consequences. Despite this complicated ending, the period of the Bourbon Reforms was, overall, one of economic and cultural prosperity that was not to be seen again in the next hundred years.

FROM INDEPENDENCE
TO CONSOLIDATION OF THE REPUBLIC

JOSEFINA ZORAIDA VÁZQUEZ

THIS CHAPTER COVERS THE PERIOD from 1808 to 1876, that is, from independence and the founding of a nation-state to its consolidation as a republic after defeating the French Intervention and the final attempt to establish a monarchy. It was a transitional period in which liberalism and nationalism began to make themselves felt on the world stage and new nation-states were forged, a phenomenon in which the Ibero-American countries were pioneers.

The American and French Revolutions, which later wielded a great influence on the Ibero-American colonies, introduced new principles into political life and the relations between states. These new principles, considered "liberal" in 1812, rejected absolute monarchy and posited that sovereignty resided in the people, and therefore that the people's representatives should elect the government, which was to be divided into three distinct branches—legislative, executive, and judicial—as a means for guaranteeing individual rights and freedoms. In granting adult men the right to elect and be elected as representatives, they ceased being subjects and became citizens. These tenets affected a nation's organization and domestic relations, but also had an impact on international relations, which were no longer exchanges among dynasties based on the sovereignty of monarchs and the exclusivity of markets. Instead, they were grounded on the principles of free trade and protection of the individual and of private property, promoting religious tolerance, reciprocity in relations, and the maritime rights of neutral countries, even in wartime. It was natural that such a drastic change would require a long period of transition to take root, and this was the context in which the Ibero-American independence movements occurred.

In New Spain, the "modernizing" changes imposed by the Bourbon Reforms had already altered the social, political, and economic relations built up over more than two centuries. This created a general malaise and caused the people of New Spain to yearn for autonomy, a desire that would inevitably be heightened in the face of increasing demands for revenue from the Spanish metropolis that affected all social groups. In this way, the breakdown of the monarchy in 1808 and the Spanish Liberal revolution, which will be discussed later in this chapter, created circumstances that favored independence by allowing American-born Spaniards to express their grievances and experience Spanish liberal constitutionalism, an influence that would permeate political thought in Spanish America during the first four decades of national life.

As in other Spanish viceroyalties in the Americas, in New Spain independence was achieved after a long struggle and, as a result, when the Mexican State was born it was frail, in debt, with a paralyzed economy and divided society, and in a state of complete disorganization. To top it all off, its reputation for enjoying prosperity and wealth made it a target for the ambitions of new commercial powers. Nevertheless, optimism about recovering its former splendor fostered the emergence of two different concepts of nationhood that were to compete for dominance, until the liberal republican regime triumphed at last.

THE REVOLUTION FOR INDEPENDENCE

New Spain's society was a human mosaic. Only 17.5% of the population consisted of European-born Spaniards and their descendants, the Creoles, most of whom were city dwellers. The number of the former was minuscule, and was comprised of government employees and permanent residents. The Creoles were the most educated and 5% possessed great fortunes, and some even had titles of nobility. But the majority were *rancheros*, merchants, business people, government officials, members of religious orders, and mid-level military men who aspired to higher rank. Indians accounted for about 60% of the population and maintained their corporate structures. Caciques, governors, hacienda owners, and traders came from the small group of indigenous nobles who spoke "Castilian" Spanish, but most Indians spoke only their native language, served as the bulk of the labor force, and paid tribute. Periodic climate changes and the development of haciendas had led many Indians to seek protection by becoming peons. Nearly 22% of the population was made up of *castas*—mixtures of Spanish, Creole, Indian, Black, Mulatto, and Mestizo—who owned no land and were barred from holding government positions or becoming masters in guilds. They worked in every activity not expressly denied them: they were miners, servants, artisans, overseers, mule drivers, and *mayordomos* (substitutes for absentee hacienda owners). Some had moved north to seek their fortune, while others were beggars, lepers, and delinquents who swarmed through the cities and mining centers. Just 0.5% of the population was Black, some of whom were slaves on sugar plantations.

Mexico City was enjoying a tranquil period when on June 8, 1808, the news arrived that Charles IV had abdicated in favor of his son Ferdinand. Preparations for celebrating the event had hardly begun when more news arrived that changed the mood: the Crown had fallen into Napoleon's hands. Astonishment was followed by anxiety about the consequences the change would have for New Spain.

The event had occurred within a complex setting in which Napoleon was trying to impose a continental blockade on his enemy, Great Britain. To accomplish this, he had forced Spain to allow French armies to cross its territories to conquer Portugal, which was allied with the British. Before delegating the Spanish Crown to his brother Joseph, Napoleon convened an assembly of representatives and conceded to the Spaniards a constitutional charter that guaranteed them certain rights and granted equality to the people of the Americas.

The Spanish people, however, rejected the imposition and rose up in armed rebellion. To mount their offensive they formed regional *juntas* (councils) which joined together in a supreme council to meet the needs for coordination and representation. But the council was unable to accomplish its task and named a regent who called for elections of the Spanish *Cortes* (States General), that is, a meeting of representatives of the nobility, the clergy, and the people, so that they could debate how the empire would be governed in the absence of the legitimate king.

Although the people of New Spain had sworn allegiance to Ferdinand VII, like those of other parts of the empire the Mexico City Council decided that since there was no king, sovereignty had reverted to the kingdom, which made it essential to call a meeting of the city councils to decide on its governance. Viceroy José de Iturrigaray granted his consent, but the *oidores* (high court judges) of the *audiencia* (court of justice over which the viceroy presided) opposed this, fearing that it was actually a move for independence. It was true that certain individuals sympathized with that viewpoint, convinced that the kingdom had the resources to provide for the welfare of its people, but the vast majority aspired to the autonomy to which they felt they were entitled.

While the kingdom convened a council similar to those in Spain, some European-born government employees and merchants prepared a coup d'état. At midnight on September 15, 1808, around 300 men under the command of wealthy hacienda owner Gabriel de Yermo burst into the palace and took the viceroy and his family prisoners. The leaders of the city council were also imprisoned. At the same time, in the official deliberation room the oldest military man in the kingdom was declared to be the new viceroy. Not only was the coup illegal, but it also showed a willingness to use violence. The Spaniards' stubbornness frustrated the Creoles, who hatched conspiracies at a time when a drought was causing a grain shortage. After the *Junta de Sevilla* (Junta of Seville) appointed Archbishop Francisco Xavier Lizana as the new viceroy, the first conspiracy emerged in Valladolid. It was soon discovered, but the archbishop-viceroy showed leniency and just exiled the people involved. However, the conspiracy had already spread to Querétaro, a prosperous crossroads. In 1810, "literary circles" were organized at the home of *corregidores* Miguel Domínguez and Josefa Ortiz de Domínguez that were attended by Captains Ignacio Allende and Juan Aldama, some priests and merchants, and the parish priest from Dolores, Miguel Hidalgo, a man of the Enlightenment and former rector of the Colegio de San Nicolás de Valladolid. The conspirators planned to start an insurrection in December, while the San Juan de los Lagos fair was in progress. But their plans were exposed, and so Allende, Aldama, and Hidalgo had no choice but to throw themselves into the fight. Since that September 16 was a Sunday, the priest called people to mass, but once the faithful had gathered he urged them to join forces to "fight against misrule." Peons, peasants, and artisans, with their wives and children in tow, took up their slings, sticks, and farm implements or weapons—when available— and followed the priest.

That same night, the horde following Hidalgo occupied San Miguel el Grande and a few days later, in Celaya, they named Hidalgo "generalissimo" (commander in chief) and Allende, lieutenant general. At the sanctuary in Atotonilco, Hidalgo gave that army its first flag: an image of the Virgin of Guadalupe. Two weeks later, the insurgents were at the doorstep of the wealthy city of Guanajuato. Hidalgo summoned the *intendente* Juan Antonio Riaño to surrender, but he decided to barricade himself in the Alhóndiga de Granaditas (a public granary) with his wealthy neighbors and their riches. Hidalgo gave the order to attack, and after resisting for a long time, the multitude invaded the granary and furiously embarked on a bloody massacre and looting that Hidalgo and Allende could not control. The unfortunate incident would reduce the number of the movement's sympathizers and delay its triumph.

About that time in the capital, the call had been received to elect 17 deputies who were to represent New Spain in the *Cortes* of Cádiz, which caused great social ferment. The archbishop had been replaced by Francisco Xavier Venegas, who had the bad luck of taking office as the viceroy a few days before the independence movement erupted. That obliged him to organize a defense without knowledge of the kingdom. He immediately ordered General Félix María Calleja to march on Mexico City and bring the Virgin of Los Remedios to the capital.

Despite fear sparked by the violence, inequalities and injustices caused the insurrection to spread throughout the territory of New Spain. José María Morelos, the priest of Carácuaro, appeared before Miguel Hidalgo and received orders to take Acapulco. José Antonio Torres attacked Guadalajara, and similar action was repeated elsewhere. In contrast, Manuel Abad y Queipo, bishop-elect of Valladolid and a great advocate of a just solution for New Spain's social problems, rejected the movement's violence and excommunicated Hidalgo. When he learned the rebels were marching on Valladolid, the bishop-elect fled while the authorities turned the city over to the insurgents to avoid the fate met by the people in Guanajuato, and the local cathedral chapter reversed Hidalgo's excommunication.

By the end of October, Hidalgo's army was in the Las Cruces Mountains in the outskirts of Mexico City. On October 30, that diverse mob met and defeated a thousand royalist Creoles. The city shuddered. Hidalgo sought an audience with the viceroy, but finally ordered a retreat, although we do not know why. Was it caused by a lack of support from the *pueblos de indios* (pueblos) in the Toluca Valley? Was it inspired by fear that the excesses of Guanajuato would be repeated? Was he afraid of being surrounded by Calleja's troops? We only know that the string of victories had come to an end, since a few days later the rebels ran into the royalist army in Aculco and were defeated. Allende, disagreeing with Hidalgo's decision, marched toward Guanajuato, while the priest continued on toward Guadalajara.

That city received Hidalgo enthusiastically. Disregarding his precarious situation and now bearing the title of Alteza Serenísima (His Most Serene Highness), Hidalgo organized his government, worked to broaden the movement, ordered the publication of the newspaper *El Despertador Americano*, and decreed the abolition of slavery, Indian tribute payments, and government monopolies. In addition, he declared that communal lands were for the exclusive use of the Indians. Unfortunately, he also authorized the execution of the Spaniards being held prisoner. Allende soon arrived, defeated, at the same time as the troops led by Calleja and José de la Cruz, who had recently arrived from Spain, advanced on Guadalajara. Although he was convinced of the impossibility of defending the city, Allende set about organizing the best defense he could. The disaster culminated on January 17, 1811, at the Battle of Calderón Bridge, where 5 000 disciplined royalists defeated 90 000 rebels.

The rebel leaders managed to escape and decided to march north to seek aid from the United States. At the Hacienda del Pabellón, Allende and Aldama wrested command from Hidalgo, and in Saltillo, they decided to leave Ignacio López Rayón in charge of the fight. But a traitor made it possible for Allende, Aldama, Hidalgo, and José Mariano Jiménez to be captured and taken to Chihuahua, where they were tried and condemned to death. In his two trials, Hidalgo honestly admitted he was guilty of unleashing the violence and ordering the death of many Spaniards without trial, although "there was no reason for it, since they were innocent." The four leaders were beheaded and their heads were sent to Guanajuato where they were placed at the corners of the Alhóndiga de Granaditas. But the movement had dealt a mortal blow to the viceroy's rule by breaking down the colonial order and profoundly affecting the economy and fiscal administration.

Meanwhile, the Spanish *Cortes* met in Cádiz to decide on an imperial government in the absence of the legitimate king. The debates and news of the *Cortes* in Spain were consumed voraciously by the people of New Spain, and they became politicized. After long discussions, the deputies of the *Cortes* promulgated the Constitution of 1812, which took effect in Mexico in September. The new supreme law of the land established a constitutional monarchy with a division of powers, freedom of the press, the abolition of tribute payments, and the creation of *diputaciones provinciales* (provincial councils; six in New Spain) and constitutional town councils in all settlements with populations of 1 000 or more. These settlements were required to organize civilian militias to maintain order and contribute to the defense of the country in case of danger. The position of viceroy was abolished and replaced with political chiefs. The Constitution satisfied some of the Creoles' desires for freedom and representation, but did not grant them the equality and autonomy they dreamed of.

The Creoles took advantage of freedom of the press to spread libertarian ideas in newspapers, flyers, and pamphlets, prompting Venegas to do away with it. Meanwhile, Calleja's plan to defeat the insurgents had enjoyed some success, which ensured that he would be named the political chief to succeed Venegas. Calleja publicized the Constitution as a counter-revolutionary document, yet celebrated its abolition when Ferdinand VII returned to the throne in 1814, since it restricted his powers. In any event, the people of New Spain had experienced becoming citizens.

Leading the rebellion, López Rayón installed a Supreme Governing Junta of America in Zitácuaro. The insurgents had the support of a secret society of "Guadalupes," which sent them money, information, and advice, but it did not take Calleja long to drive them from Zitácuaro. About that time, the priest Morelos began to stand out as a great caudillo. His background as a mule driver had familiarized him with the people and the roads, and his natural military talent led him to form a small army, but one that was disciplined and trained, while his common sense enabled him to extract some benefit from the precarious conditions he was operating under. With Hermenegildo Galeana and Mariano Matamoros—his invaluable collaborators—and loyal followers like Nicolás Bravo, Manuel Mier y Terán, Guadalupe Victoria, and Vicente Guerrero, he managed to take Chilpancingo, Tixtla, Chilapa, Taxco, Izúcar, and Cuautla. In the latter he held out for two months against a siege by Calleja, and then miraculously managed to escape and regroup. Once the insurgents had gained control of a large area, Morelos brought together a Congress to establish sovereignty and organize a government. The Congress took office on September 14, 1813 in Chilpancingo, with the reading of the "Sentiments of the Nation" in which Morelos declared that the Americas were free, that sovereignty derived from the people and that the government should be divided into three branches, with the same laws for everyone, and that "they should moderate opulence and poverty." After signing the Declaration of Independence, the Congress conferred the presidency on Morelos, who took on the title of "The Servant of the Nation." The constitution that Congress drew up, largely inspired by the Spanish Constitution of 1812, was promulgated in Apatzingán on October 22, 1814. Unfortunately, Congress appropriated all power to itself and deprived Morelos of his freedom to act. The fighting continued. Although he managed to take Acapulco, Morelos was defeated in Valladolid and, cornered, was taken prisoner on November 5, 1815. After facing trial and being stripped of his priesthood for heresy, he was shot by a firing squad on December 22 in San Cristóbal Ecatepec.

By now, the kingdom showed the ravages of years of war. Its center was devastated by poverty and in ruins. The insurgents' domination over broad areas had dismantled the administration and the tax collection system. The necessities of war had led both the insurgents' and the Crown's military leaders to wield broad fiscal and judicial powers that would serve as the basis for their future political strength. Be that as it may, since New Spain appeared to have been pacified, the Spanish government chose to try a policy of reconciliation. Juan Ruiz de Apodaca was appointed viceroy in 1816 and immediately offered the insurgents amnesty, which many accepted. Amid circumstances which made it appear that order had been restored, in 1817, Fray Servando Teresa de Mier and the Spanish Captain Francisco Xavier Mina led a fleeting attempt at liberation. With 300 mercenaries, Mina marched as far as the Bajío, but was defeated by royalist troops and executed on November 11 of that year. Mier was jailed in San Juan de Ulúa.

The Crown's former prestige had been eroded due to its inability to restore order, when in January 1820 circumstances arose that favored consummating the struggle for independence. In Spain, commanding officer Major Rafael de Riego came out at the very beginning of January, 1820 in favor of restoring the Constitution of 1812 and forced the king to swear to it, causing the whole empire to do so and a call to be made for elections to the *Cortes*.

By then, ten years of strife had transformed New Spain to such an extent that even the Spanish-born population supported independence, although each group did so for different reasons. The upper echelons of the military and church hierarchies favored independence because they feared that the radicals in the new *Cortes* would take away their privileges, among them their immunity. Other groups wanted a constitution appropriate for New Spain, while still others preferred establishing a republic. For the time being, the constitutional order liberated the imprisoned insurgents, and the freedom of the press then prevailing allowed subversive publications to see the light of day. This, together with the election of deputies to the *Cortes*, provincial councillors, and constitutional town councils again began to alter the mood of the people.

In this context, a plan for independence emerged within the ranks of the royalists. Its author, Agustín de Iturbide, was a military man and a Creole born in Valladolid. He sympathized with those wanting autonomy, but had rejected the violent course of the rebel movement. As of 1815, he had said that independence could easily be achieved if the members of the two warring armies banded together. Don Agustín had never been defeated in battle, but an accusation against him had interrupted his career and, although he was exonerated, he chose to return to private life. The experience of war and his withdrawal enabled him to reflect on the situation, and his access to a broad range of groups within the population familiarized him with the differing viewpoints of people in New Spain, which he combined in a plan to consummate independence in a peaceful way. His prestige caused the group opposing the constitution to try to win him over, but contrary to traditional interpretation, Iturbide did not join that current of thought, but rather sought a consensus solution. When Ruiz de Apodaca offered him the southern command to get rid of Vicente Guerrero, Iturbide saw the opportunity to meet his objective, so he reported his plans to New Spain's deputies who were traveling to Spain.

Iturbide was confident he could defeat Guerrero or persuade him to accept amnesty, but as the venture became more complicated, he invited him to join with them. For his part, Guerrero was aware of his isolation and had reached a similar conclusion: independence was only possible if he joined forces with a royalist officer. At first he distrusted his former enemy, but the plan and the assurances that Iturbide offered ended up convincing him, so he asked his troops to recognize Iturbide "as the commander in chief of the national armies."

To build consensus, Iturbide had based his plan on three guarantees: religion, union, and independence, which summed up the goals of the Creoles in 1808 and those of the insurgents. The guarantee of union was designed to pacify the European-born Spaniards. The plan was unveiled on February 24, 1821, in Iguala. Copies were sent to the viceroy, all of New Spain's civilian and military authorities, and both the royalist and insurgent leaders. The plan was enthusiastically received by the people and the army, with the exception of the military leaders and authorities in the capital and some of the European-born Spanish commanders.

Meanwhile in Madrid, New Spain's deputies had managed to have the liberal Juan de O'Donojú appointed the *Jefe Político* (political leader) of the colony. Also, in a last attempt to achieve autonomy within the Spanish Empire, they presented a federalist proposal in June 1821 that was not even considered, so they withdrew. O'Donojú arrived in Veracruz in July, when the Iguala movement had already spread throughout the viceroyalty, which convinced him that independence was irreversible. Therefore, he reported to the government that it was inevitable: "We ourselves have experienced what a people can do when they want to be free." Thus convinced, he decided to meet with Iturbide, with whom he signed the Treaty of Córdoba, which recognized the independence and the establishment of the Mexican Empire, but salvaged the union with Spain by having the new empire headed by a member of the ruling dynasty. O'Donojú immediately demanded the surrender of the army that occupied the capital, which made it possible for the city, decorated with triumphal arches, to give an enthusiastic welcome to the liberator Iturbide, Guerrero, and the Army of the Three Guarantees on September 27, 1821. There were parades, fireworks, and songs to celebrate independence and the liberator, while widespread optimism masked the contradictions that existed between the royalists and the insurgents.

THE MEXICAN STATE IS BORN

The war and the 1812 Constitution had fostered the breakdown of organization in New Spain, whose vast territory, which lacked means of communication and had a sparse and heterogeneous population, was exposed to U.S. expansionism on its northern border. Although full of optimism, the empire—divided, disorganized, bankrupt, with a huge debt of 45 million pesos and a population that lacked political experience—was established on a shaky foundation. O'Donojú's recognition made the path towards the creation of a new State seem expeditious, but he died in October and deprived the nation of his experience and the legitimacy he personified. So, once the festivities were over, the nation faced the arduous task of taking control of its territory, resuming regular tax collection, inspiring loyalty among its citizens, and achieving international recognition to regularize its relations with the world.

Iturbide created a *Junta Provisional Gubernativa* (Provisional Governing Junta) made up of individuals who sympathized with a variety of ideas, but without the insurgents, who also lacked representation among the five members elected by the Junta as regents. Iturbide, as President of the Regency, immediately called an election of deputies to serve as representatives in the National Congress that was to draft the empire's constitution. But, ignoring the 1810 call to elect deputies to the *Cortes*, he opted for corporate representation that favored the elites. Once the deputies were elected, Congress began its work on February 24, 1822. At that time, the welcome news had arrived of the annexation of the Captaincy General of Guatemala, which—bankrupt and threatened with breaking into pieces— sought a way out. But another piece of less satisfactory news also arrived: the *Cortes* in Spain had refused to recognize the Treaty of Córdoba. The monarchists immediately began to take issue with the group that favored Iturbide's coronation.

The situation was complicated. The reduction in taxes and disorganization in efforts to collect them—together with the perception that independence had freed people from having to pay taxes—made resources scarce. The urgent need to pay the wages of government employees and military men meant that Congress had to legislate how the public treasury and the army would be structured, not to mention writing the Constitution, but the deputies' lack of experience caused them to become distracted with formalities. Iturbide, equally lacking in expertise, did not know how to deal with the situation either, and after a confrontation with the members of Congress, threatened to resign. Given his popularity, the rumor about his resignation prompted Sergeant Pío Marcha to instigate a mutiny in the Celaya Regiment of the army on the night of May 18, uttering the cry "Long live Agustín I, Emperor of Mexico!". The mob in the capital wasted no time in joining in, demanding that Congress discuss the proposal. Instead of refusing outright, Congress spent the night deliberating amid shouts and cries and, since many deputies supported the petition, a majority voted in favor of Iturbide's coronation.

While the republican insurgents suffered privations and were dissatisfied, Iturbide was crowned on July 21, although with fewer powers than he had had when he was President of the Regency. This discontent and the arrival of Mier, who had been released from San Juan de Ulúa prison, gave rise to conspiracies. The emperor proceeded to jail suspects, thereby creating such a critical situation that several deputies advised him to dissolve Congress. After doing so on October 21, Iturbide replaced it with a *Junta Nacional Instituyente* (National Founding Junta) elected from among the members of that same Congress.

This event, together with the provinces' fear of the centralism that Iturbide favored and the imposition of involuntary loans, had produced unrest that the young Brigadier Antonio López de Santa Anna would turn to his advantage to pronounce himself in charge. On December 2, 1822 in Veracruz, Santa Anna refused to recognize Iturbide's authority and demanded Congress be reinstated and that a republican government be established. The plan received very little support, but paradoxically created a situation in which secret societies or Masonic lodges formed a coalition among the troops sent to defeat Santa Anna and on February 2, 1823, issued the Plan of Casa Mata. This plan required election of a new Congress and, since it recognized the authority of provincial deputations, garnered regional support. Iturbide, confident that the plan was not an attack on him personally, limited himself to reinstalling the Congress that had been dissolved. But since the unrest did not dissipate, he abdicated on March 22, and on May 11 sailed with his family on a voyage to Italy. Congress not only declared that the empire was illegal, but also that Iturbide would be arrested if he touched foot on Mexican soil. This decree led to Iturbide being shot by a firing squad when he tried to return to Mexico in 1824.

Now that the political experiment to create a monarchy had been a failure, the nation was leaderless. The reinstated Congress had no qualms about assuming all power, and on March 31 appointed a triumvirate made up of Pedro Celestino Negrete, Guadalupe Victoria, and Nicolás Bravo to serve as the Supreme Executive Power. The provincial deputations and the army refused to obey that power and demanded that elections be held for a new Congress in accordance with the Plan of Casa Mata.

In colonial times, Central America had been administered separately, and was the only entity to separate itself from Mexico permanently. However, Guadalajara, Oaxaca, Yucatán, and Zacatecas declared themselves free and sovereign states, making it appear that Mexico's disintegration was imminent. The ruling triumvirate appointed Lucas Alamán as Minister of the Interior and Foreign Affairs. To prevent the country's fragmentation, Alamán mobilized the army against the most aggressive of the provinces, Guadalajara. Representatives of Guadalajara and Zacatecas agreed to acknowledge the authority of Congress on the condition that the country be organized as a federation. Congress was reluctant to do so, but the fear of the country being torn apart, as had happened in the viceroyalties further south, prompted it to give in and call for the election of a new Constituent Congress.

In November 1823, the new Congress was sworn in with a federalist majority that was willing to maintain the union. Thus, the act passed on January 31, 1824 created the "United Mexican States," and—after long debate—by September Congress had readied the text of the Constitution of 1824, which was adopted in October. The Constitution established a representative, popular federal republic made up of 19 states, four territories, and a Federal District. It kept Catholicism as the State religion and would tolerate no other, and divided government into three branches, with the Legislative Branch holding the most power. A president and vice president were made responsible for the Executive Branch, and the Judicial Branch was entrusted to the courts and a Supreme Court of Justice. The electoral system instituted by the Spanish Constitution was kept in place. Since it was an indirect system, voting was restricted, although at the lowest level almost all adult men voted. The Mexican president was elected by the state legislatures. This Constitution was influenced by the United States Constitution, but its primary basis was the Constitution of 1812.

Due to traditional regionalism, Mexican federalism was more radical than the United States' version, because the federal government was deprived of the right to tax citizens, but was left responsible for paying the debt, defending the nation, maintaining order, and gaining international recognition. To do all this, it was only allocated payments that had to be made by the states—and few states complied—plus import duties and some minor fees.

The presidential election favored former insurgents Guadalupe Victoria and Nicolás Bravo for president and vice president. They took the oath of office in an atmosphere of optimism and confidence that the new political regime would ensure progress. This was in contrast to actual conditions in the country: in debt, disorganized, and in need of credit and international recognition to function. The empire had only been recognized by Gran Colombia (Great Colombia), Peru, Chile, and the United States, but urgently needed Great Britain's acknowledgment. Owing to the latter's political and financial dominance, it was the only power capable of neutralizing the threat of re-conquest and providing the necessary loans. Since Great Britain was interested in Mexican silver and commodity markets, in 1825 it extended recognition and in 1826 signed a treaty that fostered friendship and trade. Speculative fervor on the part of British bankers had made it possible for two loans to be extended before recognition was obtained. Although conditions were grossly one-sided, the loans allowed the first presidency to function and to expel the Spaniards from San Juan de Ulúa, their last redoubt in Mexican territory. Unfortunately, Mexico was unable to pay the interest on the loans, with the consequent loss of creditworthiness and the nightmare that debt represented for all governments.

The free trade that people had longed for began with independence and enabled European and U.S. merchants to move in. Trade remained virtually paralyzed for the first decades, depressed by economic stagnation, poor communications, insecurity, the high cost of mule transport, and lack of flexible currency. Iturbide had resorted to printing paper money, but this stopped when he was deposed. So letters of credit (called *libranzas*) served as a substitute. In 1829, copper money was introduced for use in small transactions, but since it was quickly counterfeited on a large scale, it was withdrawn in 1841, causing the public treasury enormous losses.

The high hopes that had been placed on free trade were soon dashed by a reality that destroyed the incipient industrialization which had begun at the end of the eighteenth century. In any case, the large packet boats that arrived in Mexican ports with merchandise from Europe and the United States fostered some types of transactions. The British soon dominated wholesaling in inexpensive cloth, yarn and thread, tools, and machinery, while trade in luxury items became the preserve of the French. International treaties reserved retail trade for Mexicans, but it was impossible to prevent the French and Spaniards from getting into the business, which caused serious diplomatic problems that forced the government to eliminate the prohibition in 1842. Free trade also had political consequences, since some merchants were consuls or vice consuls representing their home countries who meddled or instigated insurrection, especially in Veracruz and Tampico, to take advantage of tax discounts that rebel forces gave them.

Silver continued to be Mexico's primary export, although the country also exported logwood, indigo, vanilla, cochineal, henequen, and sugar. Most trade occurred by way of Veracruz, Tampico, Matamoros, Campeche, Sisal, Mazatlán, Guaymas, and San Blas, and was riddled with contraband. Some routes set up in the North, especially between Chihuahua, Santa Fe, and the United States, were particularly successful. But, unfortunately, they served to whet the territorial ambitions of Mexico's northern neighbor.

Despite economic stagnation, memories of the splendor of New Spain, ambitions awakened by the publication of Alexander von Humboldt's book, and the vital supply of Mexican silver inspired the arrival of British and German investment in mining. But the injection of capital and the introduction of steam engines were not enough to maintain production at former levels, and it fell to half. Except in Zacatecas, the recovery of mining was slow, but Mexico did manage to export an average of 15 million pesos of silver every year legally, plus an additional amount that was smuggled out.

Agriculture, badly affected by the smaller labor force, lack of security, and cost of transportation, was also slow to recover. The haciendas remained in Creole hands, and their owners continued to diversify their business interests to defend themselves against economic fluctuations. To produce sugar, coffee or henequen for export, large haciendas invaded pueblo lands, which caused rural insurrections.

Nor could the dream of building railroads to solve communication problems be realized. It was blocked by a lack of financing, and only 18 km (11 miles) of rails were laid. The formation of a merchant fleet fell victim to the same difficulties; only Yucatán had a flotilla of small ships for coastal trade.

Nor did political life achieve stability. The plague of factionalism produced by the Masonic Lodges and military uprisings would quickly send peace up in smoke, although it must be noted that with the exception of the revolutions of 1832 and 1854, only limited areas were affected. The Scottish Rite Masonic Lodge, introduced by the Spanish Army, had become popular among the upper classes, so the radicals decided to found another for the masses. President Victoria favored this because he felt it contributed to "balance," and the first U.S. Minister to Mexico, Joel R. Poinsett, registered this organization in the United States. That society, known as the York Rite Masonic Lodge, adopted the anti-Spanish rhetoric that was popular with the lower classes and grew in strength with the discovery of Father Joaquín Arenas' conspiracy, which sought a return to the colonial order. This event increased confrontations among the masons, bogging down government activity and prompting Vice President Bravo in 1827 to come out against the lodges and Minister Poinsett's political interference. Bravo's defeat and exile secured the dominance of the York Rite and the passage of laws expelling the Spaniards.

In a tense atmosphere, an election was held in 1828 for the first presidential succession, and Mexico did not pass the test. The state legislatures' votes favored Manuel Gómez Pedraza, but in Veracruz General Santa Anna declared his support for Guerrero. After a mutiny of radicals in Mexico City supported this uprising, Pedraza resigned. Without constitutional authority, Congress appointed Guerrero as President and Anastasio Bustamante, Vice President.

During his brief and unfortunate presidency and with an empty treasury, Guerrero had to carry out the expulsion of the Spanish and confront the expedition to reconquer Mexico led by Isidro Barradas. Generals Mier y Terán and Santa Anna managed to defeat that aggression. This success was followed by promulgation of a decree abolishing slavery, although its unpopularity was not neutralized. In December 1829, the army reserves that had been stationed in Jalapa to support national defense refused to recognize Guerrero's presidency and, in January 1830, Vice President Bustamante took over the Executive Branch with Lucas Alamán serving as Minister of the Interior and Foreign Affairs.

Bustamante's administration was determined to end the military rebellions, put public finances in order, normalize the payment of debts to Britain, and foster economic development. Alamán succeeded in putting financing on a sounder footing and renegotiated the foreign debt, in addition to working to promote economic development and industrialization. To that end, he founded the *Banco de Avío* (a government-financed loan bank) and imported textile machinery, cotton seeds, goats, and vicuñas. His efforts and the spread of practical knowledge in newspapers like *El Mercurio* encouraged the creation of textile factories which, by mid-century, would manage to turn out a modicum of production, without competing with that from Britain.

Although everyone recognized Alamán's competence, people distrusted his political maneuvering, which had enabled him to eliminate enemies of his regime in some states. This provoked fear among the state governments that he aimed to centralize administration. Moreover, people were unhappy about the execution of General Guerrero and other radicals in 1831. Santa Anna, who aspired to be president himself, decided to take advantage of this discontent and led a rebellion against Bustamante in January 1832. This unleashed a revolution so costly that it forced the government to borrow money from the Church, mortgage revenues from customs, and lease the mint and salt mines, all of which ended up leaving it at the mercy of usurious lenders in order to be able to function at all.

Santa Anna, aided by the militias and customs revenue from Veracruz and Tampico, triumphed over Bustamante and the army. The states lent their support on the condition that Gómez Pedraza return and serve out his term of office. When the 1833 election was over, Santa Anna and Valentín Gómez Farías were the victors, along with a radical and inexperienced Congress. Since Santa Anna was constantly away at his hacienda or on a military campaign against the revolt championing "religion and privileges" that had broken out against the governors of Michoacán and the State of México, Vice President Gómez Farías ran the presidency for almost the entire first year.

The radicals were determined to undertake a liberal reform. To ensure they did not have any major opposition, they passed a law that condemned a list of suspected opponents to exile. By

October 1833, in the midst of a cholera epidemic, Congress began promulgating laws that affected the Church. They eliminated use of the police for collecting tithes and enforcing monastic vows. They decreed the provision for vacant parish priest positions by the government, closed the university, and secularized higher education. Gómez Farías suspended the provision regarding priests because he considered it impolitic, but Congress demanded the measure's implementation and condemned any bishops who put up resistance to exile. This measure, together with the banishment of citizens, led to an outbreak of popular unrest.

The religious reforms had enjoyed Santa Anna's approval, but when Congress began to debate reorganizing the army, he took advantage of the general outrage against the vice president and radicals to resume his role as president. General Santa Anna appointed a moderate liberal cabinet and suspended the reforms, with the exception of the elimination of the tithe payments, a step that favored hacienda owners.

In fact, from 1829 onward the Constitution was null and void. Congress had violated the supreme law of the land several times, the presidency was operating using extraordinary powers exclusively, and the weakness of the federal government made it difficult for government to function. In other words, constitutional reform was urgently needed. In 1835, during a critical situation in which Texan colonists were preparing to secede, the Mexican Congress passed a decree that cut back the civil militia. The State of Zacatecas and the State of Coahuila and Texas decided to challenge the law, and Minister of the Interior and Foreign Affairs José María Gutiérrez de Estrada made a futile attempt to convince the Zacatecas government of the legality of the law and the impossibility of making exceptions to it. Zacatecas readied its militia to resist the decree, although when the Mexican army arrived, the commanding officer, militia, and governor fled, making it possible for the state's capital to be occupied without a shot being fired. Nevertheless, events seemed to indicate that the enemies of federalism were right.

FACING THREATS FROM ABROAD, MEXICO EXPERIMENTS WITH CENTRALISM AND DICTATORSHIP

Due to the challenge from Zacatecas and the threat of Texan secession, the perception that federalism was fostering the disintegration of Mexico's national territory became more widespread. Thus, although the Congress elected in 1834 began to debate amending the Constitution, it ended up giving in to the clamor for the legislature to become a Constitutional Congress and adopt a "form more analogous to its needs and customs." Therefore, while Santa Anna set off on an expedition to Texas, the members of Congress began to draft a new constitution. The deputies proceeded to carefully study the "errors" of the country's first constitution and debate how to correct them.

The "Seven Laws," Mexico's first centralist constitution, was ready in December 1836. Although the federalists claimed it was conservative, it actually had a liberal bent, since it preserved representation and the division of powers among branches of government, to which it added a fourth, the "Supreme Conservative Power," which was responsible for overseeing the other three. The perception that broad representation caused instability led to limitations being placed on it. Thus restricted voting was established, similar to that prevailing in all the countries that had representative government. In other words, the only people who could vote or hold office were those who paid taxes or owned property. Election continued to be indirect. The states lost their autonomy and became departments, with governors chosen by the federal executive from a slate of three candidates presented by the departmental councils. State legislatures became departmental councils consisting of just seven deputies, while town councils were cut back to those that existed in 1808, plus councils of pueblos with more than 8 000 inhabitants and ports with a population of over 4 000. Presidents were to be elected in a more complicated way. It was determined that the Senate and the Supreme Court of Justice would present their slates of candidates from which the Chamber of Deputies (equivalent to the House of Representatives) would select three, and that list would be sent to the departmental councils. The vote of each departmental council would be considered by the Chamber of Deputies, whose chairman would declare the winner. The public treasury was centralized to strengthen the national government. However, although the president's term of office was extended to eight years and the vice presidency was eliminated, the Executive Branch continued to be very weak, since it was subject to the Supreme Conservative Power, the Congress, and the Government Council. Although the Seven Laws were adopted after the Texas disaster, the Mexican people—always believing in miracles—elected General Anastasio Bustamante president in an atmosphere of optimism that saw the system as "a new and promising beginning."

The uninformed attribute Texas' independence to centralism, but the loss of Texas was determined by the arrival of colonists from Mexico's expansionist neighbor and the United States' interest in purchasing it, which had been expressed since 1825 by U.S. Minister to Mexico Poinsett. The Spanish Crown had authorized the entry of the first Anglo-American colonists in an attempt to populate the territory and provide a safe haven for its former subjects living in Louisiana and Florida (which had been lost); these subjects were authorized to move to Texas with certain privileges. When Mexico became independent, the government maintained that policy because it wanted to populate the North. It set the condition that Anglo-American immigrants had to be Catholic, but increased their privileges in hopes of making them loyal citizens. Land grants for huge areas were given to some "entrepreneurs" who promised to populate them with honest colonists that would receive land almost for free, paying the entrepreneurs only for the boundary survey and division of the plots. The State of Coahuila and Texas charged for giving title to land and a symbolic payment. Unfortunately, the long border, great distance, and lack of resources led to a Protestant majority that favored slavery coming in and breaking the law, such that illegality prevailed in the colonies.

It is true that the Constituent Congress of 1824 created many problems by making Texas a part of Coahuila, but by 1834 most of these had been resolved. The real sources of friction were slavery and the installation of customs offices once the tax exemption periods had expired. From the time the state constitution was being debated, Anglo-American businessman Stephen Austin had "blackmailed" deputies who wanted to abolish slavery, asking them where the money would come from to pay slave owners for the value of their "property." As a result, the Constitution of 1827 limited itself to declaring that "in the state no one is born a slave." In 1829, Guerrero declared the abolition of slavery in Mexico, but exempted Texas on the condition that not a single additional slave be imported into the state. But the fact that slavery would disappear in the near future worried the Texan colonists.

In any event, it was the colonization law of 1830 prohibiting the immigration of Anglo-Americans that caused discontent to spread, and it grew further with the opening of the first customs office in 1832. That caused an uprising in the town of Anáhuac which led to the meeting of the first Anglo-American convention. Annexationist speculators, who arrived in the late 1820s, made skillful use of "these grievances" to stir up peaceful colonists. A second convention decided to send Austin to Mexico City to present some petitions to Congress. Austin, who had many friends among the radical deputies in 1833, managed to get the prohibition against Anglo-American immigration repealed, to extend the period of tax exemptions, and to have Coahuila make changes to increase Texas' representation. The use of English in administrative and legal proceedings was authorized, as well as trial by jury, that is, courts in which the accused would be judged by citizens.

But the reopening of the customs office in 1835 when the new period of tax exemption expired again caused great restlessness. The military commander-in-chief did not know how to resolve these problems, and the annexationists were again manipulating the colonists' fear of Mexican anti-slavery measures to curry their support for independence. In order to strengthen their movement, the colonists called on the people of the United States to join their fight for "freedom." As a result, thousands of clubs were formed in the U.S. that recruited volunteers and gathered weapons and funds. President Andrew Jackson declared "neutrality" regarding an internal Mexican problem, but his actions belied his words.

The government chose to send an expedition under the command of General Santa Anna to put down the Texan rebellion. Lack of public funds and the ad hoc nature of the army led to it being poorly organized and supplied, but the campaign started off successfully and, in a bloody battle, they won back the fort at the Alamo. That did not, however, prevent the Texans from declaring independence on March 6, 1836. They appointed a provisional government in which Lorenzo de Zavala, a Mexican, was named vice president. Santa Anna began the fight against this government and in a moment of carelessness was taken prisoner. The second in command, General Vicente Filisola, obeyed the imprisoned president's order to retreat beyond the Rio Grande (which later became known in Mexico as the Río Bravo). This clinched Texas' independence and its claim that the river would be the new Republic's border. Mexico's lack of funds stood in the way of sending another expedition, but did not keep the goal of recovering Texas from becoming an obsession that would prevent the Mexican government from heeding British warnings to recognize Texas' independence in order to avoid even greater losses.

It did not take long for centralism to crush the hopes it had inspired. It had no sooner been put into practice than the elimination of many town councils and imposition of a tax that all residents had to pay (a head tax) caused rural rebellions and federalist uprisings in the North. Thus, the centralist decade became the most unstable one in the century and further paralyzed the Mexican economy. The national government's weakness encouraged foreign interventions, which were justified by demands that Mexican administrations had neglected to meet. Most were unfair or exaggerated, as would be proven by international arbitration in the case of U.S. demands, which were reduced to only 15%. In 1838, France used Mexico's failure to meet its demands as an excuse to bombard and blockade Veracruz and Tampico, obliging the nation to go into debt to pay very unjust reparations.

The scarcity of funds exacerbated the government's indebtedness and forced Congress to impose a 15% tax on imported goods, which drove many foreign and some Mexican merchants into bankruptcy. As a result, before the first presidential term of office could be completed, some sought to solve the country's problems with a monarchy, "with a foreign prince," or with a military dictatorship. José María Gutiérrez de Estrada, convinced that a conspiracy was afoot to create such a dictatorship, dared to suggest the alternative of a monarchy. The army skillfully provoked a great republican outcry that would open the way for dictatorship. In 1841, foreign merchants urged Generals Antonio López de Santa Anna, Mariano Paredes, and Gabriel Valencia to pronounce themselves against the government, and in October a military dictatorship headed by Santa Anna was established. Moderate federalists supported the dictatorship on the condition that a new Constitutional Congress be convened. Santa Anna complied, and the federalists achieved a majority, which sealed its outcome. In December 1842, the government dissolved the Constitutional Congress and replaced it with a Board of Dignitaries that drafted the *Bases Orgánicas* (Organic Laws). The new centralist Constitution eliminated the Supreme Conservative Power, strengthened the Executive, and expanded representation and the powers of departmental bodies, which were called legislative assemblies. But the bankruptcy of the public treasury also made it impossible to enforce the new laws.

After the *Bases Orgánicas* had been adopted and the 1843 election had been held, Santa Anna was elected president, with a Congress of moderate federalists determined to make him comply with the Constitution. Therefore, when Santa Anna tried to dissolve the Congress in November 1844, it put up resistance and on December 5, 1844, stripped Santa Anna of his privileges with the support of the courts, the city council, and the mob of the capital. The chairman of the Government Council, José Joaquín de Herrera, became the interim president in accordance with the law. Herrera appointed a cabinet of distinguished moderate federalists and set about to create an honest government that would reconcile differences among the factions. The moderates realized the impossibility of going to war and chose to negotiate recognition of Texas in order to avoid doing so.

However, both national and international circumstances were adverse. Mexico was not only threatened by the United States, but also by Spain, whose ruling family had organized a conspiracy to install a monarchy in Mexico, to which France and Great Britain had agreed. Salvador Bermúdez de Castro, the Spanish minister in Mexico City, organized the project, which involved the collaboration of influential citizens such as Alamán.

This effort to install a monarchy fragmented the political scene even further. And to make matters worse, by the 1840s the asymmetry between Mexico and its neighbor had grown much more pronounced. The United States population reached 20 million, while Mexico had just over seven million people and lacked the wherewithal to confront a dynamic nation with abundant human and material resources. Unfortunately, Mexico's proposal to begin negotiations for recognition of Texas was poorly timed, and in June 1845, Texas approved the United States' offer of annexation. This caused the radical federalists to accuse Herrera of attempting to sell Texas and California.

Against this sensitive backdrop, the monarchists approached General Mariano Paredes y Arrillaga, commander of the army reserves, who took advantage of their support to seize power. Paredes' reputation for honesty and efficiency had enabled him to obtain government resources needed to reinforce his division, an essential measure for supporting the defense of the threatened North. Nevertheless, when he received orders to march toward the border, instead of obeying them, Paredes proceeded to refuse to recognize Herrera's authority and marched toward the capital to mount an attack on the presidency. His military dictatorship was a great failure, since it neither reduced corruption nor reordered public finances nor strengthened the country's defenses. As could have been expected, a federalist uprising soon broke out in Guadalajara. Yet despite the fact that the U.S. Army was advancing on Mexican territory, Paredes diverted army units to fight the federalists.

Paredes also tried to avoid war, but U.S. President James Polk was determined to acquire California at any cost. Polk preferred to avoid war in order to prevent stirring up regional problems. He therefore attempted to bribe Santa Anna, who was in exile in Havana, and offered to buy the territory. At the end of 1845, Polk's envoy arrived in Mexico City with a variety of offers to purchase territory, but was not allowed an audience. As soon as Polk received news that the mission had failed, he ordered General Zachary Taylor to march toward the Rio Grande, that is, toward Mexican territory or territory that at the very least was in dispute. After learning of a violent incident in March, Polk declared war on May 12, 1846, accusing Mexico of having "spilled American blood on American soil," a charge that was false.

By then, the first Mexican defeats had already occurred on May 8 and 9. The news stunned the Mexican people and discredited the Paredes dictatorship and centralism. Ignoring the disadvantages of a change in political system in the middle of a war, on August 4, a federalist *pronunciamiento* (military declaration and uprising) deposed Paredes and restored the Constitution of 1824. The change of government at that moment was an obstacle to organizing the nation's defense. On the one hand, the Constitution deprived the central government of powers and left it practically alone to prosecute the war. On the other, the scrambling for city council positions and the election of state and federal powers distracted attention from events at the front.

Once the war had started, the outcome was predictable. Mexico lacked everything: its weaponry was obsolete; its officers were unprofessional; its soldiers, poorly trained. Its army faced one that may have been smaller, but was professional, with access to supplies and sanitation, modern long-range artillery, and a flood of volunteers who could be trained and periodically replaced. While the Mexican Army was moving from the south to the north, the United States detached various units and attacked on several fronts simultaneously. At the same time, the U.S. Navy blockaded and occupied Mexican ports, depriving the government of revenue from customs duties, which the invaders used to support the war. Since tax payments were reduced, trade picked up. To prevent its ports from being occupied, Yucatán declared neutrality in the war.

By January 1847, the United States had annexed New Mexico and California, which were sparsely populated and almost totally lacking in defenses. U.S. superiority ensured victory and occupation of the North and, later, of the Veracruz-Puebla region. The Mexican army, ill-fed, poorly armed, and demoralized by the enemy's technological superiority as well as by the abandonment of their wounded, continued fighting against well-fed and well-supplied soldiers, although their sacrifice was almost futile. Monterrey and Veracruz resisted, suffering costly losses, and in La Angostura the Mexican Army fought a heroic battle for two days (also known as the Battle of Buena Vista), but when they had to fall back it became a defeat.

The army that disembarked in Veracruz wasted no time in occupying Puebla, which made the fall of Mexico City inevitable. After four defeats in the Valley of Mexico, Santa Anna ordered the army to retreat from the capital to prevent greater hardships. When the people heard that the U.S. Army was advancing, however, they tried to defend the city, which caused blood to flow through the streets and a state of siege to be declared. On September 14, 1847, the U.S. flag flew over Mexico's National Palace.

The following day in the town of Guadalupe, Santa Anna resigned the presidency, which was transferred to Manuel de la Peña y Peña, president of the Supreme Court of Justice, who moved the government to Querétaro. Despite the radicals' and monarchists' active opposition, the moderates managed to convene Congress and bring together several governors, giving the government a certain appearance of normalcy.

Meanwhile, in the United States its victories had led to a strident form of expansionism that called for absorbing all of Mexico. Polk had sent Nicholas Trist to negotiate peace, but given the U.S. triumphs, Polk ordered him to return to demand more territory in the peace treaty. The order posed a moral dilemma for Trist. He had already accepted a communiqué from the Mexican government with the names of the envoys with whom he would negotiate: Luis G. Cuevas, Bernardo Couto, and

Miguel Atristáin. At the urging of the British ambassador and General Winfield Scott, the commanding officer leading the army that had marched from Veracruz to Mexico City, Trist decided to disobey the order and begin the difficult negotiations that culminated on February 2, 1848, with the signing of a peace treaty in the town of Guadalupe. Trist would confess to his family the shame he felt "in all our meetings [facing] ... *the iniquity of war*, which was an abuse of power on our part." In the treaty, Mexico acknowledged the loss of more than half its territory. An "indemnity payment" of 15 million pesos was accepted for damages and a prorated amount for the portion of Mexico's foreign debt that corresponded to the lost territories, since they had been conquered by force of arms. The envoys managed to save Baja California and Tehuantepec and to ensure the rights of Mexicans living in the lands that had been lost. In Article XI, the only one favorable to Mexico, the United States made a commitment to defend the border against the attacks of Plains Indians, but it never actually did so. When he presented the treaty to Congress, De la Peña stressed that it had been signed in order to recover the occupied areas and see to it that "the republic survived its disgrace."

Despite hostility from the monarchists and radicals, the government conducted an election and managed to get the Congress that met in Querétaro to approve the treaty in May. Herrera won the presidency and re-established the government in Mexico City in June. He began reorganizing the country in an atmosphere of generalized depression, amid threats of monarchist and federalist *pronunciamientos*, while coping at the same time with Indian revolts in several states, particularly Yucatán. But that was not all; the country also suffered attacks from Indians living north of the U.S.-Mexico border and U.S. filibusters who sought to carve out new pieces of land for themselves.

The Herrera government managed to reorganize the administration and cut the size of the army, but could not overcome the political polarization between the moderate and radical federalists and the monarchists, not to mention General Santa Anna's followers. Bitterness led the political factions to blame each other for the defeat, which at least forced them to define their principles. Thus, in 1849 the Conservative Party emerged with a platform put together by Alamán, which prompted the federalists to define themselves as the Liberal Party.

In 1851, Herrera peacefully handed the presidency over to his successor, Mariano Arista, who was less fortunate and succumbed to attacks and uprisings that obliged him to resign. After an interim period with the chief justice of the Supreme Court serving as president, a military agreement imposed General Manuel María Lombardini to rule until the states conducted an election for a provisional president, who would convene a Congress. By that time, all the parties had reached the conclusion that a strong government was necessary. As a result, when the election was held, General Santa Anna, then exiled in Colombia, received the most votes.

That irresponsible man from Veracruz returned to power on April 20, 1853. The conservative Alamán presented him with a plan that focused on the need for a strong but responsible government, without any representation, with a respectable army, united under a single religion and benefiting from European support. The liberal Miguel Lerdo de Tejada presented an alternative plan that emphasized economic measures for development. Santa Anna, accustomed to mediating among parties, adopted the conservative plan of Alamán, who headed his cabinet, but also attempted to implement the policy suggested by his radical *paisano* (person from the same state of the country) Lerdo, whom he appointed as *oficial mayor* (senior official) of the new Ministry of Development, Colonization, Industry, and Commerce.

Santa Anna instituted a policy of repression and exiled former president Arista. Given that the conservatives considered the dictatorship to be a transition to establishing a monarchy, they began a search for a candidate. This had scant success given the sensitive context of European politics, which were focused on problems in Turkey. Alamán died in June 1853, and without this moderating influence, Santa Anna increased censorship and exiled more liberals. He also soon regained his taste for power and declared himself dictator for life, adopting the title of Most Serene Highness.

The dictatorship faced the perennial problem of scarce resources and indebtedness. Since the dictator's capricious and fickle nature had not changed, to raise money he established new and absurd taxes. Nonetheless, the dictatorship did accomplish some things, including publishing the first Commercial Code and benefiting from the Ministry of Development's work to encourage machinery imports and the creation of libraries and better communications.

Santa Anna again had to confront U.S. expansionism, which remained ravenous despite having already swallowed half of Mexico's territory and was applying pressure to obtain the Isthmus of Tehuantepec, Baja California and, if possible, the northern states. The new U.S. ambassador James Gadsden, aware of the Mexican government's shortage of funds, believed it would be easy to convince it to sell a good part of its remaining territory. The U.S. government utilized as pretexts a mistake on a map employed to negotiate the Treaty of Guadalupe Hidalgo and the need to use the Mesilla area for building a railroad.

The Mexican government was not able to finalize any European alliance to counteract the U.S. threat and, fearing another war, Santa Anna agreed to negotiate in December 1853. The U.S. took advantage of the signing of another treaty (known in the U.S. as the Gadsden Purchase) to obtain the Mesilla mesa and void the clause that ensured defense of the border against Indian attack. The ten million U.S. dollars paid served to keep Santa Anna in power, but the treaty's political cost was high and the dictatorship was completely discredited. Furthermore, the hopes placed in a "strong" government had evaporated and, one year after it had taken power, repudiation of the dictatorship had become widespread. The by-now customary *pronunciamiento* erupted in March of 1854 with the Plan of Ayutla, promoted by Juan Álvarez and Ignacio Comonfort. The plan did not recognize the Santa Anna government, repudiated the sale of the Mesilla, and demanded election of a Constituent Congress that would reinstate a representative federal republic.

Although they had the moral support of exiled liberals living in New Orleans, their lack of resources confined the rebels to a guerrilla war, while the Mesilla payments enabled Santa Anna to fight back effectively enough to remain in power until August 1855.

LIBERAL REFORM, THE FRENCH INTERVENTION, AND THE DEFINITIVE TRIUMPH OF THE REPUBLIC

Santa Anna's dictatorship caused the polarization of political positions. Although the two parties shared a goal of progress, their ideas about how to achieve it differed. The conservatives believed that progress could only be achieved through a system of monarchy and a corporate society, supported by a strong church and army. Meanwhile, the liberals thought that only a people's federal representative republic similar to the U.S. model could ensure such an aspiration. They therefore believed in the urgent need to wipe out the entire legacy of the viceroyalty, eliminate corporate entities and privileges, and disentail the Church's property and communal land to turn Mexico into a nation of small-scale property owners. But disagreement about how to accomplish this task kept the liberals divided. The moderates wanted to do it slowly to avoid violent resistance and so they favored reinstating the Constitution of 1824 with some amendments. But the purists favored drastic reform and, as a consequence, a new constitution.

The Ayutla movement had been able to sustain itself owing to the protection of the southern mountains and the access to the sea provided by Acapulco, but a pressing need for funds sent General Comonfort on a trip to the United States to raise money, with little success. Political circumstances were favorable to him, however. In 1855, a moderate movement emerged in the Bajío followed by another monarchist movement in San Luis Potosí that sought to put the grandson of Agustín de Iturbide on the throne of a new empire. This led to a coalition of purist and moderate liberals and the return of exiles. At the same time, Álvarez's host of supporters, which had been gradually growing, were on the march and caused Santa Anna to flee on August 17, 1855.

By September 16 the liberals had occupied the capital. On October 14, a council of state representatives elected Juan Álvarez as provisional president. He formed a cabinet of purist liberals: Melchor Ocampo, Benito Juárez, Miguel Lerdo, Ponciano Arriaga, and Guillermo Prieto, all members of a generation that was beginning to distinguish itself. Almost at once reform was instituted with the passage of the Juárez Law, which did away with military and clerical immunities, thereby making it possible for all citizens to be equal before the law. The Church, which had been reorganizing since the 1840s, began to counterattack.

Juan Álvarez resigned the presidency on December 11 and was replaced by the moderate Comonfort, who immediately filled the cabinet with moderates. However, when Comonfort sent troops to fight the Puebla pro-religious and pro-immunity movement, he did not hesitate to make an example of them by imposing punishment once they were defeated: he expropriated the bishopric of Puebla's property. He also passed two reformist laws: the Lerdo Law, which disentailed the rural and urban estates of civil and religious corporations, and the *Ley Iglesias*

(Iglesias Law), which prohibited the Church from charging the poor parish fees for services. The Archbishop of Mexico repudiated these laws, considering them an attack on the Church.

Once the election had been held, the Constituent Congress met on February 14, 1856. Although moderates were in the majority, the purists dominated the debates, which were very heated. The most controversial subjects were education and religious tolerance. The liberals wanted to control education in order to shape the citizens of the future, but—consistent with their convictions—they compromised on the freedom of teaching. They did not dare declare themselves in favor of religious tolerance because of a widespread fear of a popular uprising, but did do away with Catholicism as the state religion and stated that no prohibition existed against "the exercise of any religious belief." Some liberals wanted to adopt the Anglo-Saxon model of trial by jury as a democratic institution, but this was not approved. Agrarian reform was also debated, but in the end the Constitution only included the Lerdo Law, which ensured individual property rights to land.

The Constitution adopted on February 5, 1857 was not radical, but did systematically introduce the "rights of man": freedom of education and work; freedom of expression, petition, association, transit, and property; equality before the law; and the guarantee of not being detained for more than three days without justification. The Constitution ratified the sovereignty of the people constituted within "a representative, democratic, and federal republic made up of states that are free and sovereign with regard to their internal governance," with a government divided into three branches, with a unicameral legislature as the dominant power. It maintained the indirect system of elections and simplified election of the president, which would be "indirect in the first instance and by secret ballot." In other words, the president would be elected by the representatives chosen by the citizenry.

The election gave Comonfort the presidency, but he had no resources and had to abandon the liberals' hope that sales of church property would solve the government's financial problems, since the Lerdo Law had produced paltry results because of the easy payment terms, discounts, and acceptance of payment in the form of bonds that lacked any value. The law was designed to make stipulations regarding real estate benefit tenant farmers and occupants of dwellings, but their honesty or poverty ensured that the properties ended up in the hands of speculators.

Despite its moderate approach, the Constitution displeased the conservatives and was not enough to satisfy the purists. This situation disheartened many politicians and favored the position taken by Benito Juárez, who owing to the strength of his convictions was willing to risk everything for the Constitution. Juárez belonged to a non-Spanish-speaking ethnic group (Zapotec) in the mountains of Oaxaca and had been educated in a seminary and in the Institute of Sciences and Arts of that state. His career had been supported both by the radical federalists and the centralists. His election as a deputy to the Mexican Congress in 1847 allowed him to play a role in the nation's political life, although he returned to Oaxaca to serve as governor from 1847 to 1851 and again in 1856. After being elected president of the Supreme Court of Justice that year, he returned to Mexico City in 1857.

Pope Pius IX condemned the liberal government's actions and prompted Bishop Antonio Pelagio de Labastida to lead a conservative rebellion, for which he was sent into exile. This caused many liberals to advocate the need for a liberal dictatorship to provide a transition. Within this context, in December 1857 General Félix Zuloaga led a *pronunciamiento* demanding a new Constituent Congress. President Comonfort, who questioned the feasibility of governing under the Constitution, supported him and jailed Juárez, who refused to recognize this coup d'état. When a few weeks later Zuloaga refused to recognize Comonfort as the president and assumed the presidency himself, Comonfort resigned and freed Benito Juárez, who under the Constitution was his legal replacement. The existence of two presidents made civil war inevitable.

The country split into two camps. The governments of the states of Colima, Guerrero, Guanajuato, Jalisco, Michoacán, Oaxaca, Querétaro, Veracruz, and Zacatecas declared their support for the Constitution, but most of the army and the clergy aligned themselves with Zuloaga, who was recognized by foreign representatives because he held the capital city. Juárez was convinced that the rule of law was essential to achieving lasting peace. He left for Guadalajara, but a conservative threat there made him sail for Veracruz. In addition to being a liberal city, Veracruz could provide him with revenues from the customs office.

Since the army supported the Conservative Party, the liberal forces consisted of members of the lower and middle classes who had been part of the National Guard troops mobilized to defend Mexico in 1846. But this lack of formal structure had its limitations, and the conservative armies dominated the central region of the country, especially after General Miguel Miramón replaced Zuloaga as president. Miramón's strategy was to focus his attacks on Veracruz, which he subjected to two sieges. The failure of the first siege led him to plan a simultaneous attack from both land and sea, for which purpose he acquired a ship to attack from the water while he surrounded the port on land. Juárez took advantage of the fact that the United States had withdrawn recognition of the conservative government —because it had refused to sell it Mexican territory—to ask the U.S. Navy to arrest Miramón's ship as a pirate vessel. Although the U.S. commander did not have the authority to do so, he did as Juárez requested and caused the defeat of the siege. However, a U.S. court later ruled that the seizure had been illegal.

To secure the support of the purists and the business class, which was very interested in the Church's properties, Juárez and his cabinet of purists chose to consolidate the reform and on July 12, 1859, began passing the *Leyes de Reforma* (Reform Laws). These mandated nationalizing (confiscating) church property, separation of Church and State, suppression of religious orders (brotherhoods, congregations, and orders), civil registry of births and marriages, secularization of cemeteries and, finally, freedom of worship.

A lack of resources led the two factions to commit the nation to agreements with other countries. Washington was willing to support the liberals in exchange for a new purchase of territory, but this was rejected out of hand. The liberals agreed to sign the McLane-Ocampo Treaty under which the Mexicans, in exchange for a loan of two million pesos, would allow the U.S. free transit through the Isthmus of Tehuantepec with trade privileges and the possibility of military intervention, if needed. Fortunately, the U.S. Senate refused to ratify the treaty.

For their part, the conservatives sought European support. They signed the Mon-Almonte Treaty with the Spaniards, which recognized the Convention of 1853 Santa Anna had signed, under which questionable debts were accepted as being owed. In addition, they took a loan under onerous conditions from the Swiss banker Jean-Baptiste Jecker and appropriated to themselves money from the British Embassy. This discredited them abroad and increased claims against the Mexican government, as well as its indebtedness.

The failure of the siege of Veracruz paved the way for a liberal triumph. Victories at Silao and Calpulalpan opened the doors of the capital for the liberals. Juárez entered the city on January 11, 1861, but peace was far from being won. Bitter over their defeat, the conservatives hatched an increasing number of plots in Europe and resorted to assassination, to which Ocampo, Leandro Valle, and Santos Degollado fell victim. Juárez decreed the expulsion of the apostolic delegate, the archbishop, and several bishops and ministers from Spain, Guatemala, and Ecuador who had supported the conservatives.

Juárez won the election and at once reorganized the administration and education and declared that the country would adopt the decimal metric system. But a lack of funds forced him to suspend payment of government debts, including both interest on the British loans and those based on Spanish and French claims. Mexican monarchists living in Europe took advantage of this development to interest Napoleon III, Emperor of France, in a project to establish a monarchy in Mexico. The French emperor dreamed of building a "Latin" empire that would serve as a retaining wall against Anglo-Saxon expansion, and so he saw the suspension of payments as an opportunity to intervene and summoned Great Britain and Spain to discuss the matter. On October 31, 1861, in London the three countries signed an agreement that committed them to blockading Mexico's Gulf ports to force resumption of payments without intervening in the country's domestic politics.

The Spanish fleet arrived in Veracruz in December, and the French and the British, in January. When Juárez received their ultimatum, he sent Minister of Foreign Affairs Manuel Doblado to negotiate with the interventionists. To prevent their catching tropical diseases, Juárez authorized them to disembark their troops and advance inland on condition that they again board their ships if no agreement was reached. Doblado assured them that the suspension was temporary and that payments would be resumed as soon as possible. The British and the Spaniards accepted this. The French not only refused, but instead of reboarding their ships, they sent more men ashore, among them some Mexican monarchists, such as Juan N. Almonte, who was Morelos' son.

The French began their advance on April 17. Under these critical conditions, Juárez declared amnesty for the conservative army and authorized the formation of guerrilla groups. Ignacio Zaragoza prepared to defend Puebla against the best army in the world. The Count of Lorencez, confident of the complete superiority of his troops, failed to heed Almonte's warning, and on May 4 and 5, Zaragoza's "gangs of rabble" defeated him. The humiliation only served to prompt Napoleon to send 30 000 more troops under a new command.

One year later, Mexican troops were concentrated in Puebla without General Zaragoza, who had died of yellow fever. After a long siege, the city fell to the French. Juárez was forced to abandon the capital, which was occupied in June. The French convened an assembly of dignitaries that proclaimed the establishment of an empire on July 19 and announced that Maximilian of Habsburg would be invited to occupy the throne of Mexico. The governing body appointed—which was comprised of some outstanding generals, civic leaders, and clergy, among them Archbishop Labastida—turned out to be mere window dressing. Marshal Achille Bazaine was the real decision-maker, following instructions from Napoleon III. While waiting for the emperor to arrive, the French army began occupying the cities of Mexico one by one due to their military superiority. However, liberal guerrilla raids, as well as a hostile populace inflamed by the arrogance of the French troops, made it difficult for the French to maintain their positions, and towns had to be retaken again and again.

Maximilian, who was the brother of the Austrian emperor and was married to Carlota Amalia, daughter of the King of Belgium, received the Mexican monarchists at the Castle of Miramare. The archduke conditioned his acceptance on the Mexican people calling him to serve, a condition the monarchists met by collecting thousands of signatures. Once these were presented on April 10, 1864, Maximilian accepted the throne.

The emperor signed two treaties with Napoleon III, who made sure that Mexico would pay the cost of this adventure.

France would maintain 28 000 soldiers and grant a loan of 175 million francs, of which Maximilian would receive only eight million, with the rest dedicated to paying off the inflated debts owed to France, the costs of war, and interest. The secret treaty provided that the army's numbers would reach 38 000 and then would begin to be cut back after 1865.

After an audience with the pope, the emperor and empress set off for Veracruz, where they arrived at the end of May, 1864. The liberal port gave them a cold welcome that would contrast with the enthusiasm with which they would be received by "the cream of society" in Orizaba, Puebla, and Mexico City, where people were only too eager to overwhelm the royal couple with their attentions.

Many moderate liberals collaborated with the imperial government, hoping that it would be able to resolve the problems that had plagued the country since 1821. Maximilian, a confirmed liberal, announced that he would exercise royal patronage, would not suppress freedom of worship, and would not reverse nationalization of the Church's property as the papal nuncio was demanding. This decision deprived him of the support of many conservatives and served as the source of jokes among the liberals. Mexico City seemed to take on new life in becoming home to the imperial court. The capital was beautified and streets were aligned and adorned with ash trees and gas lighting. The great avenue of the empire was formed, which would later be rechristened by the liberals as *Paseo de la Reforma* (Reforma Avenue) and Chapultepec Castle was refurbished. The emperor dedicated himself to the work of legislating. He began by drafting the Imperial Charter, which was adopted on April 10, 1865, followed by a proposal for a civil code and agrarian and labor laws that would return their former lands to the *pueblos de indios* (pueblos) and give lands to those who had not had them previously. This law provided for a maximum work day of ten hours, cancelled debts of more than ten pesos, prohibited corporal punishment, and limited company stores where customers paid in scrip. Education and scientific research also merited his attention, while the empress promoted instruction for girls and women. Maximilian decided to divide up the territory into 50 departments and concerned himself with economic development, signing a contract for construction of a railroad from Mexico City to Veracruz and authorizing the operations of the Bank of London, Mexico, and South America to facilitate trade.

The French occupation forced Juárez to move north. The president had to cope not only with the French, but also with traitors within his ranks. During 1864, the republicans dominated the northern states, Colima, Guerrero, Tabasco, and Chiapas, but by 1865 they only held small isolated redoubts. At this critical juncture, General Jesús González Ortega, a minister of the Supreme Court of Justice who was then in the United States, demanded that Juárez turn the presidency over to him, since Juárez's legal term of office had expired. Don Benito, using the convincing argument that the country was at war, extended his mandate to the length of time the country was occupied, a decision that caused him to lose the support of many purists.

At the end of 1865, circumstances began to change. With the end of the Civil War in the United States, Mexican liberals managed to obtain a loan of three million pesos and the U.S. decided to protest against the intervention in Mexico. The republican guerrillas, who had become a real army, began to advance.

With the money from the French loan spent, the empire was beset by the country's perennial financial problems and disturbed by the rumor that Napoleon III would withdraw his troops in light of the threat posed by the consolidation of the German Confederation. Maintaining control over such a large country was difficult, so collapse was virtually inevitable. Maximilian tried to form a national army and recalled the conservative generals he had sent to Europe on diplomatic missions. His brother Franz Joseph agreed to send him 4 000 Austrian troops, but a protest from the United States prevented them from sailing. The empress offered to travel to Europe to demand fulfillment of treaty terms, but neither Napoleon III nor the pope paid any attention to her pleas, which drove her insane. The news convinced Maximilian that he had no alternative but to abdicate, but his ministers made him hold off, although they later abandoned him to his fate.

By early 1867, the rapid advance of the republicans had reduced the empire to the states of Puebla and Veracruz. The emperor fell back to Querétaro, where he was joined by Miguel Miramón and Tomás Mejía. When Porfirio Díaz took the city of Puebla on April 2, Miramón proposed abandoning Querétaro, but Maximilian refused to flee and decided to withstand the siege. A traitor made his arrest possible. Juárez and Sebastián Lerdo de Tejada took it upon themselves to apply the law of 1862, so the emperor was tried by a court-martial. Two famous attorneys defended him, but could not prevent his being sentenced to death. Petitions for clemency for the Habsburg prince arrived from around the world, but Juárez held firm. Before his death, the emperor maintained great dignity. After writing to his mother and his wife, he faced the firing squad that would execute him together with Miramón and Mejía on the *Cerro de las Campanas* (Hill of the Bells) on June 19, 1867. Before being shot, Maximilian expressed his wish that his blood would bring an end to "the misfortunes of my new homeland."

With the fall of the empire, on July 16, 1867, Juárez returned to Mexico City. This time the people, who appreciated his fight to preserve national sovereignty, received him with genuine jubilation. The triumph of the republic finally eliminated the monarchist alternative, although it did not put an end to the disorder and uprisings, which were now the result of infighting for political power among the liberals.

Juárez acted quickly to call an election in August. The disappearance of the Conservative Party from political competition left three liberals as candidates: Juárez, Sebastián Lerdo de Tejada, and Porfirio Díaz, the military hero of the war. Although Juárez won, his enemies multiplied, both because of his reelection and because he favored amending the Constitution, which seemed to contradict his previous efforts to defend it. Juárez's political experience was undoubtedly unique, since he had governed for nearly ten years in wartime using extraordinary powers and virtually without a legislature. That had enabled him to strengthen the presidency, but he now found himself in a different situation. The Constitution of 1857 maintained the supremacy of the legislature which, because it was unicameral, was more to be feared. Juárez therefore advocated restoring the Senate to achieve greater balance. In appointing a cabinet of civilian constitutionalists, Juárez had offended the military men who felt they deserved credit for victory and favored Porfirio Díaz. With so many enemies, Juárez and his ministers became fodder for satires and political caricature, despite which they maintained complete freedom of the press throughout the restoration of the republic.

Nor did winning the war make the situation less complex. The long struggle had renewed the old confrontation between the regions and the central portion of the country, given that it had fragmented power as military leaders had taken on broad fiscal powers. To do away with these ad hoc powers and impose order, Congress supported Juárez and decreed them null and void. Furthermore, the punishment of conservative officials ignited resentments. Juárez tried to mitigate them in order to begin a reconciliation process, and in 1870 declared a far-reaching amnesty that allowed the return of Archbishop Labastida, who was treated with full respect.

The Mexican Republic showed the ravages of years of war and needed to invigorate the economy. Trade again fell victim to disorder, although creation of a free trade zone at the northern border had encouraged activity and created a pole of development. For part of the U.S. Civil War, cotton from the South was exported to Mexico through Matamoros, and flour, food, and a variety of Mexican products were sold to the United States. This fueled the growth of Monterrey, Piedras Negras, Laredo, and Matamoros.

The republic was also beleaguered by a lack of funds. The sale of church property had not borne the fruit that was hoped for, although it had contributed to putting public finances on a sounder footing by absorbing a large part of the bonds representing domestic indebtedness that were in circulation. For the pragmatic Juárez, general reorganization and lending order to the public treasury were top priority and indispensable for obtaining the monies needed to promote development. His ministers José María Iglesias and Matías Romero conducted a broad-based study of public finance and the debt. After analyzing the 450-million-peso debt and reducing it to 84 million by repudiating debts incurred by the empire, they set a new payment schedule. They also achieved savings, including by reducing the army to 20 000 men. By 1870, Romero had managed to summarize the ups and downs of the public treasury since independence and, with a clear idea of revenue and expenditures, drew up the first federal government budget.

As a good liberal committed to development and progress, Juárez wanted to foster all branches of production: investment, communications (especially telegraph lines, roads, and railroads), and colonization. He not only approved certain U.S. investment projects, but also honored the contract that the empire had signed to build a railroad from Veracruz to Mexico City. His cabinet member Romero dreamt of founding a national bank and a mint to create a uniform currency, but the lack of funds made this impossible, and he had to settle for the operation of the Bank of London, Mexico, and South America.

Because of his own personal history, Juárez gave priority to education. From the beginning, he demonstrated his willingness to promote it as the means for achieving the growth he desired, integrate Indian ethnic groups, and provide them with a respected place in the nation. Thus, in 1867 he passed a law that established free mandatory elementary education and founded the National Preparatory School.

Normalizing Mexico's relations abroad was another of his fundamental concerns, since the war had caused a break with Great Britain, France, and Spain. Yet he ran up against an unfavorable international situation. Distance and lack of communication were obstacles to maintaining contact with Ibero-American countries, plus there were border problems with Guatemala. For these reasons, Juárez tried to avoid letting anything cloud relations with the United States. In spite of differences and a lack of U.S. support during the French Intervention, relations between the two countries were as good as they had ever been. After the Civil War, U.S. industrialization had refocused the drive for territorial expansion toward financial growth. But there were two problems between the nations: roving bands and bandits crossing the border and claims for reparations. The first was left pending, because neither Juárez nor Sebastián Lerdo authorized U.S. citizens to cross the border in pursuit of "guilty parties." Juárez tried to resolve the question of claims and agreed to the formation of a binational commission to settle them. The commission ruled on the U.S. claims, but left the Mexican claims in limbo. In 1869, the opportunity presented itself to strengthen Mexico's ties with two new States: the Kingdom of Italy and the North German Confederation.

In the 1871 election, Don Benito was reelected, although his popularity had declined. But this time Díaz did not resign himself to defeat and declared himself in rebellion, supporting the Plan of La Noria on November 8 "against indefinite reelection." Despite his connections with regional leaders, Díaz's movement progressed slowly, and the generals supporting Juárez were able to contain it. Juárez's political skills enabled him to take advantage of division among the liberals to stay in power in this last season of his life, in spite of personal adversities and frail health. Juárez died sitting in the presidential chair on July 18, 1872.

Following the Constitution, Sebastián Lerdo de Tejada, president of the Supreme Court of Justice, became President of Mexico and granted a general amnesty that ended the La Noria coup attempt. He immediately called for an election and was elected in an overwhelming landslide. Don Sebastián Lerdo shared many of Juárez's principles, and his skill enabled him to reinstate the Senate and integrate the Reform Laws into the Constitution. He showed less flexibility in religious matters and expelled the Sisters of Charity, disregarding their essential work providing hospital services. His anticlericalism made him the target of attacks and sparked popular rebellions. These were in addition to the uprisings among the Yaqui of Cajeme and that of the terrible Manuel Lozada in Tepic, who was shot by a firing squad in late 1873. Lerdo also had a confrontation with the Great Mexican Workers' Circle over textile and mining strikes, and with commercial interests because he refused to grant concessions for construction of a railroad uniting Mexico City with the United States, even though the Veracruz-Mexico City railway had already been put into service in 1873.

Presidential succession again became the source of discord. Lerdo was running for reelection, but this time Díaz did not wait for the election to be held and instead made a *pronunciamiento* (a declaration of rebellion) ahead of time with the Plan of Tuxtepec, in which he accused Lerdo of "violations of the Constitution." Díaz had learned the lessons of his earlier defeat with the La Noria movement and this time prepared very carefully. He took advantage of Lerdo's intervention in an election in Oaxaca to consolidate a state alliance against him. Assured of Oaxaca's support, Díaz went to Brownsville in late 1875, and from there invited governors and regional military commanders to join his struggle. But because the movement was centered in the Northeast and Oaxaca, he changed his plan and offered to recognize the military titles and honors of anyone who supported his movement, thereby multiplying the number of centers of rebellion.

General Mariano Escobedo held the rebels in check. When the 1876 election was held in September, Lerdo was declared the winner. At that moment, to the Tuxtepec movement was added a refusal to accept the election results already expressed by the president of the Supreme Court of Justice, José María Iglesias, "because of fraud." Iglesias incited an uprising in Salamanca. Although Iglesias received little support, his rebellion helped Díaz's cause. On November 11, Díaz led his army to victory over federal troops in the village of Tecoac. Lerdo created confusion by fleeing, since several governors had already recognized Iglesias as president, so negotiations between the two contenders were necessary. Díaz offered to recognize Iglesias as provisional president if he divided his cabinet between supporters of the two of them and named Díaz Minister of War. When Iglesias refused, Díaz chose a more drastic course and on November 23 led an army to occupy Mexico City. A week later he assumed the presidency.

THE NATION SLOWLY BECOMES A REPUBLIC

The six-and-a-half million residents of the territory of New Spain that had become an independent nation in 1821 constituted a heterogeneous group united by historical experience and religion. Only a minority among them spoke Spanish. To a greater or lesser degree, almost all of the population had seen their lives turned upside down during 11 years of battle and witnessed how the order in place for 300 years had been distorted and a long period of changes had begun. Spanish liberalism had introduced new concepts, whose meaning was often made to accommodate traditional ideas. Due to their disenchantment with this dependence on Spain, the elites and middle classes viewed the promises the new order offered with optimism—an optimism that painful events would soon obliterate.

The sparse population, which was concentrated in central Mexico and in the South, inhabited an enormous territory that had reached its greatest extent during the Iturbide Empire: 4.5 million km^2 (1.74 million square miles). It had been incapable of growing, affected by periodic epidemics and wars, such that by mid-century the population was just over seven million, and by the 1870s it had risen to nine million. Nevertheless, the capital had a quarter of a million residents, followed by the much smaller cities of Puebla, Guanajuato, Querétaro, Zacatecas, and Guadalajara. The inability to populate the northern region, combined with political changes and threats from abroad, had caused the land area to shrink: Guatemala separated from Mexico in 1823, Texas became independent in 1836, the United States conquered New Mexico and Alta California between 1846 and 1847, and the Mesilla area was sold in 1853. Thus, at the end of the period the republic had been reduced to 1 972 545 km^2 (761 604 square miles). Mexico's 19 states, four territories, and Federal District had by 1869 become 28 states and one territory.

Although there was some continuity, from the very beginning independence and establishing the republic had affected the notion of corporate society. The fighting itself allowed a certain amount of mobility, especially for Creoles and Mestizos. In any event, equality remained a mere promise, given the people's crushing poverty, which was shameful in light of the ostentatious opulence of a rich minority. Furthermore, political change affected everyone. A lack of order and unsafe roads led to losses for merchants and very low productivity on haciendas.

The abandonment of many mines caused them to flood, and a lack of resources caused them to be sold or joined in partnerships with foreign capital. With independence, government employees lost their job security, to the extent that the hope of receiving overdue wages or recovering one's job led civil servants to favor changes of government. Professionals, with the exception of some prosperous physicians and attorneys, came to swell the ranks of the bureaucracy. In any event, the departure of the wealthy European-born Spaniards and laws mandating their expulsion allowed the Creoles to monopolize the upper echelons of society.

Mine workers lost the advantages they had enjoyed, and those holding technical jobs were replaced by Europeans. The entry of coarse cloth affected the workers in old textile mills. The rest of the population adjusted to the limitations of the times, while the dregs of society took advantage of disorder to loot what they could.

The clergy felt the loss of its members who had fought for independence, while the slow secularization of daily life thinned the ranks of religious orders. Moreover, the Church was a favorite target of governments of all stripes and saw its income and capital grow smaller over four decades. What wealth it possessed continued to be enjoyed by ten bishops and 177 canons, while the regular and secular clergy, which were reduced to 3 500 priests in 1825, lived in poverty, even though their parishioners suffered from the payment of fees for services.

The group that really benefited from the wars and uprisings was the army. Owing to a lack of financing, the 75 000 soldiers in the ranks in 1821 shrank to 30 000, an inadequate number to oversee such a large land area. Since the livelihoods of a good part of the officer corps were in the realm of politics, their promotions came from their participation in rebellions, which hampered their professional training and made the number of generals excessive for the small number of troops. Like government employees, soldiers suffered from a constant lack of timeliness in the payment of their wages, so that officers were always seeking *contratas* (special agreements for provision of supplies and services) for the army, while the levied troops tried to desert at every opportunity.

The new rituals and civic festivals that legitimized the new order and tried to compete with religious celebrations were gradually adopted. In reality, the most notable changes occurred in the ports and the capital with the arrival of foreigners. The mooring of packet boats not only meant the entry of merchandise, but also of novelties, fashions, and inventions, as well as making travel to the United States or Europe easier. The new stagecoach company reduced the duration of travel within Mexico: a trip from Mexico City to Veracruz took seven days; to Guadalajara, 13; and to Santa Fe, one month.

The faith in progress that had inspired the Enlightenment was maintained, and people were confident that education would resolve the nation's ills. The job of making the population literate was entrusted to the Compañía Lancasteriana (after Joseph Lancaster, of Britain), which was founded in 1822 by some leading citizens. Foreign teachers also arrived to offer their services as tutors or to start private schools. In contrast, the universities lost their prestige and were replaced by academies responsible for disseminating scientific knowledge and by new institutes of the arts and sciences promoted by the republicans, which would educate the generation that would enter politics at the middle of the century.

Calendars and almanacs played the role of disseminating historical and scientific news. The politicization that began in 1808 and the new nation's Constitution encouraged the printing of newspapers, pamphlets, and flyers of a political nature, which were the favorites of large groups of people who were anxious to hear the news. Printed matter passed from hand to hand, or people listened to it being read out loud in *pulquerías* (pulque bars), cafés, and public squares. This interest in politics led to greater interest in history, which was very well represented by Servando Teresa de Mier, Carlos María de Bustamante, Lorenzo de Zavala, José María Luis Mora, and Lucas Alamán. Literature was also developing and would bear witness to social change in the works of José Joaquín Fernández de Lizardi, Manuel Eduardo de Gorostiza, and Fernando Calderón. The arts, on the other hand, took longer to recover their brilliance, although the government granted some scholarships for study in Italy or Germany.

It would take half a century for real change to arrive when the secularization of society was firmly in place. The Church, which with independence had lost the social control it had wielded throughout the colonial period, during the Reform would have to forfeit its role in maintaining records of births, marriages, and deaths, as well as its property. All this made it impossible for the Church to continue offering the social services it had provided in its hospitals, schools, and orphanages and other shelters. With the sale of its real estate, many convents were torn down or put to uses other than those originally intended. When some churches were given to Protestant denominations, public disturbances became common. Private religious schools did not disappear, but public education was secularized to a great extent.

Political confrontations obliged intellectuals, most of whom were originally journalists, to dedicate themselves to challenging censorship or opposing dictatorship. The exercise of journalism made detailed analysis of national problems possible and, as a result, liberal intellectuals of stature published major works on social issues. Thus, Manuel Payno, a well-known author of novels of regional customs and manners (called *costumbristas*), conducted in-depth research on the public debt, disentailment of church property, and the Reform. Miguel Lerdo de Tejada did the same for trade and the economy, while Melchor

Ocampo studied problems of Church and State. It is therefore not surprising that during the 1860s and 1870s, the press would achieve great maturity and liberal administrations would respect freedom of the press despite its excesses, allowing it to assume its role as the "Fourth Estate."

The deep rupture caused by the wars led those who restored the republic to give high priority to bringing the nation together through education and culture, as a way of preventing yet another controversy from dividing the Mexican people. That is why when Mexico City had just been recaptured, the Minister of Justice hastened to present a plan for public instruction that led to the laws of 1867 and 1869, which put great emphasis on elementary education and founded a model institution for secondary education: the *Escuela Nacional Preparatoria* (National Preparatory School). The school adopted Auguste Comte's positivist method to do away with traditional education by replacing religious and metaphysical explanations with logical and scientific ones. This was designed to clarify the thinking of the leaders of the future. Juárez and Sebastián Lerdo did not limit themselves to making changes in laws, but also tripled the number of elementary schools. Juárez's determination to teach the Indians Spanish in order to integrate them into national life aroused great opposition, while the official adoption of positivism in secondary and higher education triggered an intellectual debate that evolved during the years of the restoration and the Porfiriato, because many liberals considered this contrary to their principles.

In addition, the French Intervention awakened a brand of nationalism that would permeate all forms of culture, art, literature, and music. Ignacio Manuel Altamirano was its primary advocate in his literary gatherings and his magazine *Renacimiento*, whose pages gave exposure to liberal and conservative writers like Manuel Payno, Ignacio Ramírez, José Tomás de Cuéllar, Vicente Riva Palacio, Francisco Pimentel, José María Roa Bárcena,

Guillermo Prieto, and Anselmo de la Portilla. This setting encouraged the founding of academic societies, such as the Mexican Geographical and Statistical Society, the Mexican Lyceum, and the Mexican Academy of the Spanish Language.

Nationalism caused novels of regional customs and manners and historical novels, which began to be published as serials, to flourish. The study of history held its privileged place and the need to promote national consolidation led to the appearance of the first school textbooks on the history of the "fatherland." Conservatives such as Francisco de Arrangoiz, Manuel Orozco y Berra, and Joaquín García Icazbalceta, as well as liberals Guillermo Prieto and Vicente Riva Palacio, interpreted the "national" past. Depending on their ideological bent, they preferred to study current events or to delve into and reinterpret the distant past of both colonial and pre-Columbian history.

Thanks to a lottery, the Academy of San Carlos was renovated during the war with the United States, and the visual arts gradually recovered their importance. Juárez renamed it the National School of Fine Arts, and the sculptor Manuel Vilar and the painters Pelegrín Clavé and Eugenio Landesio continued to teach European techniques and styles there. They could not resist the nationalist fervor, however, and ended up adopting it. As a result, landscapes and historical subjects replaced religious themes, while lithography and caricature became instruments of attack in the political arena. Without a doubt, José María Velasco, with his splendid Mexican landscapes, was the most outstanding one. Of course, while the latest trends captivated artists in the capital, in the provinces artists maintained their freshness with still lifes and portraits, as was the case of *costumbrista* painters José María Estrada and Hermenegildo Bustos. Sculpture benefited from the commissioning of statues of national heroes to adorn the *Paseo de la Reforma* (Reforma Avenue). Architecture, which had declined considerably during the first decades of Mexican nationhood—to the extent that the only buildings constructed were the National Theater, a few markets, and some prisons—would be reinvigorated by the knowledge of the use of iron that the architect Javier Cavallari would bring.

Music also began to come into its own. When the republic triumphed, the Mexican Philharmonic Society, founded in 1866, was given the building that had housed the then-closed University for its home. It taught classes and gave concerts and lectures there. The marches of the popular Aniceto Ortega expressed the nationalist spirit in music.

It is possible that this nationalism inspired the effort to describe all of the new country's physical attributes, which fostered the study of Mexico's land and resources. The status given to the sciences and the introduction of positivism gave great impetus to this study, and specialized academies multiplied and cultivated the professionalization of these disciplines when the former University was definitively closed down in 1865.

Scientific research also benefited from the work of doctors, naturalists, geographers, chemists, and geologists, encouraged by the Mexican Commission for Science, Letters, and the Arts (1864-1869) by fostering contacts and scientific trips to the Old World. Although it would not bear fruit until later, the publication of translations and reports in the Bulletin of the Mexican Geographical and Statistical Society laid the foundation for its subsequent development.

* * *

The long journey begun in the early 1800s had profoundly affected society by the last third of the century. The old corporate society had disappeared with the secularization of the Reform, such that the country began to be a true republic. With the change of customs, the life of society was different, and the disruptions themselves—*la bola*, as they were popularly called, with their forced conscriptions that drove citizens from place to place throughout the country—had spread knowledge of Spanish, which was now taught in public schools that imposed the use of "the national language."

The failure of political experiments, as well as military defeats in the face of foreign threats, had also left their imprint. Society was now more skeptical and cautious, although hope for progress had not been abandoned. With the republic and liberalism triumphant, Mexicans were anxious to achieve a peace that would allow for material development; as a result, they were prepared to accept a project that would ensure order and progress and to pay whatever the price, a keen desire that Porfirio Díaz would know how to use to his advantage.

THE PORFIRIATO

Elisa Speckman-Guerra

Porfirio Díaz governed Mexico for 30 of the 34 years between 1877 and 1911, and that is why this era is known as the Porfiriato. Two political events marked the beginning and end of this period. It started in 1877, when Díaz began his first term as president just a few months after defeating the Lerdo and Iglesias factions. It came to a close when Díaz abandoned the presidency and went into exile in 1911, just a few months after the outbreak of the Revolution.

A hero in the battle against conservatives and imperialists, Porfirio Díaz was born in Oaxaca in 1830, which means he was younger than Benito Juárez and Sebastian Lerdo de Tejada. He also differed from them in that he pursued a military career, rising to the rank of general. He ran for the presidency three times, but was defeated by Juárez and by Lerdo. He twice refused to recognize the legitimacy of the election and rose up in arms: the first time in 1871, with the Plan of La Noria; and the second time in 1876, with the Plan of Tuxtepec. Both times he hoisted an anti-authoritarian and anti-centralist banner, rejecting the excessive power of the President of the Republic vis-à-vis the Legislative and Judicial Branches and also the state governments. In addition to opposing reelection, he fought to limit the powers of the Executive Branch to those stipulated in the Constitution and, as a counterpart to this, he favored strengthening the state and pueblo governments and respecting the pueblos' right to elect their own municipal officials and make decisions regarding their internal affairs.

As a defender and representative of regional interests and groups, he had the support of the caciques or local leaders, as well as of the military men who had been displaced by Juárez or Lerdo. Similarly, he gained the favor of the pueblos and peasant collectives that were trying to defend their political autonomy and, in some instances, even acquiesced to disentailment of their land or the division of land among their members as long as that was done according to their customs and needs. Lastly, he gained the support of urban groups, who believed he was the only man capable of preserving Mexico's unity and sovereignty and ending the state of war that had afflicted the country for more than 50 years.

In November 1876 he entered Mexico City in triumph and, after an election victory, took office as president in 1877. During his first term of office, he held to his anti-reelection position: in 1878 he promoted a constitutional amendment that prohibited consecutive terms in office and in 1880 turned power over to his *compadre* (close friend) Manuel González. By doing so he increased his political sympathies, which continued to grow during the González administration as he established new ties and alliances. Then, again running unopposed, he won election to his second term as president (1884-1888). This time, however, he did not plan to leave the presidency: in 1884, a new constitutional amendment allowed two consecutive terms, that is, for the president to be reelected once. That enabled him to serve from 1888 to 1892. In 1890 all restrictions on reelection were eliminated from the Constitution, and in 1903 the president's term of office was extended to six years, making it possible for Don Porfirio to proclaim his electoral victories for the 1892-1896, 1896-1900, 1900-1904, and 1904-1910 terms without any significant opposition.

Many changes occurred during those years, so many that it is impossible to speak of a single consistent Porfiriato. Instead, we must talk about at least two Porfiriatos, plus the crisis years.

POLICIES OF THE PORFIRIATO

The first stage

The first stage of the Porfiriato started in 1877 and ended with the beginning of Porfirio Díaz's third term as president (1888), or when all legal restrictions on being elected an indefinite number of times were eliminated (1890). This was a period of building, pacification, unification, conciliation, and negotiation, but also of repression.

Once he took power, Don Porfirio had to confront a variety of challenges. The State and the nation were far from firmly established. The Constitution adopted in 1857, as well as the liberal concept of government and society, had not been fully respected. As mentioned in the previous chapter, the Constitution provided for a society of individuals who were equal before the law and whose rights were guaranteed. In order to avoid a concentration of power, it also divided authority among three branches: the Executive (responsible for carrying out laws), the Legislative (for making laws), and the Judicial (for ensuring proper application and enforcement of the law). It also gave the people responsibility for electing the members of government (the president, governors, legislators, ministers of the Supreme Court, and magistrates of the local superior courts of justice). Lastly, the Constitution provided for the separation of Church and State and, to ensure religious freedom, placed activities like education and social welfare in the hands of the government.

Application of these provisions, however, had been thwarted by the war between the Constitution's defenders and its detractors. The obstacles did not disappear with the republican victory of 1867, since different concepts of "nation" and "society" persisted. There were also other hurdles to overcome. There was the problem of governance. For example, the balance of powers as set down in the Constitution did not favor the Ex-

ecutive, which made it difficult for the president to control opposition of the corporations or to overrule regional powers.
That is why Juárez and Lerdo exerted greater power than was
provided for in the law. On the other hand, in some aspects the
Constitution (inspired by the liberal model and committed to
modernization) did not correspond to traditional institutions
and practices.

This discrepancy was pointed out by numerous intellectuals who, based on this, proposed postponing the application of
certain items of the Constitution. Among other things, they ar-
gued that equality before the law, which was in keeping with a
society comprised of individuals, was not how one could describe Mexican society which, in fact, was heterogeneous and
whose members continued to see themselves as part of a *cuerpo*
(institutional body) within society and acted on behalf of that
entity, or that total observance of individual rights should be
enforced only once society had achieved both order and peace.

It was also necessary to have a political system that demonstrated its effectiveness. Although Juárez, Lerdo, and Díaz had
enjoyed great popularity in some regions, it was still necessary
to preserve legitimacy and consensus and to extend that consensus throughout the country. Above all, it was essential to create
cohesion among the political and regional forces and put an end
to the risk of uprisings or the fragmentation of Mexico's territory.

Nor was there a fully coherent national identity. Some population groups remained isolated and did not feel that they were
part of a socio-political unit larger than themselves whose governors were very removed from or disinterested in their problems. To top it all off, the borders were porous, and the threat
of foreign interventions persisted.

Porfirio Díaz's challenges, then, were to unify and create
cohesion among political and regional factions, to confer legitimacy and legality on the regime (respecting or appearing to
respect the Constitution), and to gain international recognition.

He basically used two strategies. First he used conciliation or negotiation, preserving the loyalty of groups that had supported him and won over former opponents. Thus, he incorporated into the army the soldiers who had defended the Plan of Tuxtepec, but also included those who had been dismissed by Juárez and Lerdo, and even soldiers who had fought for Lerdo and Iglesias. He married Carmen, the daughter of former Lerdo supporter Manuel Romero Rubio and, in doing so, sealed his commitment with that faction. He included in his cabinets liberals with a military background—men who had been excluded during the Restored Republic—, but also liberals who were politicians or intellectuals, regardless of their affiliation. For example, in 1884 only one cabinet minister could have been called a Díaz loyalist. Yet there were two Juárez supporters, two Lerdo supporters, and one who supported the empire. So, in addition to unifying the liberal factions, Díaz attracted some supporters of Maximilian's Empire and the Catholic Church.

At that time, the Church as an institution was very weak. It was prohibited from owning property and its revenues had been cut back, making it economically dependent on the State. Furthermore, it had lost part of its membership, since only secular clergy was allowed. And it had also lost its role in society, because worship was not permitted outside of church buildings, and the clergy was prohibited from managing or controlling schools, welfare organizations or hospitals. This changed under the Díaz administration. Porfirio did not repeal the anticlerical laws, but neither did he enforce all of them. He allowed the Church to own property again, for the regular clergy (monks and nuns) to be strengthened, and the founding of congregations involved in the community that were dedicated to education and to caring for the sick and needy. By the same token, the wives of government officials, including Carmen Romero Rubio, attended religious services, and church festivals were celebrated publicly and at times ostentatiously, such as the coronation of the Virgin of Guadalupe in 1895. In exchange, the church hierarchy supported Díaz and refused to recognize popular uprisings that occurred under a religious banner, while some of its congregations participated in pacifying and evangelizing the Yaqui and Mayo Indians. Moreover, in resuming its social welfare and educational work, the Church provided services that the government would have been hard-pressed to supply using its own resources.

Díaz's relations with peasant collectives, as well as with caciques or regional leaders, were more complex and variable. In some regions, the president honored his agreement with the pueblos, respected their political autonomy, and put an end to disentailment. In other places, he stopped neither the breakup of collectively held property nor colonization, which was intended to bring uncultivated lands into production and into the marketplace, and the government gave one-third of these lands to surveying companies that reported them. The problem was that those companies also reported lands that were being farmed, but whose owners —including some pueblos—lacked title to the property and so lost out.

Porfirio's way of interacting with governors and caudillos also varied. In general, for heading state governments, the president sought men who were loyal to him and who enjoyed consensus support among other local groups. If his supporters, who were often caciques, fulfilled both conditions, he took away their military power but helped them become or remain as governors. If they did not meet his requirements, he removed them from the political sphere, but offered them means to become wealthy. In this way he won over or weakened local leaders and managed to have governorships occupied by men loyal to him, whom he allowed a certain amount of freedom by not intervening in how they ran things as long as they ensured their regions were at peace.

Porfirio Díaz also took a conciliatory approach abroad and achieved his third goal: gaining international recognition. He reestablished diplomatic relations with France, Britain, Germany, and Belgium, which had been broken off as a result of the moratorium Juárez had decreed. He also curried favor with the United States. Relations with Mexico's northern neighbor entailed a diverse array of problems: Mexico's foreign debt; border Indian tribes and cattle thieves crossing into Mexico being pursued by the U.S. military; the tax-free zone Mexico had opened on its border to attract colonists and the contraband this generated; and the migration of Mexican workers to the United States. Despite this and owing to payment of the debt and compensation and special terms granted to investors, among other things, in 1878 the United States recognized the Díaz government. Nevertheless, Mexico's president firmly defended national sovereignty.

When he could not achieve results through conciliation or negotiation, Porfirio Díaz chose a second approach: force and repression. This meant using the army, the police, and the *rurales* (members of the Mexican Rural Guard). For example, in 1879 the governor of Veracruz ordered that nine rebel Lerdo supporters be shot, perhaps going beyond the president's instructions. Díaz had asked him to punish the leaders of the uprising who were also naval officers, although there are those who say that another telegram existed with the blunt instruction: "Kill them on the spot." Agrarian rebellions in Sonora and Yucatán, which will be discussed later, were also brutally repressed. In addition, highway robbers and bandits, among them Jesús Arriaga ("Chucho el Roto" or "Chucho the Dandy") and Heraclio Bernal ("El Rayo de Sinaloa" or "The Thunderbolt of Sinaloa"), were captured or shot "while attempting to escape."

We now come to the problem of the regime's respect for the law, i.e., its consistency with or divergence from constitutional standards. Just as he intervened in appointing governors,

Don Porfirio also manipulated or negotiated elections of deputies (congressmen), senators, and federal judges. These elections were indirect, which means that males (women were not allowed to vote) who were born in Mexico, were children of Mexicans or were naturalized foreigners, older than 18 if they were married or 21 if not, who "earned an honest living" voted to choose the electors, who in turn voted to elect the representatives. Nevertheless, voting for federal office tended to be a farce. On election day the polls were practically deserted, and ballots were not filled out by voters. But elections were always held. It was a ritual that sought to demonstrate the political system's effectiveness and legitimized the regime. The same occurred in some state elections which, in certain cases, were also indirect. Thus, although in electoral matters the laws were not always obeyed, there was interest in providing a semblance of legality or at least in observing the formalities. The same was true of other areas. Another example is that of the anti-clerical laws; they were not always enforced either. Despite the insistent pleas of the church hierarchy, these laws were not repealed and represented a constant threat to the Catholic Church. For instance, the government showed greater tolerance towards religious orders, but from time to time the authorities would close down a "clandestine" monastery or convent.

In summary, the regime alternated between legality and the appearance of legality. Furthermore, besides the legislative changes and the use of force, thanks to negotiation and conciliation, in this first phase Porfirio Díaz gained international recognition and increased national cohesion by establishing ties with people from different parties, regions, and social sectors. Given that the traditional way of doing politics was for individuals to represent collective groups (their family, pueblo, hacienda or profession), in attracting individuals the president brought whole groups to his side. He took advantage of his supporters' ties and managed to place himself at the top of a pyramid of loyalties. As a result, instead of influential groups potentially becoming elements that divided the country, Díaz linked the chains of allegiance to bind his political structure.

The second stage

The second phase of the Porfiriato, which began between 1888 and 1890 and ended around 1908, was characterized by an increase of the centralism and the personal and authoritarian form of government run by Díaz and the state governors.

The change of approach was accompanied by a turnover in the people involved in politics, since many of the men who had been with Díaz during his rise to power and the first years of his rule had died. But this was also due to a new interplay of forces. Three figures—Joaquín Baranda, José Yves Limantour, and Bernardo Reyes—fulfilled important roles in the friction between the members of the elite of the Porfiriato and divisions among them, and each represented a different group and region, approach to politics, and idea of the nation.

Baranda, the first to join the cabinet, served as Minister of Justice from 1882 on. Previously, he had been governor of Campeche and had strong ties in this region. He also enjoyed influence in the states of Tabasco and Yucatán thanks to his brothers, as well as in Veracruz due to Governor Teodoro Dehesa. Baranda represented the liberals of the Reform Era who were civilians and not military men, and wanted full application of the Constitution and a limited political apparatus.

The second to join the cabinet—but the last to become part of the political scene—was Limantour, who served as Minister of Finance from 1893 to 1911. He was a member of the *científicos* (literally "scientists" or "those scientifically oriented," these were a circle of professional advisors to Porfirio Díaz), a group comprising people like Justo Sierra, Miguel and Pablo Macedo,

Rosendo Pineda, Joaquín Casasús, and Francisco Bulnes. They were outstanding professionals, some members of wealthy families and others linked to those families, who had originally been brought together by their association with Manuel Romero Rubio and were founders of the Liberal Union. That union was a group which defended government by institutions and fought to strengthen existing institutions, proposing reforms such as the creation of the vice presidency. As followers of positivist philosophy, the *científicos* believed that the scientific method should be applied to studying society and solving social problems. In other words, they believed that a systematic analysis of society would enable them to understand the patterns that govern its functioning and act on them in ways that would make it possible to eliminate obstacles to social progress. Their insistence on adopting "scientific policy" based on this method and entrusted to a group trained to conceptualize and apply it, led to their being called *científicos*. They also believed that the country needed a strong government, one capable of developing the economy and reforming society; hence their interest in promoting health care and educational programs. As for their affiliations, they represented economically powerful groups in Mexico City, but had less contact with other parts of Mexico and with the middle and lower classes.

Bernardo Reyes was the third to join the cabinet, although when he did so he already had much experience in politics. In 1876 he was already a colonel, in 1889 he served as governor of the State of Nuevo León, and from the beginning of the Porfiriato he was a highly influential figure in northwestern Mexico. He served as Minister of War between 1900 and 1902, and represented the classic Díaz loyalists: military men from the provincial middle or lower classes who were in close contact with the states. In addition to having the army's support, he was a favorite of the groups he had backed during his term as governor of Nuevo León: businessmen, the petty bourgeoisie, and the middle classes, plus organized labor, because he had promoted a policy of protection for workers.

For a few years, Díaz was able to mediate between the groups, but a rupture took place when the time came for him to choose a successor. This happened in 1898. He selected Limantour and believed that Reyes and Baranda would acquiesce. However, Baranda, then Minister of Justice, was opposed to that choice and had to resign from the cabinet, for which reason his group lost influence, even though it was weak in any event and much less powerful than the other two factions.

Two years later, the president continued trying to govern with *científicos* and Reyes supporters, maintaining a balance between them, but also taking advantage of the weakness caused by their constant confrontations with one another. In other words, he wanted to exploit the benefits each side contributed: the *científicos* provided skill in developing the economy and their ties with the capital's businessmen, bankers, and investors; and the Reyes supporters contributed with their influence in the Northwest and with the army, as well as their ability to meet the expectations of businessmen, but also those of the middle class and workers. At the same time, he capitalized on the division between the two factions, because their constant disagreement prevented them from growing stronger and meant they needed a mediator. That is why he appointed Reyes Minister of War and Limantour, Minister of Finance.

Once the decision had been made in favor of one faction, conflicts became more pronounced. In 1902, Limantour refused to furnish resources for renewing and modernizing the army and also criticized the Second Reserve, a corps created by Reyes composed of an increasing number of civilians who received military training on the weekends. Fearful of the power that a professional army and a civilian militia could give the minister of war, Don Porfirio asked Reyes to return to the governorship of Nuevo León, made changes in the army, and de-mobilized the Civil Guard.

By 1903 or 1904, the *científicos* were already clearly in charge. The men in the cabinet who had been with Díaz during his rise to power—liberal intellectuals and military men—had been replaced. Furthermore, the *científicos* imposed their candidate for the vice presidency in the 1904 elections. It was the first time elections were held for the post of vice president, who would succeed the president should he be absent or die, which—considering that Díaz was 73 years old—was fairly probable. Thus, in electing a vice president, Díaz's successor was being chosen. Limantour proposed Ramón Corral to fill the position, and Díaz put him in.

The elite had been splintering into factions, and the president could neither ensure their cohesion nor make peace among them. In favoring the *científicos,* replacing the old liberals, and making enemies with some groups within the military, he lost his contacts with the regions and groups that were left on the sidelines of the political game. A variety of newly emerging groups had also been left out and found no place in a paralyzed political system where almost everything was already agreed to, negotiated, and handed out. Similarly, the pact with the governors or regional powers obliged the president to renege on his commitment to the pueblos and to peasants in general. His relationships with investors and businessmen led him to neglect workers' demands. All this explains why he had to increasingly resort to imposition, authoritarianism, and repression.

Moreover, in this second phase the violation of the autonomy of the legislative and judicial powers—although nothing new—became more apparent. As previously mentioned, the president intervened in the designation of both federal and local legislators and judges, who were reelected again and again. Thus, they lacked autonomy. As a result, Congress presented few initiatives of its own and tended to support decisions made by the Executive. For its part, the Supreme Court abstained from participating in politics and functioned only as a last resort in the judicial system when, rather, it could have set itself up as a constitutional tribunal to ensure the legality or correct enforcement of federal laws, including electoral laws which, thanks to the *amparo*, it could have done, albeit by resolving individual cases.

The state governors also lost their autonomy. They did conserve some margin for action (for example, in electing deputies they could choose among candidates selected by Díaz or name alternates, who were often the ones attending sessions), and did not always accept decisions handed down by the federal government (for instance, they defended their right to legislate regarding education and accepted a standard curriculum, but gave it a regional flavor). Yet clearly, there was growing intervention from the central government in the regions' politics and economies and, with that, tension between the President and local elites heightened.

In addition, centralization was replicated within the states. The governors named *jefes políticos* (political chiefs), authorities situated between state governments and municipalities and who were useful to them as go-betweens. With broad spheres of competence, these political chiefs began to concentrate power and increasingly intervene in town council matters. Overall, the autonomy of the pueblos was further reduced during this phase and municipalities retained some of their independence only in certain regions.

Parallelly, control and repression of the regime's opponents were increasing. Partisan political opposition emerged that harked back to the origins of the Mexican Liberal Party. Opposition also surfaced in the press. There were pro-government newspapers like *El Imparcial* that received government subsidies, focused on news, and abstained from editorializing. Thanks to modern machinery, the low purchase price of copies, sensationalism, and the use of graphic images, it managed to increase the number of its readers, and its circulation by far surpassed that of older daily newspapers. But there were also non-official newspapers that were liberal, Catholic or pro-labor, some of which modernized much like *El Imparcial*. Others continued to print small numbers of copies using old equipment. All, however, had one thing in common: they published items critical of Díaz's policies and were therefore subject to repression. Their directors, editors, and even printers were often jailed. There is no better example of this than Filomeno Mata, director of *El Diario del Hogar* (*The Home Journal*), who was imprisoned so many times that legend has it that when he was asked his address he gave both his home address and that of Belén Prison, because he never knew at which location he would be.

Repression also grew against an increasing social protest, as we will explain later. Discontent took on a variety of forms: street demonstrations, attacks on public buildings, looting or banditry, labor strikes, and agrarian rebellions. And more than at other times, force was used to put them down. This was the phase during which hundreds of Yaqui men, women, and children were taken by force to labor camps in Oaxaca and Yucatán, and miners in Cananea and workers in Río Blanco were killed.

Finally, Díaz reoriented his relations with other countries. From the beginning he had demonstrated caution toward the United States and was aware of the threat of its expansion, which was now focused more on economics than on land. This wariness, expressed in the famous saying "Poor Mexico, so far from God and so close to the United States," was accentuated for two reasons: the United States' increasingly powerful influence in the Caribbean and Central America, especially in Guatemala (with which Mexico had long-standing problems related to the border and the movement of people), and its growing importance to Mexico's economy. To keep U.S. interference in check, he cultivated diplomatic and economic relations with Britain and France. On the other hand, he opposed the United States' becoming the guardian of Latin America in confronting the European threat or being the arbiter among the nations of the Americas, maintaining that those nations themselves were capable of handling these tasks.

The final years

A variety of factors led to the demise of Porfirio Díaz's regime. In fact, instead of speaking of a crisis, one must talk about several crises that dated back to the first years of the century which, as will be seen later, affected economic, social, and cultural matters and also influenced politics.

The Díaz regime was getting old: the president was 80; the cabinet members' average age was 67; and the situation was similar for governors, judges, and legislators. Don Porfirio was not the only one who had been in power for so many years, since reelection occurred at all levels of government. This was true for the state governments: Teodoro Dehesa governed Veracruz for 18 years, Mucio P. Martínez ruled for 17 years in Puebla, and both Francisco Cañedo in Sinaloa and Joaquín Obregón González in Guanajuato were in power for many consecutive terms. As mentioned, the regime was also paralyzed because it had lost the ability to conciliate and accommodate new political or social groups. And as if this were not enough, the regime itself had divided into factions. The rift between the *científicos* and Reyes supporters not only failed to disappear with Reyes' return to Nuevo León, but re-emerged on the eve of the 1910 elections.

In 1908, Díaz granted an interview to a U.S. journalist named James Creelman. In the interview he said that he would not run in the upcoming election and would allow the election to take place in full freedom, because he believed that Mexico was ready for democracy. This stirred up public opinion and roused political debate although, to all appearances, to the men close to the caudillo it was clear that this statement was meant for foreign consumption and that once again, the position in play was that of vice president. At that time, as the president grew ever older, the vice presidency promised to provide the path to succession.

In 1909, the *científicos* again nominated Corral, with Díaz's support. The Reyes supporters mobilized to nominate Reyes and set up clubs throughout the country made up of partisans from the middle and working classes. However, perhaps out of loyalty to Díaz or due to his reluctance to lead or even promote any armed movement that might end the peace, Reyes discouraged his followers and accepted a mission that the president assigned to him in Europe.

The opposing factions then became radicalized, including Reyes' supporters (who continued the movement even after Reyes left to go abroad), the liberal opposition, and supporters of Madero. These groups differed greatly from each other, both in the backgrounds of their leaders and supporting forces and in their platforms. But at that time they had several demands in common: adherence to the Constitution and the law, respect for the vote and the principle of non-reelection, plus varying degrees of legal protection for peasants and workers.

Despite this atmosphere, elections were held in the traditional way and Díaz and Corral were declared the winners. The Mexican Revolution broke out less than six months later, and less than a year later, in May 1911, Don Porfirio had to abandon not only the presidency but also the country and sail for France. This ended the Porfiriato since (as was explained earlier) its beginning and end were set by political history and, concretely, by the rise and fall of Porfirio Díaz.

This era turned out to be extremely important for the consolidation of the nation-state, despite the fact that Porfirio Díaz did not fully carry out the program he proposed, nor did he meet all of its challenges. The regime's two mottos were "order and progress" and "less politics, more administration." A certain degree of order was undoubtedly achieved, although not without some uprisings or rebellions, but a great deal of political skill was required to achieve it. And while Porfirio Díaz resorted to the use of force, he managed to get into and maintain power owing to his personal and clientelist ties, negotiating skills, and ability to conciliate and make political actors dependent on his intervention. Thus he made great progress in incorporating political party and regional interest groups. Granted, he did not adhere to the law, respect electoral laws, or enforce all the antiecclesiastic laws, and he violated individual rights (such as the freedom of speech) or failed to guarantee them (he allowed debt peonage to persist, which infringed upon the freedom of choice of work and even one's birthright since debts were inherited). At the same time, nevertheless, he advanced the implementation of other areas of the liberal model and even of the Constitution. For example, he enforced major aspects of the Reform Laws and secularization project (such as respecting freedom of religion), and continued the process of establishing modern laws and justice (he finished the task of codifying and regulating writs of *amparo* (appeal for legal protection in the case of violations by government officials of individual guarantees) and took decisive steps to further the economic goals defended by the liberals. Lastly, he made progress in unifying the country by creating a national identity and defending its sovereignty.

So we can affirm that this era gave birth to or strengthened many of the political institutions of the twentieth century. And the same can be said of innovation with regard to the economy, society, and culture.

PUBLIC FINANCES AND ECONOMIC DEVELOPMENT

Porfirio Díaz inherited a bankrupt public treasury. Debts abroad and to Mexican moneylenders were considerable; customs revenues were turned over to the nation's creditors; some tax revenues belonged to the states and did not benefit the federal government, and taxpayers opposed creating any additional tax burdens. To put finances on a sounder footing, the ministers of finance (most notably Matías Romero, Manuel Dublán, and José Yves Limantour) used a variety of strategies. They cut public spending and carefully administered resources. They exercised greater control over revenues. They created new taxes which —in contrast to those in the previous phase—did not fall on or cripple commerce. Lastly, thanks to a new loan, they restructured the domestic and foreign debt, which in turn enabled them to gain the confidence of lenders abroad and of investors both in Mexico and other countries and obtain additional loans and investments. Part of the debt was paid with money coming in from abroad and for the rest they negotiated with creditors to defer payments and establish fixed interest rates, converting it into a long-term debt. As a result of all these actions, over time expenses ceased to exceed revenues and, beginning in 1894, they even achieved a surplus.

In addition, a surprising transformation took place in production systems. In response to a favorable international climate, both Díaz and Manuel González sought to establish ties between Mexico and the international economy through exports of agricultural or mining products. But they also fostered development of industry and domestic trade. At the beginning of the Porfiriato, the Mexican market was small, and isolated regional and local economic units subsisted, producing almost everything they consumed and, therefore, they bought and sold very little. It was essential to increase production several-fold and to stimulate trade relations throughout the country and beyond its borders. This required legal infrastructure, investments or credit institutions, money in circulation, and means of transport and communications.

Let's begin with the legal system. In this phase, a commercial code was issued that provided clear and coherent regulations brought together in a single document. Furthermore, the *alcabala* (a tax on the transit of merchandise through a given area), which had made products more costly and discouraged long-distance trade, was eliminated. Also, the government implemented policies that subsidized industry or the construction of public works and transportation infrastructure, as well as a protectionist policy that taxed foreign products in competition with Mexican ones during some years and in some industries.

Obtaining government or private funds posed a greater challenge. In the early years, the State had no economic resources. It was able to undertake public works and communications projects only during the second phase of the Porfiriato, once surpluses had been achieved. Although large fortunes were amassed in different parts of Mexico and invested in works in specific regions, even these were scarce. Therefore, during the first phase it was imperative to secure money from abroad. The federal and state governments offered generous concessions and legislation that provided the opportunity for high profit margins. As a result, they attracted a considerable amount of investment.

Many of these funds were used to build ports and especially railroads. When Díaz came to power, the only rail line was the one connecting Mexico City and Veracruz, which was 640 km (398 miles) long. Other transportation routes had to be traversed by horse or mule, making travel slow. This mode of travel was only possible during certain times of the year and was subject to bandit attacks. During the Porfiriato, rail lines grew by 12% a year: in 1885, they covered 5 852 km (3 636 miles), and by 1910 that figure had risen to 19 280 km (11 980 miles). In order to attract investment, the federal government gave grants per-kilometer-built, and state governments often also supplied tax exemptions and land. Rail lines were built primarily with capital from the United States (42%), but to counteract U.S. influence and ensure competition, the government sought contracts with Britain (which eventually controlled 35%). Moreover, between 1902 and 1903, the government bought the *Ferrocarril Nacional Mexicano* (Mexican National Railroad) and the *Ferrocarril Interoceánico* (Inter-Ocean Railroad), and in 1906 it bailed the *Ferrocarril Central Mexicano* (Central Mexican Railroad) out of bankruptcy. These acquisitions together formed the National Railways of Mexico and paved the way for government control of railroads.

Ports and railroads favored foreign trade, but helped domestic commerce as well. Mexico traded with the United States, Europe, and the Caribbean. It exported increasing amounts of metals and agricultural products, the value of which rose from 40.5 million pesos in 1877 to 287 million pesos in 1910. Mexico also imported an increasing amount of machinery, tools, manufactured goods, and some foodstuffs. The rail routes laid out by foreign companies were in fact determined by the interest in developing trade with the United States. Nevertheless, railroads also brought enormous benefits for domestic commerce. Linking areas with rail lines made low-cost commerce possible year round, which led to growth in trade and made it possible to produce for distant markets, thereby favoring regional specialization.

Trade expansion occurred hand in hand with greater agricultural, mining, and industrial activity. Agriculture experienced its greatest increase in exports of henequen, rubber, and coffee. These products were cultivated on haciendas that benefited from subsidies, credit, railways, and modern farming techniques. In contrast, food production suffered a setback because that of wheat, barley, beans, and chili peppers was the same in 1910 as it had been in 1877, despite considerable population growth. As a result, food became more expensive and products like corn had to be imported.

Mexico also underwent impressive development in mining for export, which was concentrated in the states of Sonora, Chihuahua, Sinaloa, and Durango. Thanks to foreign investment, extraction of gold and silver increased, and production was diversified as new technologies and less expensive transportation made copper, zinc, and lead mining profitable. European and North American industries were creating great demand for these metals. Oil exports were added to these in the early twentieth century.

Industry comprised another sector of major importance that was transformed at the end of the nineteenth century. Artisanal workshops managed by master craftsmen employing a few workers using unsophisticated tools subsisted during the Porfiriato, particularly in some regions. But these workshops were gradually replaced by manufacturing industries that were often family owned, operated with machinery or specialized tools, and organized by dedicating workers to specific phases of production. After 1890, these were joined by modern industries owned by businessmen's associations that operated using equipment powered by water, steam or electricity, making them more productive. In general, factories were concentrated in Nuevo León, Jalisco, Puebla, Veracruz, and Mexico City, and were dedicated to the production of pottery, cigarettes, shoes, beer, textiles, paper or glass. Light industry related to the production of consumer goods was the branch that developed the most. Although the industrial sector was efficient and grew gradually, its development was limited by an ineffective financial system, a scarcity of raw materials or inadequate consumption capacity in Mexican society. Industry was also crippled by a lack of machinery and capital goods, given that heavy industry developed later and to a lesser degree. The *Fundidora de Fierro y Acero de Monterrey* (Monterrey Iron and Steel Foundry) is noteworthy in this area: it was established principally in response to the demand created by the railroads.

The contrasts between agriculture for export and for domestic consumption and between light and heavy industry reflect one aspect of the inequality that prevailed in economic matters. There were also geographic differences, since some regions developed more than others, including the North, which had a diversified economy (agriculture, livestock, mining, and industry) with a mostly urban population, modern wage relations, and the highest literacy rate in Mexico. There was also an inequality between time periods, since prosperous eras were eclipsed by times of crisis: for example, the panic in the 1890s caused by a drop in the price of silver, or the 1907-1908 crisis brought on by capital flight and a decline in export prices as a result of a worldwide recession.

In short, during this phase, Mexico became a major exporter of raw materials and also witnessed its first industrial revolution. However, development was uneven and benefited only some sectors, regions, and groups.

RURAL AND URBAN SOCIETIES

Changes in the makeup of society were no less important. There was unprecedented population growth: Mexico had a population of approximately nine million in 1877, while in 1895 it had grown to more than 13 million and by 1910 had risen to 15 million. Demographic growth was affected by the end of civil strife, expansion of markets and better food distribution, and—for some sectors of society—advances in hygiene and medicine.

It was both a growing and dynamic population, since this was an era of immigration. Some states in the North (Chihuahua, Coahuila, Durango, Nuevo León, and Tamaulipas), in central Mexico (the Federal District and Puebla), on the Gulf Coast (Veracruz), and in the North Pacific (Sonora and what was later to become Nayarit) received many immigrants, who came primarily from the states of México, Guanajuato, Jalisco, Michoacán, Hidalgo, Zacatecas, and San Luis Potosí.

Although immigrants tended to settle in cities, a large percentage of the population continued to live in villages of fewer than 15 000 inhabitants. For example, 90% of the population lived in this type of settlements in 1900. Most Mexicans resided in and made a living from the countryside, distributed among haciendas, small villages or towns, and ranches.

Haciendas and agrarian property were concentrated and expanded in size at the expense of communal landholdings. Nevertheless, communal landholdings persisted or owners looked for ways to keep their land. Communities were left with the least fertile and most isolated lands. In other cases, pueblo lands were divided up to secure ownership, but labor continued to be distributed according to tradition. Another variation was that they took the form of owners' associations or unions comprised of private landowners, which were permitted by the law. Furthermore, although disentailment and boundary surveys favored the hacienda owners, wealthy peasants and also usurers took advantage of this process as well, perpetuating the existence of medium-sized holdings. Thus, small or large haciendas, medium-sized properties, and communal landholdings coexisted.

In rural society, or rather rural societies—the situation differed from one place to another—, hacienda owners were at the top of the social pyramid. Some were Mexican, while others were foreigners, and not all lived in the countryside. Many left their properties in the hands of an administrator and resided in the cities. The middle of the pyramid was occupied by *rancheros* (ranchers) or small landowners, merchants, artisans, and some hacienda employees, such as administrators, foremen, and farm equipment mechanics. Landless peasants were at the bottom of the pyramid, working for prosperous *rancheros* and, in most cases, for large hacienda owners. This group included resident peons who lived in the hacienda or around its main compound on a permanent basis and received a fixed wage, and also laborers who were contracted only when extra hands were needed, who had to travel around the countryside following the harvests. In fact, temporary or seasonal labor was advantageous for the landowners but not for the "contract workers." Lastly, there were tenant farmers or sharecroppers, to whom the large hacienda owners rented the least fertile lands in exchange for money or part of the harvest.

These peasants' working and living conditions varied by region. Nothing could better illustrate this than the difference between the North and the Southeast of Mexico. In the North, large landholdings were farmed by day laborers or tenant farmers who enjoyed better conditions than those in central and southern Mexico. The owners had to offer them better wages or accept lower rents because laborers were scarce owing to the small population, but also because there were other job opportunities, since men could work in the mines or emigrate to the United States.

The situation was very different on the tobacco haciendas of Valle Nacional or the henequen haciendas of Yucatán. Many workers were linked to their employers by ties not involving their wages. To keep their peons, hacienda owners resorted to a system of indebtedness: they paid their workers with scrip that could be used at the company store, which also granted credit. The peons' wages were never enough to meet their needs, much less repay any debt, so they remained tied to the hacienda for the rest of their lives and sometimes debts were inherited. The southern hacienda owners also resorted to giving workers an *enganche*, or initial sum at their place of origin that they had to repay, ensnaring them in debt from the start. Owners also used prisoners and the Yaqui and Mayo Indians who had been deported. With no chance of leaving the hacienda, peons had to tolerate dismal working conditions.

Hence it comes as no surprise that many agrarian uprisings occurred during the Porfiriato. In general, the rebels opposed seizure of their communal lands, forests, and waters, and were defending their political autonomy. In some cases they were also fighting to preserve their cultural and ethnic identity, because since independence Mexican governments had tried to make the population more homogeneous and impose Western culture. They sought to establish a single language and set of customs; some even promoted *mestizaje* (crossbreeding or interracial marriage) with a view—as they said at the time—to "whitening" the Indians, who were considered lazy, uncivilized, and superstitious. So many communities fought to preserve their lands, their right to elect their representatives and make their own internal decisions, and even to practice their traditions and speak their own languages. The Maya rebellion in Yucatán, the Yaqui uprising in Sonora, and the rebellion of the residents of Tomochic are noteworthy examples.

While throughout this era Mexican society was eminently rural, urban centers experienced impressive growth during the Porfiriato. The most outstanding example is the capital, but Guadalajara, Puebla, San Luis Potosí, and Monterrey (see Table 1) also merit mention. In addition, there was major growth in other

Table 1. Population Growth in Cities

City	Population in 1877	Population in 1900	Population in 1910
Mexico City	240 000	345 000	720 000
Guadalajara	65 000	101 000	120 000
Puebla	65 000	94 000	96 000
San Luis Potosí	34 000	61 000	68 000
Monterrey	14 000	62 000	79 000

cities; in 1877, only ten state capitals had populations of more than 20 000 (out of a total of 28 cities), while in 1910 there were 19 state capitals of this size (the data on the other cities with over 20 000 inhabitants varies greatly according to the source, and ranges from 20 to 79 cities). Some settlements grew up around mining centers (such as Cananea and Santa Rosalía), whereas others were the result of industrial development (Monterrey and Torreón), others were more dependent on trade (the ports of Tuxpan, Progreso, Guaymas, and Manzanillo), and still others were towns the railroad passed through (such as Nuevo Laredo and Ciudad Juárez). Several of these factors came together in the capital, which was the seat of federal power, the destination of the main rail lines, and home to 12% of the country's industry.

Government officials and the elites wanted the cities to reflect the nation's prosperity and progress and to resemble the metropolises of Europe and the United States. In order to make their cities beautiful and comfortable, they built gardens and wide avenues similar to the Champs Élysées in Paris. They also wanted cities to be safe and clean. But the cities were not prepared to receive so many immigrants. Most urban residents lived on dirty, flooded streets and suffered from a lack of housing, drinking water, and food. All this created serious health problems that led to very high mortality rates. Moreover, crime and prostitution increased.

To solve these problems, and as part of a modernization project, government officials issued penal and sanitary codes and police regulations and reformed health and penal institutions. They built drainage works and paved streets to control flooding; they constructed sewers for wastewater and installed pipes for drinking water. Lastly, they waged a crusade to improve the cleanliness of cities and their inhabitants: they cleaned streets, established garbage truck routes and public urinals, and forced slaughterhouses and especially cemeteries to locate outside the city limits. To control or prevent epidemics, they isolated the sick and burned their belongings. At the same time, they promoted advances in medicine and founded institutes to study bacteriology and pathology. Thus, the Porfiriato was an era of building public works, founding institutions, and establishing rules. The government regulated many aspects of people's lives, from their commitments to institutions and society to their conjugal and family relationships, habits of hygiene, and forms of entertainment.

Nevertheless, not all areas of these cities nor all social groups benefited from government programs or modernization. In fact, the urban landscape evidenced marked social stratification: in commercial areas and neighborhoods where privileged groups lived all services were available, while in poor neighborhoods they were completely lacking. Wealth was concentrated among small groups made up of hacienda owners, businessmen, owners of commercial enterprises, bankers, and eminent professionals, all of whom were united by family relationships, friendship or business dealings, and who also invested in trade, industry or real estate. Within the middle classes, which grew tremendously as a result of expanded trade and services, there were professionals, people employed in government, commerce or transportation, and prosperous artisans. Finally, the lower classes accounted for the majority of the urban population and were composed of diverse groups including servants, local shop assistants, artisans, laborers, and street vendors.

Laborers deserve a special mention. Industrial expansion caused their numbers to multiply and gradually replace artisans. As occurred in other countries, no legislation protected workers, because economic liberalism dictated that the government should not intervene in the economy, and wages should be set by the law of supply and demand. As a result, although there was freedom of association, strikes were not allowed. Men, women, and children worked 12- and 14-hour days, some of them seven days a week; they could be fired for no reason, and were not protected against accidents. Low wages, whose purchasing power was constantly eroded by inflation, were further reduced by arbitrary docking and payment in scrip usable only at company stores.

Workers organized themselves into mutual benefit societies, contributing dues that went to help the wounded or sick, widows or orphans, or to pay for funerals. They also created lending and food supply cooperatives, as well as organizations that fought to improve working conditions and wages, which in some cases were influenced by socialist or anarchist ideas.

Díaz was more tolerant of mutual aid organizations, which he subsidized and for which he provided meeting spaces, because their members attended public events celebrated in his honor and thereby gave his regime legitimacy. But he was less broad-minded when it came to more radical organizations and movements. Throughout the Porfiriato there were constant conflicts and strikes, which became more numerous after 1900. Díaz sought conciliation between workers and employers, but when an agreement could not be reached, he resorted to force. The best examples of this are the conflicts in Cananea and Río Blanco. In 1906, the miners in Cananea in northern Sonora rebelled, demanding that a maximum number of working hours per day and a minimum wage be established, and also asked for treatment and compensation similar to those given to U.S. workers employed in the same company. Their demands were rejected and a strike broke out that was followed by a rebellion. To put it down, U.S. volunteers were brought in, supported by the Mexican army.

Months later, textile workers in Orizaba, Puebla, Tlaxcala, and the Federal District went out on strike to protest poor working conditions. Employers drafted a set of regulations and, in reaction, workers wrote their own. In an attempt to conciliate, Porfirio Díaz presented a proposal that included a wage increase, an end to docking of wages, a fund for orphans and widows, and the prohibition of child labor, but he made its implementation voluntary, relying on management's goodwill. Workers in some factories accepted the agreement and returned to their jobs, but those in Río Blanco rioted and looted the factory and its store, taking the toll of many lives.

In short, urban society demonstrated deep divisions of class and even ethnicity. The elites were concerned about the visibility of low-income and marginal groups, especially those who dressed in indigenous attire, since they believed that this tarnished the city's image. Their concern grew on the eve of festivities or commemorative events. To prevent foreign visitors from seeing this evidence of poverty and "barbarism," they distributed clothing to the neediest. Thus, longstanding and deep-rooted social and racial prejudices persisted, which some groups now upheld on the basis of "scientific" ideas.

CULTURE

During the Porfiriato, a variety of ways of understanding the nation, society, and the individual coexisted, including liberalism, positivism, and conservatism. While some held to liberal ideas and others enthusiastically embraced the premises of positivism and concepts such as Social Darwinism, many chose an eclectic approach that combined elements of liberalism and positivism. For example, they adopted the positivist idea that the scientific method should be applied to studying society and resolving its problems, and criticized the liberals for basing policy and legislation on imported theories instead of focusing on observation of Mexican society. Nonetheless, they did not want to replace liberal institutions or the Constitution of 1857, and were willing to postpone implementation of the latter until such time as Mexicans were judged to have achieved the necessary level of development. By the same token, they believed education and science should be promoted as the best means of achieving national progress.

Others sympathized with conservative ideas and the doctrine of the Catholic Church. But there were differing groups among them. Some opposed separating the temporal and spiritual realms and defended the supremacy of sacred laws and the moral authority of the Church over society, while others accepted secularization and concentrated on restoring its role in social life. In addition, there were those who favored Social Catholicism or believed that Catholics should participate in guiding national politics, and especially in resolving the social problems that plagued Mexico. Those sympathizing with this group, which grew in strength at the beginning of the twentieth century, were concerned about inequality and social injustice, demanding that the State issue legislation to protect workers and that owners treat workers decently.

Regardless of ideology, Catholicism had not lost its place among religions. Most Mexicans were Catholic. In 1910, for example, 99% were baptized and practiced the Catholic faith. Protestantism was much less prevalent. Protestants had arrived in Mexico around 1870. Over time, 18 missionary societies were established at the northern border and in Guanajuato, Puebla, Pachuca, Mexico City, and Veracruz. They offered education and free medical services to members of their congregations. They faced a variety of obstacles to spreading their faith, however: internal battles among Protestant denominations and public mistrust, plus the opposition of the Catholic Church. At times Catholic groups openly confronted missionaries, but the latter had the support of Díaz and state governors, who used this support as a way to demonstrate their compliance with the law; moreover, they viewed the spread of Protestantism as a way to limit the influence of the Catholic Church. Thus, although the impact of the Protestant Church was minimal in numerical terms, with its adherents representing about two percent of the population if we count foreigners, its presence symbolized respect for freedom of religion and the laicity of the Mexican State.

As we have seen, in the realm of ideas there were divisions between liberals, positivists, and conservatives, but on the whole they upheld the same values. The elites, middle classes, and even some sectors of the lower classes shared the same notions with regard to the family and the role of women within the family unit and in the heart of the community. This was reflected in many writings, including legislation, legal texts, literature, publications of religious and secular associations devoted to philanthropy, conduct manuals, magazines for women and the family, miscellaneous publications, and popular literature. Mexicans believed that the family must be the outgrowth of matrimony, preferably consecrated by the Church. The husband was viewed as the head of the household, and laws allowed him to manage his wife's assets without her consent (while she needed her husband's permission to manage property held in common), and the husband was granted guardianship of children (which the woman acquired only after her husband's death, and then only with certain restrictions, since she had to answer to a counselor appointed by the husband). Each gender was assigned a different sphere of action: the man was involved in public life, that is, political and work matters, while the woman had to limit herself to private life and dedicate herself to domestic tasks. People took a dim view of women working outside the home, and this was acceptable only for widows or single women who needed the income, provided that they worked in "activities appropriate to their sex," such as sewing or teaching. As a result, laws did not give women the right to vote or to hold popularly elected office and restricted their work activities. While training in professional fields was not prohibited for them, only in exceptional cases did those of the upper and middle classes receive higher education. Nevertheless, as the twentieth century approached, women came to achieve greater participation in public life, and—among other activities—published women's magazines in which they defended their intellectual equality. An incipient feminist movement that demanded legal and educational equality with men was also developing.

In other matters, European and especially French influence was strong in literature and art, as it was in cuisine and fashion. This was evident in modernist literature, which owed much to French symbolism, as represented by Manuel Gutiérrez Nájera, Salvador Díaz Mirón, Amado Nervo, José Juan Tablada, and Efrén Rebolledo. Architecture used a variety of Classical, Romanesque, Mudejar, Gothic, Baroque, and Art Nouveau styles, which it freely combined, sometimes in a single building. This majestic architectural heritage is evident in the theaters of Mexico's principal cities: the Juárez Theater in Guanajuato, the De la Paz Theater in San Luis Potosí, the Doblado Theater in León, the Calderón Theater in Zacatecas, and the Peón Contreras Theater in Mérida.

But a national and nationalistic culture was also developing, one that reflected the country's unique characteristics and that could therefore serve to foster a sense of identity. Following an old tradition, costumbrist literature (such as novels of manners) emerged initially that was either romantic or realistic in tone, depending on whether the author was Ángel de Campo, José Tomás de Cuéllar, Rafael Delgado or José López Portillo y Rojas. Later, realist literature was also cultivated following the costumbrist legacy, but was interested in more faithfully reproducing the atmosphere and characters of Mexico's reality; for example, the works of Heriberto Frías, Federico Gamboa, and Emilio Rabasa. Another outstanding tradition was Mexican landscape painting, with artists such as José María Velasco or Joaquín Clausell, and portraits of characters, scenes, and events of daily life depicted by José Guadalupe Posada, who publicized his work in "penny" newspapers, chapbooks, and handbills published by Antonio Vanegas Arroyo's printing company.

However, to recreate a sense of a common culture, Díaz's supporters again followed the example of the rulers of the Restored Republic, believing that nothing was more effective than education and, above all, teaching the country's history, which expanded views beyond regional boundaries and inculcated in children the civic values that would prepare them to be citizens in the future. Education was therefore free and mandatory, and used official curricula and textbooks. Numerous schools were founded. Yet the educational program did not meet with the success they expected. It was concentrated in urban areas and even there fell short: in 1895, only 15% of the population knew how to read and write, a number that grew to just 20% by 1910.

Historical works were also written, such as *México a través de los siglos* [literally, Mexico Through the Centuries or Ages, not to be confused with the Diego Rivera mural in the National Palace in Mexico City] by Vicente Riva Palacio, and *México, su evolución social* [Mexico, Its Social Evolution] by Justo Sierra, which brought the indigenous and Spanish pasts into harmony and, with an evolutionist tone, presented history as a march towards nationalism, liberalism, and scientific and material progress.

Civic ceremonies were another way of promoting nationalism, Mexican history, and the veneration of heroes. There were celebrations for the nation's birth and the defense of its sovereignty, as well as for its liberal institutions—of which the Porfiriato claimed to be the heir and defender and viewed Porfirio Díaz as their champion. Thus, these special days glorified not only the country, but also its president.

To sum up, culture during the Porfiriato admired the foreign, but also evidenced national and nationalistic traits. The latter is clearly expressed by the intellectuals of the Revolution, who took up claims first made in the early years of the twentieth century by forming the "Athenaeum of Youth." This was a group made up of people like Antonio Caso, Pedro Henríquez Ureña, Alfonso Reyes, and José Vasconcelos. The members of the

Athenaeum advocated more openness to new ideas; they criticized adherence to the positivist model, because they believed that knowledge could be obtained through a variety of means, not only through the scientific method, and they defended the capacity of human beings, emphasizing freedom of action and choice; they fought to reaffirm humanistic values in culture, for an end to French influence in literature and, in general, for the recovery of all that was Mexican.

This and much more is the Porfiriato's legacy to twentieth-century Mexico, a legacy that is not limited to the cultural arena, but extends to politics (with progress in consolidating the nation-state), the economy (with the expansion of markets, transportation, and means of communication; promotion of agricultural exports; and the beginning of industrialization), and society (with population growth and urbanization). Moreover, it handed down political vices, a profoundly unequal society and economy, and a series of conflicts that gave rise to the Revolution and which would still need to be resolved in the first decades of Post-Revolutionary Mexico.

THE REVOLUTION

JAVIER GARCIADIEGO

CRITICS, OPPOSITIONISTS, AND PRECURSORS

THIS CHAPTER IS DEVOTED TO ANALYZING THE MEXICAN REVOLUTION, which was a consequence of the Porfiriato and the process that defined Mexico for a major part of the twentieth century. Although many scholars maintain that a longer period including the most significant political, socio-economic, and cultural changes was also part of the Mexican Revolution, we will limit ourselves here to the years in which there was widespread violence, although without treating the Revolution as synonymous with the armed struggle per se. Rather, we define it as a complex process by means of which the late nineteenth-century oligarchic, neocolonial State was destroyed. The institutionalization that began in the latter part of the 1920s marked the consolidation of a new kind of State and the beginning of another historical era.

After several years of economic growth and political stability, the Porfirian regime began to evidence various signs of its decline. The crisis was multifaceted and insoluble. It affected political, economic, social, diplomatic, and cultural spheres to varying degrees: the magnificent state of affairs characterizing the end of the nineteenth century started to deteriorate at the beginning of the twentieth. The problems faced by Porfirio Díaz's regime in its final years sparked criticism and op-

position movements among a variety of social classes and political groups.

The first to raise their voices were certain sectors of the
Catholic Church, influenced by the renewal of ideas on social
issues put forth by the Vatican as of 1891, when it issued the
Rerum Novarum encyclical that attempted to offer a Christian
solution to social conflicts. Despite the Church's relatively good
relations with the Porfirian regime, it mildly reproached Díaz
for preserving the liberal, anticlerical principles of the 1857
Constitution. In addition to these complaints, socio-political
criticism arose as Mexican Catholics adapted the encyclical
—which was intended for the European industrialized world—
to their overwhelmingly rural environment. Although these
critics defended private property as a natural right, they began
to object to the excessive concentration of agricultural property,
as well as the labor conditions prevalent in most Mexican haciendas. After protesting against the agrarian situation, Catholics
went on to condemn the predominance of caciques (local political bosses) and the lack of democracy. They always recognized Porfirio Díaz's great historical accomplishments; nonetheless, without mentioning him by name, the objections aimed at
his government eroded his prestige and the consensus he had
enjoyed. The socio-political impact of this critique, albeit moderate, should not be underestimated.

Around 1900, motivations in the opposite direction gave
rise to the emergence of an ideologically liberal group that included diverse sectors of the urban middle class such as professionals, journalists, teachers, and students. They claimed that
the government had distanced itself from liberal principles and
proposed to reorganize the nineteenth-century political group
known as the Liberal Party in order to pressure Díaz to put those
principles into practice. They supported anticlerical laws, but
also wanted freedom of speech, electoral democracy, the separation of powers, an effective judicial system, and municipal

autonomy. To begin this work of restructuring the party, Camilo Arriaga invited the defenders of liberal ideas to a convention in San Luis Potosí, in the very heart of Mexico. Noteworthy among those attending were the brothers Jesús and Ricardo Flores Magón, sons of a Juárez supporter from Oaxaca and residents of Mexico City, where they were studying law and published the oppositionist newspaper *Regeneración*. They soon became more radical: in 1903, they extended their attacks to the *científicos* and to Bernardo Reyes, began to question the desirability of foreign investment, and concerned themselves with the plight of workers and peasants. The government responded with repression, forcing many of them into exile in the United States.

Their experience in the U.S. was both dramatic and decisive, since some deserted, some broke away from the group, and others became more radical. For a time they continued proposing peaceful methods of opposition in *Regeneración* and remained true to liberal ideology, as evidenced by their Liberal Party Platform drafted in 1906. After gaining more leverage than Arriaga, Ricardo Flores Magón led the transition towards anarchist ideology. There are several explanations for this change: his relationships with members of U.S. socialist and anarchist organizations; the multinational nature of his new surroundings, which included Hispanics, Chinese, and Europeans; and, above all, because he was living in a more industrialized society than Mexico's. Also important was the fact that Flores Magón and his partisans tended to see the workers' movement and the middle-class intellectuals allied with it as the vanguard—an inappropriate diagnosis of the situation in a rural country—, which led them to err in their political strategies. Their connection with Mexico became more remote when the influence they might have had on the labor movement was diminished by repression of the strikers at Cananea and Río Blanco. To top it all off, their subsequent calls for armed warfare alienated any middle-class sympathizers they might have had, and they were put under surveillance. Although their influence declined from that point on (1908), their historical importance is unquestionable: they directed the most constant and well-founded criticisms at the Díaz regime, and through *Regeneración* politicized and raised the awareness of many Mexicans. Several leaders who would later distinguish themselves in the Mexican Revolution gained experience as part of their group, and the time they spent in the United States served to undermine Don Porfirio's international prestige.

Lastly, Díaz's preference for the *científicos* to succeed him caused Reyes' supporters—who until then had been Díaz loyalists—to become a very important opposition group mobilized to pressure Díaz into selecting Reyes as his vice president in the 1910 election. Very quickly groups, clubs, newspapers, and books hostile to the *científicos* and favoring Reyes appeared. The skill and strength shown by his adherents were such that Díaz, worried, sent Bernardo Reyes on a mission to Europe in September 1909. With the movement leaderless, most of Reyes' followers joined a group still in its infancy that opposed reelection and was headed by Francisco I. Madero, a hacienda owner and businessman from Coahuila. The Reyes faction was important in several ways: its defection weakened the regime; it devoted itself to discrediting the *científicos* (the group that presumably was to succeed Don Porfirio); and it strengthened the anti-reelectionist movement by adding many prestigious "cadres" with political experience comprised of a variety of individuals from urban upper, middle, and lower classes. Of all the movements that preceded the Mexican Revolution, the Reyes faction contributed the most, mainly in the figures of Venustiano Carranza, Francisco Vázquez Gómez, and Luis Cabrera, to name a few.

FROM OPPOSITION TO ARMED CONFLICT

The crises that characterized the end of the Porfiriato illustrate why Francisco I. Madero came to oppose the *científicos'* economic policy and conclude that it was necessary to create a national political party to contend against Díaz's reelection in 1910. He dedicated himself to this cause beginning in the second half of 1909, making three tours to promote the establishment of anti-reelectionist clubs that would select state delegates for a national convention to be held in early 1910. At the convention, the National Anti-Reelectionist Party was founded and nominated its candidates for president and vice president: Madero and former Reyes supporter Francisco Vázquez Gómez, a combination that sealed the alliance of these two movements.

Until then, Madero had demonstrated remarkable political skill. In a short time, he turned regional into national opposition, and his popularity grew enormously. He eventually replaced other more experienced oppositionist movements (those of Magón and Reyes) and united a large portion of their members under his leadership. Once he became a presidential candidate, he began another tour, but was soon arrested, accused of inciting rebellion, and imprisoned in San Luis Potosí. While he was in jail, the election took place and Díaz and Ramón Corral were declared the winners. Soon thereafter he fled to the United States and took refuge in San Antonio, Texas. There, Madero and a small group of collaborators drafted a plan still labeled as being from the city of San Luis Potosí in which he made a call for armed struggle. How could a pacifist that supported the fight for democracy incite people to arms? Who did he think would wage this battle? Did he foresee the possible consequences of such violence? Most of Madero's supporters were urban middle-class because on his campaign tours he had only been in contact with people of that social stratum. As could have been predicted, the call to arms was not seconded by his anti-reelectionist followers, since they were not in a position to launch an armed venture. Moreover, to be known as oppositionists while living in towns made them vulnerable: the death of the Serdán brothers in Puebla was a warning about the fate that awaited urban anti-reelectionists who got involved in the rebellion.

The impact of Aquiles Serdán's assassination was decisive, resulting in the call to arms being ignored by the original opponents of reelection. However, the rebellion was well received in the mountains of Chihuahua, and quickly spread into the neighboring states of Sonora, Durango, and Coahuila. But of course, the social status of these rebels was different: they were poor and rural, and their demands were also different. During the first three months the rebel groups were small, poorly armed and disorganized, and employed guerrilla tactics. But in February 1911, Madero finally returned to Mexico to assume leadership of the struggle and the movement's organization improved. As a result, the size of the armed groups grew, enabling them to attack larger villages and towns and engage in formal combat. Most importantly, uprisings occurred in other parts of the country, for example in the states of Morelos and Guerrero. By March and April there were groups operating on many fronts, which made them more difficult to repress. Because of Díaz's ultimate mistrust of Reyes, the federal army had been punished by having its budget cut and many pro-Reyes officers had been relieved of direct command of troops, which reduced the effectiveness of the army, already out of practice from so many years of peace. If we add to this the U.S. authorities' sympathy for Madero's cause, it is not hard to understand the haste with which negotiations to restore peace began.

The fall of the border town of Ciudad Juárez in the second week of May sped up talks between the government and the rebels. It also strengthened the rebels' negotiating power, led to many new uprisings, and paralyzed the federal army and many local authorities. As a result, there were a number of bloodless takeovers of towns and villages during the second half of May, which accelerated after the Agreements of Ciudad Juárez were signed at the end of the month. The agreements accepted Díaz's resignation and thereby ensured the movement's victory. In that initial phase, the Mexican Revolution was a mobilization which shifted from electoral opposition to armed rebellion with a different set of actors and scenarios: the urban middle-class struggle became a fight by the rural poor. New leaders arose who were better suited to rural armed conflict and had not participated in the opposition to reelection, or at least had not been major figures in it. Pascual Orozco, Pancho Villa, and Emiliano Zapata then appeared on the scene in leading roles. In social terms, this implied incorporating northern *rancheros*, members of former military colonies, farm workers, cowboys, railroad workers, miners (who were undoubtedly responsible for dynamiting the railways), laborers, artisans, and rural teachers, as well as southern ranchers—like the Figueroa brothers in Guerrero—, and many residents and traditional authorities in peasant (*campesino*) communities in central and southern Mexico, such as Zapata and his entire family environment. Contrary to the wishes of government officials, Madero himself, and others of the original anti-reelectionist leaders, lower-class groups became inextricably involved in the process of political change. Indeed, they turned it into a revolutionary process. The former group wanted political change, while the latter had social, primarily agrarian, demands.

ANACHRONISTIC LIBERALISM

The parties to the Agreements of Ciudad Juárez consented to replace Díaz in the legally sanctioned way with his Minister of Foreign Affairs, Francisco León de la Barra. His responsibilities would be to oversee the disarming and demobilizing of the rebel forces and to organize new elections. Disarmament was a very complicated process: although many rebels accepted the return to peace after receiving a payment in compensation, others were organized into new *cuerpos rurales* (rural militias). Yet the most important rebel groups opposed laying down their arms: Pascual Orozco and his adherents were cast aside once the military victory had been achieved, causing them to feel that the benefits obtained had been insufficient. For their part, Emiliano Zapata and the southern rebels refused to break up or to organize as *cuerpos rurales*; they were unwilling to surrender their weapons until the lands they believed to have been illegally seized by hacienda owners were returned to them. This position put them at odds with León de la Barra's interim government.

As for the new election, Madero decided to change the National Anti-Reelectionist Party into the Progressive Constitutional Party. He also decided that for this second electoral contest his running mate would no longer be Vázquez Gómez, but rather José María Pino Suárez, an attorney and journalist born in Tabasco but living in Yucatán (in southeastern Mexico), where he collaborated with the anti-reelectionist movement. Both decisions turned out to be questionable. In the absence of a purposeful plan for government that could muster a high degree of consensus, opposition to reelection was a unifying force, albeit a negative one. Moreover, the break with Vázquez Gómez disappointed many supporters because of the way it was done. In particular, it alienated many former Reyes supporters who had the long experience and political savvy that Madero lacked. Despite all this, Madero won a landslide victory in the October 1911 election, although he took office as president after having broken off his alliances with Reyes, Orozco, and Zapata loyalists.

Madero's presidency, which began at the end of 1911 and ended violently in February 1913, was marked by the political changes it brought about: the cabinet was comprised of young men belonging to lower social classes than those during the Díaz era, which explains why they had a different ideology. Governors were also very different than before, and the same can be said of the deputies and senators. Most significant, perhaps, was the replacement of the old political bosses by new, freely elected local authorities. In short, Díaz's departure completely upended the pyramid of power within a few months. Even politicians of the Porfiriato who managed to survive in office did so in oppositionist roles. Most important, while in 1911 and 1912 the middle classes burst into government machinery and decision-making, laborers and peasants also increased their political influence. Furthermore, Madero's presidency introduced more democratic political practices: there were free elections and freedom of speech was respected; the Executive Branch no longer dominated the Legislative and Judicial Branches; and the federal government ceased imposing its will on state and local authorities.

Together with these changes in the political sphere, Madero and his new government officials instituted innovative agrarian and labor programs. Madero, who managed a cotton hacienda and was the member of a business family, favored private ownership of land, distrusted communally-held agrarian property, and maintained that a system dominated by small and medium-sized landowners should be constructed, together with modern, efficient hacienda owners. In labor matters, he respected workers' right to organize, and sought to help them improve their socio-economic conditions without seriously affecting industrialists' finances. His administration began to assume the role of arbiter in conflicts between employers and their workers. In 1912, owing to the new political climate and industrialists' diminished power, the number of labor organizations and strikes grew. The same thing was happening in rural areas: with the peasants' enormous increase in political capital due to their participation in the armed fight against Díaz and the hacienda owners' concomitant loss of strength, that year the balance of power changed in the countryside. There were many instances of lands claimed to have been illegally seized being occupied and many requests for increases in daily wages. Unfortunately for the hacienda owners, they no longer had the authorities' unlimited support, since the former local bosses and *rurales* (rural mounted police) were no longer there to back them up.

Paradoxically, Madero's reform proposals left almost every political group and social class in the country dissatisfied, not to mention foreign diplomats and investors. Hacienda and business owners saw the reforms as setting a dangerous precedent. Workers and peasants who had formerly supported Madero—workers during the electoral period and peasants during the armed struggle—considered them inadequate. That widespread discontent was translated into open criticism and opposition movements, including armed rebellions. The Madero administration had to cope with four major violent confrontations: two led by the beneficiaries of the Porfiriato (Bernardo Reyes and Félix Díaz), and another two headed by disappointed anti-Díaz rebels (Emiliano Zapata and Pascual Orozco). These rebellions can be seen as a consequence of changes in the national balance of power. While the former fought to recover their lost influence, the latter did so to ensure that their new strength would lead to immediate satisfaction of long-standing socio-economic demands. Reyes fought at the end of 1911 because he believed that only he should govern the country in Díaz's absence. Félix Díaz started a rebellion in Veracruz in October 1912, claiming that Madero was incapable of governing. The problem was that Félix (Don Porfirio's nephew) had neither the power nor the legitimacy to solve the problem of reorganizing the nation which was mandated by the great socio-political mobilization that had taken place as of the latter part of the Porfiriato. His calls to action fell on deaf ears, a clear sign that times had changed.

The popular Zapata- and Orozco-led rebellions were radically different. The peasants of Morelos did not accept the discharge of soldiers stipulated in the Agreements of Ciudad Juárez. They stated that they would not lay down their weapons without first having the lands returned that they claimed hacienda owners had taken from them. Their position led to President León de la Barra considering them rebels. When Madero became president, they formalized their struggle in the Plan of Ayala, which demanded a solution to agrarian problems and proposed that the peasant community be the country's basic agrarian unit. The military importance of Zapata and his followers is distinct from their relevance in history. Throughout 1912, they continued their struggle, but at a low level of intensity. In contrast, the Orozco rebellion was notoriously violent. Orozco and his numerous supporters rebelled in March 1912 and issued the Plan de la Empacadora for two reasons: the leaders viewed the economic and political retribution received for their decisive participation in the victory over Díaz as inadequate, and the soldiers saw the social reforms Madero was proposing as too little, too late. Unlike Zapata's rebellion, which was mainly agrarian, Orozco's effort involved a variety of social classes, since besides the many non-peasant lower-class groups involved, the regional middle class was also a major participant. Nor was the Orozco uprising merely local in scope: in addition to taking over all of Chihuahua, including the state capital, its presence was felt in other northern states such as Durango, Coahuila, Sonora, and even Zacatecas and San Luis Potosí. It was so powerful that in the beginning people feared it would end up defeating the Madero government.

To defeat Orozco's rebels, a major contingent of men and resources was put under the command of General Victoriano Huerta. Orozco's former collaborators in his fight against Díaz were used in the battle against his forces—men who had remained loyal to the government, such as Pancho Villa, who were incorporated into the federal army as aides. The objective was to have men also skilled in guerrilla warfare who were able to identify with the local poor. Moreover, the governors of northern states organized their forces to fight off Orozco raids, including outstanding militias led by Pablo González of Coahuila and Álvaro Obregón of Sonora. The result was twofold: by incorporating the former Madero aides and state troops, the revolutionary movement recovered its strength; and with its victory, the federal army regained its confidence and found a natural leader in Huerta, a situation that would become dramatically clear soon thereafter, when he decided to rebel against the established government.

At the end of 1912 and in early 1913, Madero believed he had at last achieved stability by defeating the four rebellions. His optimism was based on a mistaken assessment of the situation: all four had suffered serious limitations; nonetheless, despite their defeat they had inflicted major damage on Madero's administration. In this dangerous political setting, with a wounded but recovering army and an administration that was isolated and had many enemies, in February of 1913 Bernardo Reyes and Félix Díaz believed that together, in the very seat of federal power, they could develop a successful counterrevolutionary movement. Although they failed a second time, the new military caudillo Victoriano Huerta assumed command of that movement, which would deliver the final and fatal blow to Madero. The agreement among the victorious coup leaders is known as the Pact of the Ciudadela, because they barricaded themselves in this "citadel" (former barracks), or the Pact of the Embassy, because it was signed in the offices of the U.S. Embassy. Simultaneous opposition from the government in Washington (perhaps because of the taxes Madero levied on oil), the federal army, Porfirian political groups, and hacienda and business owners, together with the disintegration of the anti-reelectionist front, middle-class disillusionment, and government inexperience combined to make Madero's position unsustainable, and he was assassinated during the military coup that deposed him in February 1913.

THE CONSTITUTIONALIST STRUGGLE

Huerta's government began as an amalgamation of almost all the anti-Madero political groups, including supporters of Félix Díaz, Bernardo Reyes, the *científicos*, Catholics, and even Orozco adherents. Moreover, Huerta had the unconditional support of the federal army, as well as of hacienda and business owners. As for the United States government, its support for Huerta was short-lived, because within a few weeks of his taking office the Democrat Woodrow Wilson replaced Republican William Taft as president and radically changed U.S. policy toward Mexico. Huerta's rise to the Mexican presidency provoked the angry mobilization of most of the former anti-Porfirian rebels, many of whom were also veterans of the fight against Orozco, and others who had become pro-Madero local authorities. This explains why the battle against Huerta was aimed at protecting and preserving the changes and political positions achieved during Madero's administration, as well as opposing the attempt to restore a government dominated by pro-Porfirian politicians supported by a powerful federal army that favored hacienda owners and other members of the former regime's upper classes.

From the start, the rebellion against Huerta evolved in four major scenarios, each with its own social, political, ideological, economic, and military features. The first was in the State of Coahuila, led by Governor Venustiano Carranza, a former Reyes supporter who turned against Porfirio Díaz in 1909. Carranza and the other government officials in Coahuila refused to recognize Huerta's government, declared him a rebel, and called for the creation of a Constitutionalist Army to defeat Huerta

and restore the rule of law. The anti-Huerta movement in Coahuila was characterized by its legalistic nature and by having a
governor at its head. Understandably, the second tier of leadership fell to the highest-ranking local politicians and government employees. For an army, they had veterans of the fight
against Díaz. Those unique features were reflected in the Plan
of Guadalupe. While in a military sense the Coahuila faction
played a minor role in defeating Huerta, it was fundamental to
the organization, legitimacy, and management of the battle.

In the State of Sonora, several members of the middle class
assumed leadership, men who had remained out of economic
and political favor during the Porfiriato, but who had risen to
important public positions during Madero's administration. Their
goal was to preserve the positions they had attained. The most
important of these leaders were Álvaro Obregón, Salvador Al-
varado, Plutarco Elías Calles, Manuel Diéguez, and Adolfo de la
Huerta, among others. In addition to political power, they had
some military ability thanks to their experience in the battles
against the Yaqui Indians and because many had fought against
supporters of Porfirio Díaz and Pascual Orozco. Another noteworthy aspect in this area was that the indigenous-agrarian conflicts, especially those involving the Mayo and Yaqui Indians, and
labor disputes in Cananea had led local middle-class oppositionists to form alliances with groups of the poor. Thus, in addition
to their military capabilities, the Sonorans would contribute to
this movement their experience as a middle-class group capable of establishing pacts and other agreements with groups representing the masses.

The anti-Huerta contingent in the State of Chihuahua and
northern Durango was unique in that it was led by a member of
the lower classes: Pancho Villa. In contrast to the revolutionaries
in Coahuila and Sonora, Villa was not a local official, but rather
a typical rebel. As a result, his lieutenants and second-tier commanders also came from among the poor. They took up arms

again to prevent Pascual Orozco from coming to power locally or a return to the oligarchy headed by the Terrazas family. Without taking into account military aspects, their primary contribution was to supply the Constitutionalist movement with an enormous leading contingent of the downtrodden. Owing to Villa and his followers, the northern anti-Huerta fight was not just a legalistic, middle-class struggle. Nevertheless, although Villa's army came from the lower classes, it was by no means made up exclusively of peasants. Aside from many agricultural day laborers, sharecroppers, tenant farmers, poor *rancheros*, and members of former military colonies, there were also many cowboys, miners, railroad workers, and laborers.

The battle against Huerta was not limited to the North. Huerta's rise to power changed the nature of the fight waged by Zapata's supporters and increased its intensity. To begin with, any hope of an agrarian reform being implemented vanished, since from day one it was clear that Huerta's plans for the State of Morelos were being carried out by the army and the hacienda owners. Moreover, his methods of repression were bloody and drastic, which increased the number of rebels, because members of peasant communities found themselves forced to fight more defensive battles. Zapata's supporters participated in the struggle, but did not recognize Carranza's leadership, and as a result the anti-Huerta phase of the Revolution took place in two separate regions. Also, the fundamentally political demands of 1909 and 1910 were now complemented by several social demands, particularly the return of lands that had been seized, and respect for traditional peasant communities, which were considered not only valid, but the defining feature of Mexican agriculture.

Socio-geographic differences gave rise to profound political, ideological, and military divisions. Despite the leadership conferred on him by the Plan of Guadalupe, Carranza headed a rebel army composed only of his civilian and military personnel.

In order to become the authentic leader of the entire rebellion, he began exporting his movement to neighboring states. Although this spread his scarce military resources even thinner, Carranza preferred to send his men to promote uprisings in the states of Nuevo León, Tamaulipas, Zacatecas, and San Luis Potosí. Thus he went from being a state leader to a regional one. The weakening of the forces that remained in Coahuila, however, allowed Huerta's army to retake the state in mid-1913, obliging Carranza to flee and operate from a base in Sonora. This experience enabled him to develop ties with revolutionaries who had different social backgrounds. Most importantly, it made it possible for him to become the real leader of the rebellion in two regions: the Northeast and the Northwest.

By early 1914, the rebels already dominated the North of Mexico, and as of the middle and latter part of 1913 had extended rather intense anti-Huerta activity into San Luis Potosí, Zacatecas, Sinaloa, Jalisco, Michoacán, and Veracruz. On the other hand, Mexico's Center, South, and Southeast were not heavily involved in the rebellion. Aside from the State of Morelos and its neighboring areas—which were the scene of violent warfare between Huerta's pillaging troops and Zapata's forces, the latter consisting of all the defensive units of the area's peasant communities—, in the central region of the country there was hardly any activity worth mentioning except for Hidalgo and Tlaxcala. There are several reasons for the rebellion's weakness in that region, including its proximity to the capital and the importance of the railway to Veracruz through Puebla and Tlaxcala, which created a major industrial corridor that needed protection, and hence the strategic importance of controlling and therefore repressing the rebellion there. As for the South, while there were many rebel forces in Guerrero, only a few were operating in Oaxaca. To the southeast, in Tabasco there were several minor leaders, but their actions were not sufficient to worry the government. No doubt their social structure—dominated by paternalistic farm owners and also peons and Indians—, as well as their remoteness and virtual lack of communication with the outside world, made this an area reluctant to participate in the fight against Huerta.

In March and April 1914, the northern armies began their advance toward Central Mexico to expel Huerta from the nation's capital. Together—Obregón from the west, Villa from the center, and Pablo González from the east—they constituted an overwhelming force. Huerta's defeat was inevitable, given that his army was using a defensive, static strategy, barricading itself in the largest cities. Worse yet, the fact that the government in Washington had refused to recognize Huerta and his lack of control over the northern border caused a severe economic crisis, making it impossible for him to recruit new soldiers or acquire weapons and ammunition. In stark contrast to the rebel movement, which progressed steadily from its very beginnings, the Huerta administration was constantly deteriorating. In the political arena, the broad conservative alliance that was formed after the February 1913 military coup soon fell apart, undermining Huerta's claim to representation, legitimacy, and efficiency. In the diplomatic arena, Democratic President Woodrow Wilson's inauguration and Huerta's loss of the region where the main U.S. investments were located were the reasons for the growing distance between the Mexican and U.S. governments. The beginning of Huerta's downfall can be seen in April 1914, when the northern armies began their assault on the central part of the country and U.S. marines invaded Veracruz to prevent Huerta from receiving an arms shipment from Europe.

The northern armies' advance sparked many belated uprisings in the country's central states. Furthermore, each defeat of Huerta's army triggered desertions by civilian officials. Although Villa's Northern Division Army arrived in Zacatecas in June, Carranza decided that only González's and Obregón's armies would take the capital, ordering Villa to remain in the North. This decision was the final example of a long series of disagreements between the two men that resulted from their many differences in socio-economic status, political beliefs, and ideology. A split among the Constitutionalists was about to occur, although they would ultimately reach an agreement: Villa would continue to be fundamental to the fight against Huerta, although he would remain in the North, while as soon as Carranza occupied Mexico City, he would call a meeting of generals who would decide what social reforms were necessary and who the country's next president would be.

Except for this conflict, the Revolution continued to progress without difficulties: Obregón advanced through Sinaloa and Jalisco, then occupied Guadalajara, and moved on to the center of the country. González marched through Monterrey, Tampico, San Luis Potosí, and Querétaro. The ease with which they achieved victory gave no indication of the historical importance of the process that was occurring. First, the movement ceased to be an exclusively northern one, and became a tide sweeping across at least half of the country. Their geographic expansion also broadened their base in society. Given that the revolutionary advance obliged the elites and the Huerta loyalist authorities to flee, abandoning their posts, the rebel forces appealed to the middle classes who did not support Huerta to help in reconstructing local governments, which enabled this social group to come to power. By the same token, upon their arrival the revolutionary forces established alliances with the local masses of the poor, issuing pro-labor and pro-agrarian decrees in exchange for their support. During those months, the fight against Huerta shifted into new areas and involved new participants very different from the northern rebels, who were then forced to propose an approach to reconstruction that was truly national in both a geographic and social sense. These political alliances and social commitments planted the seeds of the post-revolutionary Mexican State. While Madero's battle for free elections was carried forward by the urban middle classes and the rebellion against Porfirio Díaz had been fought by the downtrodden masses of the North led by a distant member of the elite, the Constitutionalists' war against Huerta was characterized by alliances between the middle and lower classes, all headed by a radical former member of the Díaz-Reyes political machine.

CONSTITUTIONALISTS VS. CONVENTIONALISTS

With the occupation of Mexico City and the victory over Huerta's government and army, the Mexican Revolution entered a new phase and set out on a different course. The triumph was documented in the Treaties of Teoloyucan in August 1914, converting the anti-Huerta movement into a government and turning its rebel army into a pacifying force. Another significant change brought about by contact with the country's center, which included Mexico City, was the necessity of addressing the nation's greatest concentration of industry in Mexico City itself and in Puebla, Tlaxcala, and Orizaba, as well as the regions with the most contentious relations between hacienda owners and peasant communities in Morelos, Puebla, Tlaxcala, and the State of México. This was also the moment when the Constitutionalist movement ceased to be a cause of the North alone and became almost national in scope, spreading first through the Center of the country and the East Coast, then extending into the South and Southeast.

The challenge was not a simple one. The Constitutionalists had to carry out the work of governing despite the lack of a well-defined philosophy or a political bureaucracy that was experienced or large enough in number, a situation that forced them to pull together a team primarily composed of three elements: Constitutionalist military men and politicians who had some administrative experience or ability; members of the middle classes who had been marginalized by the Díaz and Huerta governments; and the former regime's mid- and lower-level government employees who were able to adapt to the new circumstances. This was the administration they had for instituting the social reforms that had been promised, especially changes in the structure of agrarian landholdings and a plethora of pro-labor measures. In addition, they had to ensure the stability demanded by the middle classes. Establishing a government required meeting the masses' socio-economic demands without arousing fears or opposition among the middle classes and foreign investors. Moreover, the new Constitutionalist government needed to extend its rule to the country's South and Southeast, regions that had not fought against Huerta. There local elites remained strong, and cadres of collaborators or networks of partisans and sympathizers favoring change had not been developed.

The major problem was that once Huerta, the common enemy, had been defeated, the victorious rebel armies would have to deal with one another. Each group—the Constitutionalists, Villa's followers, and Zapata supporters—wanted to impose its own vision for development on the rest of the country, despite the fact that the proposals of the Villa and Zapata loyalists were narrow in both social and geographical terms. While there were attempts to resolve controversies peacefully and arrive at a shared platform, the differences were insurmountable and conflict was inevitable. Conciliatory efforts and displays of hostility both occurred during the second half of 1914. The best example was the Convention, an outgrowth of a commitment made by Carranza and Villa supporters in the Pact of Torreón to jointly define the social and political reforms the country required. The sessions began on October 1 in Mexico City, but Villa's and Zapata's supporters were absent, so the Convention was quickly suspended. They agreed to meet again in Aguascalientes, a location equidistant from the capital and the North. That second meeting was attended by fewer Carranza delegates. Instead, there were supporters of Villa and Zapata, represented by people from cities who demanded that the Convention recognize the supremacy of the Plan of Ayala (Zapata's plan for agrarian reform). This assembly undoubtedly had broader-based social representation than the previous one, since the major popular groups were present. In addition, the Convention of Aguascalientes declared itself to be sovereign, became another government, and refused to acknowledge Carranza's presidency. Carranza left Mexico City and went to Veracruz, which was a safer location than the capital. The U.S. marines controlled Veracruz at the time, and decamped so that the Constitutionalists could occupy the city.

The war had resumed: Villa's troops were advancing on the capital, where they joined with Zapata's army in early December 1914. Meanwhile, Carranza began preparing for war in Veracruz. The factions realigned: Obregón's supporters chose to remain under Carranza's leadership, whereas the Villa and Zapata factions believed that since they both sprang from the masses, they could join together and fight to impose their shared values. Throughout 1915, the nation would be afflicted by the so-called "factional war." At first, everything seemed to indicate that Villa's and Zapata's popular armies would defeat Carranza's and Obregón's armies, whose leaders came from the middle classes. However, the outcome was diametrically opposed to those expectations, owing to political, military, economic, and social factors. The Convention of Aguascalientes government was characterized by the weakness of its leaders (Presidents Eulalio Gutiérrez, Roque González Garza, and Francisco Lagos Cházaro) in confronting either or both of the popular factions. This situation terrified the middle classes, which withdrew their support for the Convention, undermining its ability to devise a government, form broad-based political and social alliances, and gain the confidence of the general public within Mexico and abroad. To make matters worse, from the beginning the Convention of Aguascalientes had been characterized by its persistent secessionist leanings and its dependence on caudillo Villa's military strength. Furthermore, the weakness of the Convention's successive presidents was twofold: in addition to having to fend off illegitimate claims to power by Villa or Zapata or their top lieutenants, the parliamentarianists prevailing in this faction always favored its principal ideologues and delegates—most notably Antonio Díaz Soto y Gama, a former liberal from San Luis Potosí who had become a Zapata supporter—rather than the president. The inability to govern and a lack of socio-political cohesion were the hallmarks of the Convention of Aguascalientes and its adherents.

In contrast, the Constitutionalist faction had a single experienced and respected leader, Venustiano Carranza. Most importantly, it was a more homogeneous group with enough discipline to maintain unity, identity, and structure. This was in contrast to the Convention faction, which was based on a recent alliance of modern popular forces from the North (under Villa) with traditional peasant groups from Central and Southern Mexico (under Zapata). Thus the Convention alliance could not last: cultural and ideological differences soon arose that undermined the alliance's ability to govern and reduced its military strength.

The Convention faction also was militarily weaker because it was composed of two armies with very different soldiers, strategies, and objectives, with little or no collaboration between them. While Villa's supporters understood that a military victory had to be won first and devoted themselves entirely to that task, Zapata's supporters were convinced that the top priority was restructuring their region's political organization and agrarian land-tenure system so that they could later export this model to the rest of the country. This is why while Villa's army was committed to a bloody war in several distant regions (the Bajío, the Huasteca oil fields, and the Northeast), Zapata's troops carried on a purely defensive struggle, trying to keep their region isolated. In addition, due to a lack of southern cooperation, Villa's forces were affected by "munitions" problems. Up until August of 1914, they had had access to the U.S. market. With the outbreak of the First World War, however, European countries friendly to the United States acquired all of the U.S. weapons production and that drove up prices. Also, the Constitutionalists were the first to occupy Mexico City and took control of the weapon and ammunition factories built by Porfirio Díaz's government and maintained by the Huerta administration.

Tactical and strategic factors also played a role in the "factional war." First, Carranza set the best timetable for doing battle: knowing that Zapata's army would take a defensive stance, he decided to attack Villa first. Moreover, the Constitutionalists had experience operating on separate fronts—at least with forces in the Northeast and Northwest—, while Villa's Northern Division Army had always fought as a unit, but now had to split up to fight in the central part of the country, the Gulf Coast, and the Northeast simultaneously. Lastly, the "cavalry charge," Villa's tactic that had won him so many victories over Huerta's army, did not work against the Constitutionalists' trench warfare. Another essential factor that determined the outcome of the "factional war" was economic. On the one hand, the Zapata forces had distributed hacienda lands, which—regardless of the justice of this strategy—dealt a severe blow to the local economy. On the other, Chihuahua was the only state in Mexico where there had been constant violence since the end of 1910, and so the wealth of that region was destroyed to a greater extent. As a result, Villa had to face the most violent phase of the Revolution without the means to recruit soldiers and purchase arms, which—to further complicate matters—were suddenly more expensive due to Europe's large demand for them.

However, the Constitutionalists' advance on Mexico's Center, East, and Southeast enabled them to control valuable regions that had not been touched by violence, such as the grain-producing areas in Querétaro and the Bajío. Similarly, by occupying Mexico City, Puebla, Tlaxcala, and Veracruz, they took possession of the country's industrial heartland. Control of the oil-exporting regions of the Gulf and henequen exports once Yucatán had been occupied turned out to be even more important. As if this were not enough, when the Convention faction occupied Mexico City from the end of 1914 until August 1915, although this was seen as a sign of military and political strength, it also made them responsible for feeding, protecting, and caring for the health of the country's greatest concentration of population.

Aside from economic resources, the Constitutionalists' expansion throughout Mexico's Center, East, South, and Southeast also gave them the opportunity to recruit fresh soldiers. This geographic expansion came hand in hand with representation of broader segments of society. Thus, while one faction was securing a national presence, the other ended up being comprised of two widely separated regionalist armies. The Constitutionalists were then able to develop a two-pronged policy: on the one hand, they promoted the rise of the middle class, and on the other, without frightening the bourgeoisie, they attracted the masses by meeting certain social demands. This explains the additions made to the Plan of Guadalupe in December 1914; the agrarian law in January 1915; and, in the following month, the pact Carranza entered into with the *Casa del Obrero Mundial* (House of the World Worker), the country's largest labor organization. Even conceding that the Carranza faction's support for these measures was not sincere and that it was merely trying to lure away the Convention faction's popular base, the fact is that Zapata and his followers were unable to incorporate peasant groups from neighboring states, nor were they interested in establishing an alliance with the proletariat in the nation's center, and Villa and his partisans soon lost much of the popular support they had enjoyed during 1914. By the end of 1915, the Constitutionalists' victory was certain: they had defeated Villa's army on all fronts and taken Mexico City from Zapata's forces. Carranza's government was recognized by the U.S. government in October 1915 and dedicated the rest of that year and all of 1916 to consolidating its triumph and fine-tuning its vision for the nation.

THE VIRTUES AND LIMITS
OF THE CARRANZA GOVERNMENT

The Carranza government was divided into two phases, before the new Constitution and afterward, May 1917 being the dividing line between the two periods. The first phase was characterized by the predominance of the military. Villa's and Zapata's forces were still active, and other armed rebellions were breaking out in several parts of the country to prevent implementation of the revolutionary model. Such uprisings occurred in the oil region of the Upper Gulf of Mexico Coast, Veracruz, Chiapas, Oaxaca, and Michoacán, among other places. Another of the major problems in 1916 was both diplomatic and military. In retaliation for Villa's incursion into the town of Columbus, New Mexico, the U.S. government sent a large contingent to "punish" Villa that achieved meager results but remained in Mexico from April 1916 to February of 1917. In 1916, Carranza also took definite steps to build institutions and moderate the attitudes prevailing in the winning faction. Since the Villa and Zapata factions had been defeated, the Carranza government no longer needed mass popular support, and so the tendency to make major socio-political concessions to those groups—which happened frequently in 1914 and 1915—began to diminish.

To move forward from waging a revolution to creating the post-revolutionary State, the winning factions had to define their vision for the nation, which they did by writing the Constitution of 1917. Although the fight against Huerta was primarily aimed at restoring legality on the basis of the Constitution of 1857, that document was no longer viable after seven years of warfare. The new Constitution had to be drawn up by representatives elected from across the country. Their number would be determined by each state's population, and no one who had opposed the Constitutionalists could be elected, which excluded Huerta loyalists and supporters of the Convention of Aguascalientes. The model for the country would be formulated by the winning revolutionaries, who were not willing to risk losing in debate what they had won on the battlefield. This exclusive participation of Constitutionalists did not create complete homogeneity. The members of the Constitutional Congress came from all regions of the country, which meant they had different backgrounds and each brought his own political experience and ideological preferences. Some were former sympathizers with Social Catholicism; others had been followers of Magón; several were former Reyes supporters; and still others had collaborated with the Madero regime. All these differences were grist for the debates that took place throughout the sessions.

The Constitution of 1917 may be seen as a watershed: it was the ideological consummation of the Revolution and set the course for the new State. In writing the Constitution, the essentially destructive process of revolution was transformed into constructive and regulatory governance. By the same token, while the armed struggle had been carried out by the rural populace, the deputies who sketched the outline for the future Mexico were city people who had been elected by their peers. Owing to both low population density in the North and continued violence in states like Morelos and Chihuahua, the regions that had been most active in revolutionary warfare had fewer representatives in the Constitutional Congress than the states which had been on the sidelines or even those that opposed the armed struggle. Chihuahua had only one deputy seated, Sonora four and Coahuila five, while Jalisco had 20, Puebla and Veracruz 18 each, Guanajuato and Michoacán 17, and Oaxaca ten.

The similarities and differences from the Constitution of 1857 were soon evident in the new Constitution of 1917. While the former was doctrinaire in its liberalism, the new one was very realistic and consistent with the country's complexity. In addition, it reflected the international conditions of its time, both the decline of aristocracies and oligarchies, and the crises occurring in liberal states. The Constitution of 1917 was written between the First World War and the Bolshevik Revolution. Mexico's complicated history and segmented society meant that the new Constitution had to affirm both individual and collective property rights, as well as the coexistence of private and government-owned enterprises. Politically, Mexico continued to be a democratic, representative, federal republic. But now the Executive Branch would be predominant, undoubtedly due to the necessity of having a single leader to direct urgently needed national reconstruction. Likewise, a statist and therefore authoritarian form of government was designed, with a State empowered to intervene in matters such as the economy, education, and religion. The new Constitution was nationalistic, since the Revolution had sought to end Mexico's status as neocolonial and because the country had just suffered the U.S. invasion of Veracruz and the "punitive expedition" at its northern border. It also made major concessions to the country's masses, guaranteeing agrarian land distribution and benefits for workers. These concessions were imperative given the military and political power acquired by these groups during the revolutionary struggle. The Constitution of 1917 was the sole opportunity to create a State capable of consolidating and regulating the transformative process the country had experienced in transitioning from the Porfiriato to the Revolution.

Post-revolutionary Mexico was formally inaugurated when the new Constitution entered into force and Carranza began his constitutionally sanctioned term of office as president in May 1917, although it would take another three years for the authentic post-revolutionary State to be established. During his presidency, Carranza confronted serious political, military, economic, international, and social problems. For a start, when the Constitution came into effect, it was necessary to implement standards and procedures with which the country was unfamiliar. After 30 years of the Porfiriato and seven of revolutionary war, Mexicans had to begin to elect all their government officials, and powerful military leaders had to obey new civilian authorities and begin respecting individual rights. Enormous difficulties were involved in building a democratic system in a country that lacked the corresponding political culture and appropriate institutions—and whose recent history had alternated between authoritarianism and chaos.

Nor did military problems disappear with the return to a legal regime. In fact, Carranza had to continue pacification efforts and bring areas under control. Had he failed to do so, several of the country's regions would have remained outside the realm of his authority and the process of change. Besides reducing Villa's and Zapata's armies, he had to undertake major campaigns against several minor groups of rebels, bandits, and what were generically termed "counterrevolutionaries." These included forces led by Manuel Peláez and Félix Díaz, who operated in the oil fields and central part of Veracruz; "sovereignist" rebels in Oaxaca; and the armies of plantation owners in Chiapas. The worst of it was that Carranza had to meet all these challenges with an army that was too small, undisciplined, and poorly armed. Military campaigns led to many political conflicts because military commanders refused to give up their wartime powers. They also caused social unrest because of many serious abuses (known as *carranceos*) committed against groups and individuals. Lastly, the military campaigns exacerbated the economic problems that devastated the country by continuing to destroy the nation's assets and requiring much of the government's budget to be allocated to military spending. A considerable part of the country's labor force had died or been left disabled as a result of the war, and another equally numerous group had emigrated or was part of one of the various armies and other armed groups. The problem was qualitative as well as quantitative: the exile of many hacienda owners, businessmen, and professionals had drained the nation's human capital. To top it all off, the First World War prevented foreign trade and investment from coming into Mexico, which further postponed national economic reactivation.

The war in Europe also created serious diplomatic problems, because the U.S. government pressured Mexico to abandon its neutrality and take action in favor of the Allies. Not only did Carranza maintain Mexico's position of strict neutrality, but he was also accused of being a German sympathizer when German Chancellor Arthur Zimmermann offered him military aid if Mexico would go to war with the United States to recover the territory lost in the mid-nineteenth century. At the end of the European conflict, several U.S. politicians demanded that Carranza be punished for his conduct during those years because it had been counter to U.S. interests. Since Carranza's term of office was to end in 1920, however, Washington preferred not to make a radical decision that could affect substantial U.S. interests and investments in Mexico, and so it allowed the postrevolutionary country to continue on its path. The U.S. applied pressure only to urge moderation, the development of institutions, and rejection of radical ideology.

A decisive change occurred in Mexico in 1920. It began with the presidential electoral campaign between Álvaro Obregón (who had distanced himself from Carranza, but enjoyed strong support from many military and civilian revolutionary groups, as well as from urban and rural and lower- and middle-class segments) and Ignacio Bonillas (a former Constitutionalist official who was then serving as Mexico's ambassador in Washington and had Carranza's support, but was unknown to the revolutionary army and the general public). Given that for several years the country's army—which was Constitutionalist until May 1917—had been the best organized and most politically powerful institution in Mexico, and given also the differences between Obregón and Bonillas in terms of the strength of their socio-political networks, prestige, and popularity, Carranza's group would have had to resort to strong-armed tactics to maintain the upper hand. The result was the Agua Prieta Revolt, which was brief and practically bloodless. Carranza's pro-civilian position prevented him from enjoying the support of his own troops, so he had to flee Mexico City and was killed in an ambush in a town in the mountains of Puebla.

During the Agua Prieta Revolt, Carranza became isolated and Obregón was quickly able to garner support. Many pro- and anti-government socio-political organizations and several rebel groups of various political stripes supported the Agua Prieta movement, which began to be seen as a "unifying revolution." The most plausible explanation is that Carranza believed his differences with his fellow former revolutionaries Villa and Zapata could only be resolved militarily, whereas Obregón, Calles, and the other leaders of the Agua Prieta movement felt that the conflict was basically socio-political, and that instead of fighting against Villa and Zapata, they should incorporate them into the new State. Aware that Carranza's model of a post-revolutionary State ran counter to their inclinations and was doomed to chronic instability, the new leaders were willing to concede to the political and social demands of the groups that had been so crucial throughout the prolonged struggle.

THE NEW STATE

The post-revolutionary Mexican State was actually born in 1920, as only then did the groups that had been fundamental to the revolutionary process accept the new reality, each with varied levels of benefits and influence. After 1920, a middle class took power that was socially, politically, and ideologically distinct from Carranza's followers, because it lacked ties to the former regime. Part of the power of these new middle classes derived from their alliance with the masses. While the urban and rural poor no longer aspired to national leadership as they had at the 1915 Convention, they obtained significant political and social concessions in exchange for their support and subordination. Overall, this alliance did not mean that the post-revolutionary Mexican State was radical. In fact, the newly empowered middle classes had also come to agreements with the counterrevolutionaries, who represented the regional elites.

The Revolution is unquestionably the most important historic event of the twentieth century in Mexico, since it produced a new State led by middle-class revolutionaries who were not radical, but saw the necessity of meeting the principal demands of lower-class groups whose participation in the struggle had been decisive. It had been both a bellicose and socio-political struggle that lasted ten years and caused the rise of the middle and lower classes at the expense of the Porfirian oligarchies. From 1910 to 1912, the Revolution was headed by dissidents from among those elites, with the support of many middle-class groups and some people from the lower class. Beginning in 1913, the middle class took over and the participation of the masses became more significant. As it emerged in 1920, the new State was not democratic, although it did have a nationalistic identity. It was authoritarian, but its legitimacy was broad-based. And it was stable because it had great popular support, the leadership of a skilled, flexible group including both politicians and the military, and the sometimes reluctant acceptance of the United States.

Álvaro Obregón served as the first president of the post-revolutionary State—legitimized by the restoration of peace and organization of new elections during the interim presidency of Adolfo de la Huerta. The issues he faced in his term of office soon illustrated the complexities of the new State. Understandably, Obregón acted as a caudillo, governing according to his vision for the nation. His main goals were to begin rebuilding the country, which depended on the widespread pacification that came about after the Agua Prieta Revolt, basically an inclusive movement, as well as to centralize and concentrate power after the years of Revolution that had had the effect of dispersing it. To build a new State, many Carranza supporters had to be replaced. However, the Agua Prieta Revolt had brought together most of the Constitutionalists and the principal anti-Carranza movements, both those favoring and those opposing the Revolution, making it evident that ideological consistency would not be one of the hallmarks of the post-revolutionary Mexican State.

In agrarian affairs, for example, while the land distribution demands of some revolutionary groups were met, it is also true that the strongest support was given to developing small and medium-sized landholdings, because many revolutionary leaders were members of the rural middle classes. In labor matters, whereas on the one hand radical institutions like the General Confederation of Workers were established, on the other the government maintained a mutually beneficial relationship with the Regional Confederation of Mexican Workers. Obregón's administration decreed that banks seized during the Revolution be returned to their owners, and allowed the exiled supporters of Porfirio Díaz and Victoriano Huerta to come back to the country. Restored peace made it possible for agricultural and mining production and the railroads to recover. In addition, the

United States began its great economic boom, which was reflected in its demand for Mexican oil.

The Obregón administration's two biggest problems were its difficult relations with the United States and a military rebellion triggered by the question of who was to succeed him. The U.S. government refused to officially recognize his presidency, claiming that he had come to power by way of a military uprising. Rather than imposing a moral judgment, the idea was to pressure the Mexican government into changing certain articles of the Constitution of 1917 that were prejudicial to U.S. interests. Instead of making the changes, the Mexican government agreed that the new legal provisions would not be retroactive. Obregón's concessions to the U.S. government and investors (made in the Bucareli Agreements) would multiply towards the end of his term of office, when he desperately needed their support, given the rebellion that the presidential succession could be expected to provoke. We could say that the form of nationalism which prevailed during those years, rather than political and economic, was cultural. That was because the country had to craft and consolidate its new cultural identity, one suited to a young country with many ancestors, nationalistic without being xenophobic, and revolutionary, but in an orderly way that employed imagination in transforming the country. Above all, it had to be a just nation, but also a firm and cohesive one.

The country's transformation during the revolutionary process was total. Its cultural changes were particularly evident. At the end of the Porfiriato, a generation emerged called the Athenaeum which criticized the prevalence of positivism and the lack of development in the humanities and the arts. Antonio Caso, Pedro Henríquez Ureña, José Vasconcelos, Alfonso Reyes, and Julio Torri were some of this generation's prominent leaders. A few years later, in the middle of the decade of war, another group came to the fore, known as the 1915 generation, with its elite "seven sages." They had been victims and witnesses of the country's destruction and, as a result, instead of dedicating them-selves to art and the humanities, they determined to create eco-nomic, political, and cultural institutions that would be useful for rebuilding the nation. In this regard, the most outstanding young men were people like Manuel Gómez Morín, Vicente Lombardo Toledano, and Alfonso Caso, or Narciso Bassols and Daniel Cosío Villegas.

As part of the new middle class coming into power in 1920, José Vasconcelos became the first Minister of Public Education. He believed the Revolution had to be a moral rather than pri-marily agrarian, pro-labor or nationalistic endeavor. He saw education as more than mere instruction, as including culture and extracurricular learning. He therefore promoted the publi-cation of books and the organization of libraries, and also ar-ranged for muralists José Clemente Orozco, Diego Rivera, and David Alfaro Siqueiros to paint revolutionary subjects on the walls of centuries-old buildings as a way to teach history com-bined with the present and the future. The epic, dramatic events of those years also inspired the birth of a new literary genre, the "novel of the Revolution," penned by writers like Mariano Azue-la, Martín Luis Guzmán, Rafael F. Muñoz, Francisco L. Urquizo, and José Vasconcelos himself. Figures ranging from anony-mous soldiers to the most famous leaders of the fight—Madero, Carranza, Villa, and Obregón—march through the pages of their works.

At the end of his term of office, Obregón decided to sup-port Plutarco Elías Calles as his successor. Calles was one of the leaders of the Agua Prieta Revolt, and had headed the Ministry of War and the Navy during the short-lived De la Huerta administration, as well as the Ministry of the Interior in Obre-gón's own government. In addition to his extensive political experience, Calles had a far-reaching network of relationships and great support among the organized sectors of the lower classes, as well as major supporters in the army as a result of being a military man himself. Many men, especially from the military, aspired to the presidency. As a result, a rebellion broke out headed by a variety of regional leaders, although the most important among them was office-seeker, former provisional president, and then Minister of Finance Adolfo de la Huerta. The outcome was determined by several factors: first, in mid-1923 Pancho Villa—who could have been expected to rebel in favor of De la Huerta—was assassinated. This left the uprising without a military caudillo with ties to the underclass. Second, the Mexican and U.S. governments had agreed to mutual recognition and support in the Bucareli Agreements; and lastly, while De la Huerta could only count on the support of part of the army and the "political class" (the National Cooperativist Party), Obregón and Calles had the backing of the United States in addition to most of the politicians and military men, as well as the vast majority of both peasant and labor organizations representing the lower class. The conflict taught some lessons. For one, after the Agua Prieta and De la Huerta rebellions—both of which took place just before elections were held—, it was clear that the former revolutionaries had to regulate how popularly elected offices would be allotted. Moreover, the rebellions warned of the urgency of depoliticizing the national army and creating a national civilian organization that would become the country's primary political institution. Another lesson was that it was clearly beneficial to maintain good relations with the United States.

Plutarco Elías Calles was less of a militarist and more a politician, although he had worked with and supported Obregón. His efforts to establish institutions, his confrontation with the Catholic Church, and his civilist zeal were the hallmarks of his presidency, which lasted from late 1924 to the end of 1928. Another feature of his administration was dual leadership, given the strong influence that the caudillo Obregón still wielded. Calles' principal objective was to afford order and rationality to the process of post-revolutionary change, which prompted him to introduce standards and regulations—and therefore limits—through national commissions, such as those he established for agrarian affairs, banking, roads, and irrigation. He also sought to reactivate and regulate the economy by creating institutions like the Bank of Mexico and the Agricultural Credit Bank, and attempted to provide the government with more revenue by making better use of foreign oil income and a more efficient tax system. In addressing agrarian issues, Calles favored efficient medium-sized landholdings, and he believed that irrigation, financing, and the use of new technologies were more effective than agricultural land distribution in solving peasant problems. As for labor, he proposed that the major unions such as the Regional Confederation of Mexican Workers cooperate with one another. Nevertheless, after the Agua Prieta and De la Huerta rebellions, Calles realized that the greatest challenge was to depoliticize, reorganize, and reduce the magnitude of what had been the revolutionary army, a task he assigned to one of his most important collaborators, Joaquín Amaro.

Owing to his emphasis on expanding and consolidating the role of the State, Calles came into conflict with the other institution that was national in scope, the Catholic Church. The confrontation was far-reaching, since it involved the cultural, educational, social, and political power to control the population, and it ended up being a battle fought militarily in the so-called "*Cristero* War." This conflict lasted almost three years, from the end of 1926 to mid-1929, devastating the countryside in several central and western states: Jalisco, Colima, Michoacán, Guanajuato, Querétaro, Aguascalientes, and Zacatecas. The *Cristeros* were defending their religious beliefs, but were also from areas that had a large number of *rancheros* who saw agrarian reform as more of a threat than a promise. Moreover, they resented the overbearing presence of northerners in almost all government positions. Their military limitations were significant: they never managed to form an army with a unified command and coordination among its units. Rather, the *Cristeros* were local defensive militias led by local residents with little or no military experience, and they also suffered from a lack of funding, which was evident in how poorly they were armed. In addition, they were unable to form an alliance with their urban counterpart, the National League for the Defense of Religious Liberty. Lastly, they were fighting against the government's army and organized forces composed of agrarianists and workers. Although they were not strong enough to overthrow the government, it was clear that the *Cristero* guerrilla fighters could not easily be defeated, and their struggle would cause chronic instability. As a result, the government agreed to negotiate with the Catholic Church hierarchy. The Church agreed to respect the government's authority and abstain from being politically active publicly, while the government accepted it would not attempt to enforce the most anticlerical provisions of the Constitution of 1917.

This agreement was one of the most important factors in pacifying the country after the Revolution. Making peace with the *Cristeros* was also urgent because of the timing, since a very significant presidential election would be held in 1929. Proving that he continued to be as powerful as the sitting president, caudillo Obregón had managed to amend the Constitution to allow a president to be reelected to a non-consecutive term of office. Two high-ranking military men close to Obregón began opposition campaigns under the banner of "no reelection," but soon met violent deaths. The Mexican society had been burned, and the political atmosphere was incendiary. Obregón was assassinated by a militant Catholic after having been elected, but before taking office. With the caudillo gone, the post-revolutionary political system had lost its great decision-maker and also its only arbiter. The choice was between waiting for a new caudillo to rise to power or creating an institution that would fulfill his role. The political crisis caused by that assassination was dire.

Naming another candidate and organizing new elections would not solve the problem. The pre-election rebellions of 1920 and 1924 and the assassination of the three candidates in 1928 clearly revealed that elections had to be made civilized and that an institution had to be created that would hold together, organize, and discipline all the former revolutionaries, as well as regulate the process of nominating candidates for popularly elected office. This political institution—the National Revolutionary Party (*Partido Nacional Revolucionario*, PNR)—was formed in March of 1929. With the creation of this political party, the end of the *Cristero* War, and the institutionalization of the army, the "rough" period of the Mexican Revolution was over. We can now say that a new historical era began, one which, albeit not free from changes and problems, was to be characterized by its considerable social harmony and political stability —although it was not democratic—and by several decades of economic growth.

1929-2000: THE MOST RECENT STAGE

LUIS ABOITES-AGUILAR

DURING THE 72 YEARS COVERED BY THIS LAST CHAPTER, Mexican society underwent great changes, perhaps as profound and radical as those of the years following the arrival of the Spanish in 1519. The most significant was undoubtedly the transition from an agrarian to an urban society, a phenomenon that occurred together with extraordinary population growth. Several periods of prosperity gave industry and services ever increasing importance in the economy, relegating agricultural and mining activities to lesser roles. Another change was political. Those in charge of the government were able to create a political arrangement that made lasting stability possible: an authoritarian regime centered around Mexico's president and the official party, using negotiation but also repression to retain its control. At the end of the twentieth century, however, both economic growth and the authoritarian regime clearly began a downward spiral, although society continued to be increasingly urban and political stability was maintained.

During these seven decades, world events and incidents affected Mexican society to a greater extent than in former times. The Great Depression of 1929, World War II, and the reforms carried out in the 1980s that dismantled the Welfare State were among the most influential episodes. In different ways Mexicans suffered, benefited from, adapted to, resisted or took advantage of these events, but they could have little bearing on their course.

WORLD CRISIS AND POLITICAL REORGANIZATION

The crisis of autumn 1929 in the New York Stock Exchange swept a large part of the world into an economic depression that took years to overcome. The price of goods and international trade plummeted. Business failures caused the unemployment of millions of workers and employees in many countries. In Mexico, the crisis meant a reduction of exports and imports, which affected federal government revenue because it was largely dependent on foreign trade. Unemployment was most noticeable in places with the closest connection to world markets, such as the mining areas of the North. Furthermore, 1929 was a very dry year. So the majority of Mexico's population, which still lived in rural areas and was devoted to agriculture/livestock, faced serious difficulties.

Confronting a world in such turmoil, governments in Mexico and elsewhere were obliged to look for options within their own borders. If Mexican products could no longer be sold abroad, there was no alternative but to sell them on the domestic market. By the same token, the idea was abandoned that foreign colonization and the arrival of repatriated Mexicans returning from the United States would solve what was then considered a serious problem: a depleted population. A total of only 16.5 million inhabitants was seen as a sign of weakness and a brake on national progress. As of that time, the State took measures to protect domestic producers from foreign competition by means of tariffs or taxes on imports, and to improve the people's living conditions, particularly in cities.

The change in orientation prompted by the 1929 crisis helps us understand the course taken by society during the middle period of the twentieth century, at least until the 1970s. But in the short term, the impact of the world crisis accelerated internal processes, weakening certain sectors and fortifying others. We will address this on the following pages.

The year 1929 was also important for its political impact. The assassination of President-elect Álvaro Obregón in July 1928 had sparked a great deal of tension among political and military groups. It had also intensified the armed conflict with the *Cristeros* and the government's antagonism toward the Catholic Church. Political stability was urgently needed. The compromise worked out between the government and the Catholic hierarchy was an important achievement that, at least formally, put an end to the conflict with the *Cristeros*, which dated from 1926. Furthermore, in coping with the divisions caused by Obregón's death, the political factions reached an agreement to establish fairly clear rules for settling differences and ensuring that the transfer of power in public office—particularly the presidency—took place peacefully. Thus, in early March of 1929, just as several pro-Obregón military officers were rebelling against the federal government, the *Partido Nacional Revolucionario*, or PNR (National Revolutionary Party) was established in the city of Querétaro. The PNR was a coalition of parties and regional groups that saw themselves as the victors of the 1910 Revolution. Their first test was the presidential election of late 1929, when the official candidate, Pascual Ortiz Rubio, won out over José Vasconcelos of Oaxaca, the first Minister of Public Education from 1921 to 1924, who led an opposition campaign in some cities.

Although the emergence of the PNR was closely related to Obregón's assassination, it may also be seen as yet another chapter in the effort to forge a strong State. As a principal ingredient, such a State required a political center capable of exercising full authority over the diverse social groups scattered about the nation. The center would be the federal government, headed by the President of the Republic. Throughout the nineteenth century, those ruling the country had failed to achieve that political objective. While the federal government had managed to increase its strength throughout the Porfiriato, the 1910 Revolution seriously debilitated and fragmented it to a large extent. How, it was asked, could a solid political nucleus be created that was capable of preventing rebellions such as the Agua Prieta Revolt in 1920, the pro-De la Huerta uprising in 1923-1924, and the pro-Escobar insurgency in 1929 without strengthening caudillos and caciques in various regions of the country at the same time?

The PNR represented a significant step forward in the country's political stabilization. But that became more apparent only when the PNR was under the leadership of General Calles who, after leaving the presidency in November 1928, remained the strongman on the national political scene, to such a degree that he began to be called the "*jefe máximo* (supreme chief) of the Revolution." Between 1929 and 1935, Calles enjoyed great influence, entering and leaving presidential cabinets and taking part in the conduct of government, thanks to the loyalty of high-level officials, his connections to the army, and his role as de facto leader of the PNR. There were four presidents during that period: Emilio Portes Gil from Tamaulipas, Pascual Ortiz Rubio from Michoacán, Abelardo L. Rodríguez from Sonora, and Lázaro Cárdenas, also from Michoacán. One noteworthy aspect of those years was the legislative effort made to replace the laws issued during the closing decades of the nineteenth century and regulate the provisions of the 1917 Constitution. The penal and civil codes for the Federal District, federal labor law, water law, and the agrarian code are examples of that effort.

In 1935, Calles' influence began a rapid decline. As the most serious stage of the Great Depression was left behind, a more economically solvent government emerged. With dissent among a variety of political and lower-class sectors growing against Calles' positions (for example, his anticlericalism and his opposition to strikes and work stoppages), that year the new president, General Cárdenas, broke with the "supreme chief." In April 1936 he forced Calles to leave the country. Cárdenas wanted to make the Federal Executive the keystone of national politics. One might say that the power accumulated by the "supreme chief" was transferred to the presidency.

To further strengthen his administration, Cárdenas reached out to low-income and radical groups, including Communists, and to other political groups and the elites that had distanced themselves from Calles. Now his own man, Cárdenas quickly took measures that distinguished him from earlier presidents. He significantly stepped up the pace of land distribution and extended it to highly productive areas such as La Laguna in Durango and Coahuila, the Yaqui Valley in southern Sonora, the Mexicali Valley in Baja California, and the henequen area of the Yucatán Peninsula.

The Agrarian Reform had begun with a decree issued on January 6, 1915 that proposed restitution of lands taken from pueblos and distribution of land to those that had none. Article 27 of the 1917 Constitution declared that all land and subsoil resources were the property of the nation. Several subsequent laws regulated land grants to peasants. The president was given the power to create *ejidos* (collectively owned lands) and determine their size. By means of presidential resolutions, a group of peasants in a given location would receive land, water, and forest resources that could not be sold or mortgaged, but could be inherited. The *ejidos* had their own local authorities, and this created rifts among and sometimes weakened municipal authorities. The reform became more radical in 1934. The new agrarian code eliminated the prohibition against including hacienda peons, whom the first laws had excluded from the right to receive *ejido* lands.

During the early years of the Cárdenas administration, *ejido* land grants increased in quality as well as in quantity, since they involved an ever greater proportion of irrigated land. The amount of credit extended in rural areas also grew, with loans granted by government institutions such as the *Banco Nacional de Crédito*

Agrícola (National Agricultural Credit Bank) and the *Banco Nacional de Crédito Ejidal* (National *Ejido* Credit Bank). In some places, these loans helped to promote *ejido* collectivism. In the same vein, socialist education was encouraged and approved by an October 1934 constitutional amendment designed not only to replace the teaching of all religious doctrine, but also to combat fanaticism and educate young people using scientific knowledge of nature and the life of society. Teachers and students also had to be involved in production and social organizations. Many teachers became promoters of Cárdenas' projects, which provoked a violent reaction among a good number of Catholics and caciques. In the cultural sphere, radicalism was the order of the day: intellectuals and artists organized, novels with nationalist and pro-indigenous content were published, and the advance of Fascism in Europe was denounced and resisted. Muralists such as Diego Rivera and David Alfaro Siqueiros, writers such as Mauricio Magdaleno, and musicians such as Silvestre Revueltas actively participated in these movements. The Mexican Revolution sought to align and identify itself with the struggle of the proletariat. But there was no unanimity. Jorge Cuesta, Salvador Novo, and Xavier Villaurrutia, who were members of a group known as the *Contemporáneos* (The Contemporaries), displayed their skepticism and distrust of the radicals and, as a result, were accused of being elitists and of letting themselves be influenced by European ways. Catholic professors and students, among them Manuel Gómez Morín, controlled the National University and tried to keep it free from socialist teachings by insisting on autonomy and academic freedom.

Cárdenas' political orientation was also expressed in international affairs. His government maintained firm support for the Spanish Republic against the conservative forces headed by Francisco Franco, which were supported by Adolph Hitler and Benito Mussolini. During and at the end of the Spanish Civil War,

Mexico took in thousands of refugees, including orphans who later became known as the "Children of Morelia."

The *Confederación de Trabajadores de México*, or CTM (Confederation of Mexican Workers)—whose ideology supported the class struggle—was created in 1936 in the midst of labor and peasant demonstrations taking place throughout most of Mexico. Its leader, Vicente Lombardo Toledano, became a close ally of the Cárdenas government. Two years later, the *Confederación Nacional Campesina*, or CNC (National Peasant Confederation) came into being, led by Professor Graciano Sánchez. Cárdenas wanted to organize the working classes and create ties between them and the government as a support and counterbalance against the pressures of other groups, such as the businessmen of Monterrey and of other countries, particularly the United States. To secure these changes, in 1938 a decision was made to dissolve the PNR and create a new entity, the *Partido de la Revolución Mexicana*, or PRM (Party of the Mexican Revolution). The main difference between the two was that the new party was not composed of regional groups and parties but rather of four sectors: labor, peasants, the lower and middle classes in general, and the military. In this form of corporate organization, the President of Mexico reaffirmed his role as leader of the party, responsible for mediating between its diverse political factions. Power struggles and conflicts of interest were aired and resolved within the official party rather than in elections.

Not everything was a matter of politics. There was also concern for the economy. In 1937, the *Comisión Federal de Electricidad*, or CFE (Federal Electricity Commission), which had been created in 1933, was reorganized to meet the increasing demand for power that foreign electric companies did not seem interested in supplying. In 1937, the federal government began the construction of three large dams: La Angostura Dam in Sonora, Palmito Dam in Durango, and El Azúcar or Marte R. Gómez Dam in Tamaulipas. The purpose of these immense projects was to increase areas under irrigation in northern Mexico. As a counterbalance to the National University, which had gained its autonomy in 1929 and which criticized government policies, the federal government founded the *Instituto Politécnico Nacional*, or IPN (National Polytechnic Institute) in 1936 to diversify education and train the technicians required by industrialization and the expansion of public works. The government also promoted construction of urban infrastructure (drinking water, sewerage, and markets) to improve living conditions in several cities.

Cárdenas' administration faced a severe test toward the end of 1937 and in early 1938. Foreign oil companies openly challenged the Mexican State by ignoring a Supreme Court ruling in favor of workers. The government's response was to expropriate the oil industry, a decision announced on March 18, 1938. The Catholic hierarchy, businessmen, workers, peasants, intellectuals, and artists supported Cárdenas' bold decision. It was at that point that the idea of "nation" acquired greater vibrancy, perhaps more than ever before in Mexico's history. In spite of efforts by foreign companies to sabotage it, the national oil industry survived thanks to the support of Mexico's workers and technicians and also, truth be told, owing to the limited support the foreign oil companies received from the United States government, whose greatest concern was the then-imminent outbreak of World War II. *Petróleos Mexicanos* (PEMEX) was founded a few months after the expropriation. It was initially so fragile that the government had to subsidize it in a variety of ways.

Cárdenas-style radicalism divided the country. The *Partido Acción Nacional*, or PAN (National Action Party) was created in 1939. It was led by Manuel Gómez Morín, a lawyer who sought to confront what were considered the socialist and collectivist excesses of Cárdenas and his followers, as well as to promote a model of society that eschewed both socialist and liberal ideals. Catholic and conservative groups regarded socialist education with misgivings. Many landowners affected or threatened by the agrarian reform joined the ranks of the discontent. There were also lower-class groups active in rural areas of central Mexico including the Bajío, such as the *Sinarquistas* (Synarchists), who opposed Cárdenas, as did foreign interests affected by the oil expropriation. These were indeed critical moments for Mexico. The broad and diverse opposition to Cárdenas' policies was strengthened by the candidacy of General Juan Andrew Almazán, who ran for president in the July 1940 election.

Facing these challenges, Cárdenas and the official party chose Manuel Ávila Camacho of Puebla as their candidate for president. He was a general of limited military accomplishments who was far from sharing Cárdenas' radicalism. Although Almazán was very popular, Ávila Camacho won in a hotly contested election. Despite violence and accusations of electoral fraud, Cárdenas managed to hand the office of the presidency over to his party's designated heir, thus establishing one of the basic mechanisms of national political arrangements in the twentieth century: the incumbent president, through the official party, selected his successor. Ávila Camacho governed from December 1940 to November 1946.

1940-1958:
STABILITY AND ECONOMIC GROWTH

The new President Camacho wasted no time in distancing himself from Cárdenas by issuing a call for reconciliation and national unity, which he justified by citing the difficult world situation. The invasion of Poland by German troops in September 1939 had unleashed World War II. Initially, Mexico declared neutrality, but this position became more difficult after the Japanese attack on Pearl Harbor in December 1941 caused the United States to declare war on Germany, Italy, and Japan. In

May 1942, after two of its oil tankers had been lost as a result of German submarine attacks, Mexico entered the war on the side of the Allies (Great Britain, the United States, France, and the Soviet Union). This is when mandatory military service was instituted in Mexico.

Unlike other countries—particularly the Soviet Union—that suffered the searing effects of the war, the impact on Mexico was, in fact, positive. For one thing, its economy received a strong boost from capital flows from abroad and the opportunity to establish new lines of business. The industrializing efforts of the 1930s were reinforced by increased domestic and foreign demand. Some private investors were positively euphoric. Since the war made it difficult to buy foreign products, entrepreneurs and government authorities joined forces to produce them in Mexico. That industrialization strategy, known as import substitution, was later bolstered with tariffs or taxes on imports that protected domestic producers from international competition.

Furthermore, World War II forced the United States government to improve relations with its Latin American neighbors. As a result, Mexico and the United States signed several agreements covering debt, trade, *braceros* (migrant workers), water, technical assistance and, of course, issues related to the 1938 expropriation of oil. An agreement that amounted to a 90% reduction in Mexico's debt to the United States was of particular importance. If we consider that the economy was booming, together with the fact that the government became more moderate—for example, by eliminating socialist education and promoting rapprochement with the United States—we can see why animosities faded during the final years of the Cárdenas administration.

The *Instituto Mexicano de Seguro Social*, or IMSS (Mexican Social Security Institute) was founded in 1943, and came to play a major role in the country's social and economic life. Its creation expressed the government's interest in modernizing labor relations, and having the cost of social security shared by workers and government, as well as employers.

Together the IMSS, PEMEX, the Federal Electricity Commission, the agrarian banks, and other government institutions such as *Nacional Financiera* (the National Development Bank) demonstrated that government spending was essential to stimulate the economy. On that subject there was no disagreement. Despite differences between Ávila Camacho and Cárdenas, and between the latter and Calles, there was clearly continuity regarding the idea that public funds should play a fundamental role in directing the course of the economy. This thinking was not exclusive to Mexico. Many countries decided to increase the role of public spending to overcome the effects of the Great Depression of the 1930s. The strategy closely followed the ideas of British economist John Maynard Keynes, which gave rise to the concept of the Welfare State. Unlike the nations intensively involved in World War II, in Mexico military expenditures diminished considerably, making it possible for investment in highways, dams, electricity, hospitals, schools, and public services to grow year after year.

In this context, the government's attention to the Southeast is noteworthy. The government emphasized the fact that the Southeast was an area rich in natural resources but backward in social terms. The objective was to exploit its wealth, not only in order to modernize the region, but also to propel the national economy forward. Through the Papaloapan and Grijalva River Commissions, which were created in 1947 and 1951 respectively, the federal government began a vast program of investment in hydroelectric plants, flood control and drainage works, and clearing of forested and jungle areas to extend the reach of farming and ranching, highways, education, and health care. It was also believed that the Southeast could relieve over-population in some areas in central Mexico and even in the

North, such as La Laguna. Several colonization projects were launched, but yielded few results.

World War II is a watershed in the history of the twentieth century. It consolidated the United States' preeminence as a great world power, although in confrontation with another great power, the Soviet Union. In Mexico, the economic consequences of the war confirmed the choice that had been made by the government, major economic interests, and public opinion in favor of industrialization and urbanization; the idea of a preeminently agrarian nation was relegated to the past. Moreover, these policies laid the groundwork for a long period of economic growth that lasted until the end of the 1960s, despite peso devaluations in 1948 and 1954. During those prosperous years, the political system was consolidated on the basis of an enormously powerful central or federal government. Let us examine these three aspects in greater detail.

Industrialization became the government's highest priority. It was believed that the modernization of Mexico depended on increasing the number of factories, technicians, and workers. Both the government and the private sector were convinced that technological innovation would lead to greater labor productivity which, in turn, would create more profits for businessmen, better wages for workers, and more tax revenues for the public treasury. The decision to rely on the domestic market as the driver of the economy, which had first been made in the 1930s, was reaffirmed.

The government supported industrial entrepreneurs with additional measures. One was control of worker discontent by means of pro-government unions and sympathetic union leaders, better known as *charros*. In exchange for keeping workers in line, union leaders received privileges and government or elected posts under the banner of the official party. The fall of Lombardo Toledano from the leadership of the CTM in 1941 was an indication of how quickly labor federations became subordinated to the State. National unity replaced the class struggle. The new leader, Fidel Velázquez, remained at the helm of the CTM until his death in 1997. Better than anyone else, he personified government control over the working class. Another means of promoting industrialization was the use of price controls on food in the cities. Several institutions were created for that purpose: the *Comité Regulador del Mercado de las Subsistencias* (Basic Foods Marketing Regulatory Commission) in 1938, the *Compañía Exportadora e Importadora Mexicana* (Mexican Export and Import Company) in 1949 and later, in 1961, the *Compañía Nacional de Subsistencias Populares*, or CONASUPO (National Company for Basic Food Products).

Urbanization was a concept closely linked to industrialization. The government and, in general, the social sectors that most influenced public opinion were convinced that the nation's future no longer lay in the countryside, but rather in the cities where new industries were located. Furthermore, with population concentrated in small geographic areas, it was easier to provide modern public services such as street lighting, drinking water and sewerage, transportation, education, and health care. Three urban areas benefited most from this process: the Mexico City Metropolitan Area, Monterrey, and Guadalajara. In 1965, the three accounted for 69% of industrial production. The nation's economic geography was being reorganized. The rise of the North and the decline of some traditionally rich centers such as Hidalgo, Puebla, and Yucatán were striking.

Agrarian activities had to be subordinated to the goal of industrialization. Although a large percentage of public spending was invested in rural development—especially in the 1940s—, the goal was to increase agricultural production and productivity to sustain a rapidly growing urban population. Irrigation districts, particularly in the North, had to produce exports (such as cotton) in order to provide foreign exchange for the purchase of industrial machinery and other inputs. In spite of the 1949-1958 drought in the North and West, Mexico's farms managed to maintain a high growth rate, such that in the 1960s Mexico almost achieved food self-sufficiency.

The rise in the population was impressive during those years of economic growth and greater public spending, particularly between 1930 and 1970. In fact, this growth became one of the principal features of twentieth-century Mexico. During those 40 years, the country's population tripled, in contrast to the nineteenth century: from Independence until the Revolution, the number of Mexicans barely doubled. As the twentieth century progressed, demographic growth increased from an annual rate of 1.72% in the 1930s to 3.28% in the 1960s. Put more simply, with the former growth rate it took a little more than 40 years for the population to double, whereas with the latter, it took 22 years for it to double again. This was to a great extent due to a significant decrease in child mortality, an achievement that in turn was explained by the control of infectious and parasitic diseases. Improvements in health care, drinking water and sewerage, vaccination campaigns, and the introduction of penicillin are a few of the many factors that played a role in population growth. Generally speaking, this increase during the twentieth century constituted the second major demographic event in Mexico's history: the first was the decimation of the native population during the early decades of the colonial period.

After 1940, the population migrated as perhaps never before in the nation's history, particularly from the countryside to the city. Urban areas offered better wages and public services. The 1960 census reported that most Mexicans lived in cities (towns of more than 2 500 people). This was an indicator of the social changes occurring in the country and throughout most of the world during that same period. People were leaving agricultural areas behind. From 1930 to 1970, Mexico's overall population grew at very high rates, but the urban population grew at a much faster rate than the population as a whole.

Mexico City is a good example of this urbanization. Its population, which was about one million in 1930, grew six-fold over the next 40 years. Drinking water brought to the capital from the Upper Lerma River, transportation routes such as the Miguel Alemán Viaduct and the *Periférico* (Beltway), the subway, and the deep drainage system begun in the 1960s, all made this growth possible. Real estate and the construction business attracted the interest of entrepreneurs and politicians alike. The inauguration of the *Torre Latinoamericana* (Latin American Tower) in 1950 in downtown Mexico City is perhaps one of the most obvious symbols of this urban-focused modernizing effort.

Within the framework of world economic expansion in the post-war period, which some call the "golden age of capitalism," Mexico's economy enjoyed years of sustained prosperity. Between 1940 and 1970, the annual growth rate of the gross domestic product exceeded 6%, a true "economic miracle," as it was called. At the end of those three decades, the growing importance of industry and services (trade and banking) was noteworthy. But agriculture's contribution to the economy steadily declined.

It is worth mentioning that this economic expansion was achieved largely using domestic resources, that is, without resorting to foreign loans. In 1959, the foreign public debt was a mere US$649 million. Despite relatively meager public financing, growth was possible largely owing to government investment in infrastructure, energy, and communications. Private investment increased due to strong protection of the economy from foreign competition.

From 1958 until 1970, the economy grew rapidly with stable prices, i.e., a low inflation rate. This is what is known as "stabilizing development." During those years, the primary indicator of positive economic performance was higher real wages, i.e., people's income had more and more purchasing power. But those rising salaries were limited to a minority of employees, almost all of them in the big cities and in the principal branches of industry. They were the same people who benefited from IMSS (Social Security) services and constantly expanding public education. Despite their small numbers, it is clear that great improvements in living conditions were achieved which gave rise to a phenomenon that helps explain the political stability of those years: upward social mobility. Because of free public education, it was not unusual for a laborer to have university-educated and professional offspring, as well as to enjoy home ownership, social security, and retirement funds. The same may be said of federal government employees. The Pensions Office was created in 1925, and in 1959 became the *Instituto de Seguridad y Servicios Sociales para los Trabajadores del Estado*, or ISSSTE (State Employees' Social Security and Social Services Institute).

In 1946, the PRM was replaced by the *Partido Revolucionario Institucional*, or PRI (Institutional Revolutionary Party). One of the main differences between the two was the PRI's confirmation of a step taken by President Ávila Camacho in December 1940: removal of the military from politics. This was further proof of the political regime's stability. Removing military leaders from politics and the military's complete subordination to the president became another defining feature of the political system. The new party's first presidential election was held in 1946. The official party candidate, Miguel Alemán of Veracruz, was the winner, the first in many years who did not come from the ranks of the army and had not taken part in the 1910 Revolution. A graduate of the *Universidad Nacional Autónoma de México*, or UNAM (National Autonomous University of Mexico), Alemán belonged to a new generation of politicians and leaders. The opposition candidate, Ezequiel Padilla from Guerrero, enjoyed far less support than Almazán had in 1940. Political power was virtually monopolized by those who called themselves heirs to the victors of the Revolution, the so-called "revolutionary family."

Alemán eagerly promoted industrialization and favored business growth, to which neither he nor some of his collaborators and friends were strangers. The construction company *Ingenieros Civiles Asociados*, or ICA (Associated Civil Engineers), led by its founder Bernardo Quintana, was created at that time and soon became an example of Mexico's new business leadership. Another outstanding entrepreneur, who took advantage of the innovation brought about by television, was Emilio Azcárraga. His fortune grew as television spread to become the far-reaching mass medium it is today, capable of reorganizing domestic life and setting the standard in ideas about leisure and ways of thinking, speaking, and consuming. Urbanization, television, readily available air transportation and telephone communications, together with increasingly obvious government moderation, nourished the ideas of intellectuals and artists alike. In 1949, Octavio Paz published *El laberinto de la soledad* (*The Labyrinth of Solitude*) in an effort to understand the Mexican character. In 1953 and 1955, as part of a countercurrent to the rising importance of life in cities, Juan Rulfo published his two masterpieces, *El llano en llamas* (*The Burning Plain and Other Stories*) and the novel *Pedro Páramo*, which depicted the rural milieu of a provincial world. In 1958, Carlos Fuentes published his startling novel *La región más transparente* (*Where the Air is Clear*), an insightful portrait of life in Mexico City. Radicalism was out. Artists such as Rufino Tamayo, challenging muralism, became famous for their contemporary paintings. The acceptance of new styles and forms coming from both the United States and Europe, as well as from other Latin American countries, diversified artistic content. Movies with urban themes (cabaret artists, the poor, masked heroes, university students) clearly illustrated how the country was changing, or at least how some of its cities were.

This period also saw a significant advance in political centralization. By 1946, new electoral legislation was passed which for the first time left the management of this sensitive civic process in the hands of the federal government. Until then, elections had been organized by local authorities. The year 1946 also witnessed the creation of the Ministry of Water Resources, which further centralized water management. The sales tax was established in 1948, creating a single uniform federal mercantile revenue tax nationwide.

These events attest to the consolidation of a political system in which the federal government and the president wielded ever-increasing power. The Legislative and Judicial Branches of government became progressively weaker. Furthermore, World War II had accentuated a previous tendency, the concentration of public revenue in federal hands, to the detriment of state and municipal finances. To a considerable degree, that concentration was due to better federal tax collection (of income tax), but it was also the result of usurping state and municipal sources of tax revenue, which the federal government had done under the rubric of standardizing and modernizing the tax system. This occurred with oil in 1922, mining in 1926, electric power in 1933, and other sectors in the years to follow. As a result, the federal government had constantly increasing resources and, undoubtedly, more obligations than the states and municipalities. The gradual but continuous federalization of education, understood in the traditional way as greater federal control, demonstrates the shift in the balance of power toward the federal government and away from states and municipalities. A similar phenomenon took place at the state level: the municipalities were deprived of their main sources of tax revenue. In general terms, municipalities were far poorer in 1950 than they had been in 1910.

Nevertheless, there were indications that not even the president or the government held all the cards. This point requires much further research, but it may be said that at least in fiscal and water resource matters, federal authorities faced limits and instances where their decisions were ignored. For example, the federal attempt to control the mercantile revenue tax was fought in the richest states (Veracruz, Baja California, Nuevo León, Jalisco, and the State of México, among others). Miguel Alemán's successor, Adolfo Ruiz Cortines (1952-1958), also from Veracruz, made repeated efforts to overcome opposition, without much success. With regard to water rights, large-scale business owners, such as the farmers along the coast of Hermosillo, never obeyed federal laws that required installing meters on their wells to record how much groundwater they withdrew. In Monterrey, industrialists organized their own groundwater supply system, which they alone controlled. That city might suffer serious water shortages, but industry continued full steam ahead. It might be said that these cases were exceptional and do not really disprove the more common view that Mexico's president had enormous power. But it is also true that these examples have been studied very little. Why did one high-level official of the Ministry of Finance say in 1972 that before that year, holding a meeting which all the states' treasurers would attend had been unthinkable?

1958-1982: IMBALANCES AND THE STATE'S RESPONSE

Economic growth and political stability were the country's main features during this period. In 1960, the administration of Adolfo López Mateos (from the State of México, he was President of the country from 1958 to 1964) was responsible for organizing the celebration of the 50th anniversary of the 1910 Revolution. The governing class was proud of its achievements in leading the nation. They could point to the advances made in health, education, and infrastructure, and to the strengthening of citizenship, since women were granted the right to vote in 1953. In health care, for example, child mortality had been drastically reduced, from 27 to 12 deaths per thousand. It was no longer as common for families to lose a child. Four million people were insured by the IMSS, and another 500 000 by the ISSSTE. Illiteracy had been cut back from 62% in 1930 to 45% in 1960. As a result of government investment, there were more than 1.4 million hectares (3.5 million acres) of irrigated lands. Since 1950, it had been possible to travel the length of the country by highway, from the Guatemalan border in the State of Chiapas to Ciudad Juárez in the State of Chihuahua. Oil production had almost tripled since 1938, and electric power generation was seven times greater than in 1930, while agriculture and industry both showed considerable progress. To increase the availability of electric power and facilitate creating an interconnected national grid, in 1960 President López Mateos decided to buy out the foreign electricity companies. In short, using a variety of criteria Mexico's top officials believed they had positive results to show for their leadership of what they time and again referred to as "revolutionary government administrations." López Mateos went so far as to claim he was "of the extreme left" within the ideology of the Mexican Revolution. Those declarations and measures such as the buy-out of the electric power industry and publication of free textbooks worried the business sector. They feared an expansion of the State that would reduce their sphere of operation and influence.

The governing elite was right. A close look reveals that the nation had changed remarkably since 1930. In addition to population growth and continued rapid migration to the cities, a large urban middle class developed, one larger than at any time in Mexico's history. This was due to increased numbers of employees and officials in both the public and private sectors, as well as more self-employed professionals and small businessmen. The middle class expanded due to economic prosperity;

public spending on health care, education, and infrastructure; and, in general, the set of policies, ideas, and values that associated the nation's growth with a widening of the domestic market. An approximate but perhaps eloquent indicator of this social dynamic was the almost 15-fold increase in the number of university students: from 23 000 in 1930 to 335 000 in 1970. Public works such as *Ciudad Universitaria* (University City), which was inaugurated in 1952, or the enormous housing development *Ciudad Satélite* (Satellite City), begun in 1953 adjacent to the Federal District, or the opening of large department stores were just a few of the many components of urban expansion. Another sign of this economic, but also social and cultural change was the 19-fold increase in the number of automobiles between 1930 and 1970, from 63 000 to 1.2 million. Telephone users multiplied by a factor of nearly 10 between 1940 and 1970: from 88 000 to 859 000. These numbers are merely indications of the changes in daily life in cities. To these we should add the purchase of washing machines, refrigerators, radios, record players, television sets, and sewing machines, which created new routines in the home. New consumption patterns, perceptions, labor practices, and forms of leisure and entertainment, as well as the expectation of upward social mobility thanks to education or to families' tenacity and discipline, combined with an entrepreneurial spirit, all contributed to creating a less provincial and agrarian society. A more cosmopolitan and urban one was taking its place.

Some dissatisfied sectors did not participate in this feverish social transformation. Economic growth benefited only part of the population, primarily people living in cities, whereas rural areas remained backward. While the middle class expanded, enormous neighborhoods of poor immigrants began to encircle the cities. Inequality was therefore a key component of national life. A calculation of income distribution between 1950 and 1963 yielded an alarming result: the richest 10% of the population held almost half of the nation's wealth.

Worker and peasant discontent had sometimes been dealt with by concessions and negotiation and, at times, with violence. For instance, in 1951 an arduous "hunger march" composed of thousands of miners and their families—who walked 1 400 kilometers (870 miles) from Nueva Rosita, Coahuila, to the nation's capital—was met with indifference. The marchers were protesting labor abuses by the United States-based American Smelting and Refining Company. In 1958, telegraph operators, oil workers, and teachers suffered repression and some of their leaders were jailed. In the states of Baja California, Chihuahua, and San Luis Potosí, huge crowds mobilized at election time, demonstrating initial erosion of the effectiveness of authoritarian methods used by the official party and the federal government in general. In 1959, a widespread railroad strike was suppressed by the army, and several of its leaders, among them Demetrio Vallejo, were imprisoned, accused of the crime of social dissolution, and remained behind bars for years. Railroad workers were accused of being Communists, reflecting the ideas prevailing in the United States and Mexico in those years because of the confrontation with the Soviet Union (the so-called Cold War). In 1962, the army shot and killed Rubén Jaramillo, an independent peasant leader, and his family.

This climate of great discontent was heightened by the Cuban Revolution. Guerrillas led by Fidel Castro seized power in January 1959, overthrowing dictator Fulgencio Batista. Tensions between Cuba and the U.S. government grew, and in 1961 Castro declared himself Marxist-Leninist. That revolutionary experience nurtured the ideals of dissident and radical Mexicans and Latin Americans in general. The *Movimiento de Liberación Nacional* (National Liberation Movement) created in Mexico in 1961, led by former president Cárdenas, tried to unite the various sectors that were at odds with government policies. In addition, the Catholic Church, using the motto "Christianity yes, Communism no," organized public demonstrations that created still greater tension. In response, the country's 30 richest businessmen founded the *Consejo Mexicano de Hombres de Negocio*, or CMHN (Mexican Businessmen's Council), an organization that would soon wield great economic and political influence. The council allied itself with older business organizations such as the *Confederación de Cámaras Nacionales de Comercio*, or CONCANACO (Confederation of National Chambers of Commerce), the *Confederación de Cámaras Industriales*, or CONCAMIN (Confederation of Industrial Chambers), the *Cámara Nacional de la Industria de la Transformación*, or CANACINTRA (National Chamber of the Manufacturing Industry), the *Confederación Patronal de la República Mexicana*, or COPARMEX (Mexican Employers' Confederation), and the *Asociación de Banqueros de México* (Mexican Bankers' Association).

In this strained political and diplomatic atmosphere, the U.S. government launched a campaign to counteract the sympathies that the Cuban experience inspired in Latin America. As part of the Cold War, between 1962 and 1964 the United States pressured Latin American governments to isolate Cuba economically and diplomatically. But Mexico refused to cooperate with the U.S. initiative, and was the only country to staunchly maintain its independent position in the Organization of American States, a move that increased Mexico's international prestige. At the same time, the United States promoted the Alliance for Progress, which was aimed at preventing new insurrections in Latin America through a variety of social and political reforms. One of these was Mexico's adoption of a system of allotment of chairs in the Congress to different political parties which since 1964 allowed a limited number of opposition party representatives to be elected to that legislative body.

López Mateos' successor was Gustavo Díaz Ordaz from the State of Puebla (1964-1970). He began his term of office confronting a protest movement by medical interns and residents at the IMSS, ISSSTE, and other health-care institutions. Soon, another conflict of a different nature arose. On September 23, 1965, a small group attacked the army barracks at Madera, Chihuahua. Although this guerrilla uprising was quickly put down, it marked the beginning of a period in which a number of armed groups, influenced by the Cuban experience, tried to change the nation by violent means. The guerrillas believed that most of Mexico's people lived in miserable conditions because of capitalist exploitation. Some groups operated in the cities while others, such as those led by teachers Genaro Vázquez and Lucio Cabañas, were active in the countryside, in this case in the mountains of the State of Guerrero.

Without question, however, the key event that highlighted problems in the nation's political system was the student movement of 1968, a year of widespread protests by young people in many places around the world. That movement—particularly when it climaxed with a massacre on October 2 in Tlatelolco in Mexico City—revealed the huge gap between an increasingly urban and diverse society and a political regime that believed its efforts to modernize the country could never produce a threat or a challenge to its authority. The repression clearly showed a political regime incapable of negotiating and settling a conflict that had begun as a simple dispute among students. President Díaz Ordaz thought he was witnessing a Communist conspiracy that threatened national stability. As the opening of the XIX Olympic Games approached—they would be inaugurated in Mexico City on October 12, 1968—the situation became increasingly complicated. In September, the army occupied and cleared out the UNAM and the IPN. The afternoon of October 2, in events that are only now beginning to be explained, students gathered in Tlatelolco Square were attacked by army units. It is now known that the army's assault was provoked by snipers located in strategic places who were following instructions from high-level government officials. Dozens of people died and hundreds more were jailed in Lecumberri Prison, among them writer

José Revueltas and engineer Heberto Castillo. Those political prisoners joined others arrested during the railroad strike in 1959 and the doctors' movement of 1965. In protest against the killings, poet Octavio Paz, who would be awarded the Nobel Prize for Literature in 1990, resigned his post as Mexico's ambassador to India.

After 1968, it was clear that the political regime was losing its ability to govern a plural, educated urbanized society of people who were, above all, dissenting and frustrated by their lack of avenues for expressing their opinions. This shortcoming was related to one of the most evident features of political life: the government's iron control of both printed and television communications media. The figure of journalist Jacobo Zabludovsky, for decades the most influential television anchorman, is illustrative of that control over information. Another attack on students in Mexico City occurred on June 10, 1971, underscoring the distance between the dissenters and opposition and the State that had developed out of the 1910 Revolution.

The Mexican State tried various strategies to recover lost ground. However, a key event in the history of the twentieth century complicated this effort. That was the end of the golden age of the post-war period, which took the form of a slowdown in the world economy. The year 1973 is considered to be the end of the post-war era and the beginning of a period of widespread crisis.

During the presidencies of Luis Echeverría (1970-1976) and José López Portillo (1976-1982), both born in the capital, the Mexican government tried to attract dissident groups by offering amnesties, opening new centers of higher education such as the *Universidad Autónoma Metropolitana*, or UAM (Autonomous Metropolitan University) in 1974, and creating new programs to support the working class such as the *Instituto del Fondo Nacional de la Vivienda para los Trabajadores*, or INFONAVIT (National Workers' Housing Fund Institute), created in 1972, as well as by reforming electoral laws and making pompous speeches about democratic openness and nationalism. There was also a noteworthy effort to create closer ties with various groups of intellectuals and artists, for example by investing in the motion picture industry. "Either Echeverría or Fascism" remarked one writer close to the regime. Nevertheless, these government efforts were far from successful. Let's see why.

To begin with, economic growth began to slow. It was symptomatic of a worn-out development model that since the 1930s and especially after World War II had been based on import substitution as a means of fostering industrialization. A drop in food production and in foreign exchange inflows revealed an exhausted agriculture and livestock sector that was incapable of supporting industrialization. The difference between what the country exported and what it imported increased constantly, resulting in a balance of trade deficit. In addition, domestic savings were no longer sufficient to finance economic expansion. Compared to other countries, the Mexican government was very poor. Since the business community showed no interest in risking its capital, the situation became steadily worse. Although President Echeverría tried to carry out fiscal reforms to increase tax revenues, businessmen opposed them outright. Facing this failure—another indication of presidential weakness—, the Mexican government decided to seek loans abroad in order to maintain and even increase public spending. The deficit in public finances, or the difference between revenues and expenditures, continued to grow. Thus, debt began to accumulate that would weigh heavily on future generations.

On September 17, 1973, the powerful Monterrey businessman Eugenio Garza Sada, owner of the Cuauhtémoc Brewery and founder of the Monterrey Institute of Technology and Higher Education (ITESM) in 1943, was murdered in a failed kidnapping attempt by guerrillas of the September 23 League. At the funeral, the mourners furiously blamed President Echeverría. That event was one of the main sources of tension between the government and some business groups. Their relationship was further aggravated by the country's serious economic difficulties. In that context, in 1975, the *Consejo Coordinador Empresarial* (Business Coordinating Council) was born, composed of organizations of industrialists, merchants, employers, bankers, and the influential Mexican Businessmen's Council.

Labor groups, particularly the electrical workers led by Rafael Galván, maintained an unyielding fight against union leaders controlled by the government. Resentment grew in several worker and peasant sectors. It was a period of activism by political groups of diverse beliefs, from Maoists to Catholics linked to Liberation Theology, that is, the Catholic faction demanding action in favor of the poor, above all in Latin America. Besides these difficulties, there was another dimension to national life that remained officially out of sight: the so-called "dirty war," the illegal repression of armed movements that continued throughout the 1970s. Making use of its legitimate right to subdue those who were challenging the government with arms in hand, the Echeverría administration, however, resorted to the torture, disappearance, and murder of dozens of militants, and intimidation of their families. At the same time this was taking place, the Mexican government boasted of its progressive positions and stand in favor of the Third World. Support for the Chilean government under President Salvador Allende, as well as for the Cuban government, was noteworthy, as was Mexico's granting of asylum to thousands of Uruguayans, Argentines, and Chileans who sought refuge from military dictatorships.

The inflation unleashed as of 1973 was a reflection of economic mismanagement. Although largely the result of problems in the world market, it was also caused by printing currency and increasing public spending without solid backing. While in the 1960s prices rose at a rate of less than 5% annually, after 1973 the rate was over 20%. A rebound in inflation led to devaluation of the peso in August 1976 from MX$12.50 to the dollar—a level it had held steadily since 1954—to MX$20 to the dollar. This was the beginning of an ongoing devaluation that caused the peso to lose 760 times its value between August 1976 and November 2000 (going from MX$12.50 to MX$9 500 to the dollar, not counting the three decimal places that were eliminated by decree in 1993). To overcome the 1976 crisis, the Echeverría administration was forced to make recourse to the International Monetary Fund, which obliged Mexico to effect severe cuts in public spending in exchange for loans.

Luck seemed to be smiling on the government and the people of Mexico in general when, at the beginning of 1978, the discovery of huge oil deposits in the Campeche Sound was announced. President José López Portillo said that Mexico must prepare itself to administer those riches. And with perseverance and the help of foreign loans, the Mexican government saw to it that PEMEX increased its productive capacity. The figures are spectacular: for example, crude oil exports rose from 94 000 barrels a day in 1976 to 1.5 million barrels in 1982. In southern Veracruz, Tabasco, and Campeche, PEMEX's presence became both a pole of attraction and a nightmare: high salaries accompanied by questionable labor practices, high demand for housing in urban areas lacking infrastructure, and damage to the environment due to the feverish rush for foreign exchange. Oil revenues soon came to pay for one-third of the federal government's expenditures.

This experience was associated with another result of the world crisis unleashed in 1973. The embargo imposed by the Organization of Petroleum Exporting Countries (OPEC) that year against the United States and other nations prompted an increase in the per-barrel oil price, which rose from less than US$3 in 1970 to more than US$35 in 1981. The world economy shuddered at the increased costs of transportation and inputs. The billions of dollars obtained by oil exporting nations poured into the international financial system, causing interest rates to drop. Indebtedness became an attractive option.

The Mexican government tried to turn these circumstances to its advantage in order to compensate for its financial weakness and launch its oil venture. In 1966, Mexico's public foreign debt stood at US$1.9 billion, but by 1982 that figure was over 30 times greater: US$59 billion. This did not trouble government officials, because they were relying on continued increases in oil prices, which were projected to rise as high as US$70 per barrel. All debts could be paid.

The expansion of public spending in the 1970s led to several positive indicators: for example, an annual growth rate exceeding 7%, a sustained increase in real wages—at least until 1976—, and the greatest expenditures on health care, education, and infrastructure since 1929. According to the experts, social and regional inequalities decreased significantly throughout the decade.

At least two changes with long-lasting effects originated in this period. The first was new demographic policies based on family planning and birth control. It was already clear that the economy could not sustain a population that was growing at ever-increasing rates. The government had to take matters in hand. The National Population Council (*Consejo Nacional de Población,* CONAPO) was created in March 1974 to take steps towards reducing population growth. Despite opposition from the Catholic Church, that government initiative had a measurable impact on population dynamics. The growth rate dropped significantly in the following decades, from 3.6% to 2.6% between 1970 and 1990.

The second change was political. In the presidential election of 1976, the only participant was the PRI candidate José López Portillo. In 1977, the López Portillo administration promoted a reform to incorporate so-called minority political forces into electoral processes, particularly left-wing groups. A system of proportional representation established two ways to elect federal deputies (uninominal and plurinominal), according to the percentage of votes obtained by each party. This allowed the Communist Party, the Mexican Workers' Party, and the Mexican Democratic Party (of synarchist origin) to take part in elections. For the first time, there were Communist deputies in the Mexican Congress. Meanwhile, the National Action Party (*Partido Acción Nacional,* PAN) managed to increase the number of its federal deputies. Although with the 1977 electoral reform the Legislature continued to be subordinate to the Federal Executive and the PRI's dominance remained untouched, it was the first step in an ongoing effort to change the electoral system and, even beyond that, the country's overall political structure.

These achievements were overshadowed, however, by the momentous economic and political events of 1981 and 1982, as we shall see.

To start with, projections for the oil market were totally wrong. Beginning in May 1981, the price of oil began to drop, while interest rates rose. With less income and higher expenses because of interest on the national debt, public finances became practically unmanageable. In August 1982, the Minister of Finance admitted the Mexican economy's bankruptcy and announced the suspension of payments to foreign creditors. Both speculators and small savers trying to protect their assets took large sums in dollars out of Mexico, forcing the price of the dollar up from MX$26 to MX$70 pesos. Inflation reached almost 100%. At that critical point, on September 1, 1982, the president announced that he was nationalizing the banks. Some applauded, but the measure fell far short of attracting widespread public support. On the contrary, a lack of confidence in the government was painfully evident.

1982-2000:
CITIZEN MOBILIZATION AND POLITICAL CHANGE

The election of Margaret Thatcher as Prime Minister of Great Britain in 1979 and Ronald Reagan to the presidency of the United States in 1980 are considered to mark the beginning of the conservative reaction to the 1973 world crisis. Less public spending and support for private enterprise were two basic building blocks of this new approach, which rejected the tenets of John Maynard Keynes and the Welfare State. Keynes' place was now taken by economists who believed that when all was said and done, economic difficulties were the result of excessive public spending. At the same time, the confrontation with the Soviet Union was exacerbated, favoring an aggressive arms strategy, particularly in the United States. The new Roman Catholic Pope, chosen at the end of 1978, involved himself actively in world affairs. Pope John Paul II made the first papal visit to Mexico in February 1979. Public enthusiasm was overwhelming.

In the face of the crisis that broke out at the end of the López Portillo administration, just when the personal computer began to be in common use in offices, companies, homes, and schools, a drastic change in the conduct of government took place which severely affected most of the population. The task of effecting this change fell to the new president, Miguel de la Madrid, from the State of Colima (1982-1988). In keeping with the positions of the U.S. and British governments and the conditions imposed by the World Bank and the International Monetary Fund for overcoming the 1982 crisis, public spending and investment shrank markedly (for example, running expenses for 1983 were cut by one-third) and the sale of many semi-state enterprises began. It was imperative to reduce the government deficit at all costs. With a rebound in inflation and the measures to contain it, salaries dropped precipitously. Unemployment, a long-standing problem, ballooned to dramatic proportions. Many families realized that they were now on their own. The result was a growth of self-employment: hundreds and then thousands of street vendors set up shop on sidewalks and in squares and streets. In other families, some of the men decided to risk their lives immigrating illegally to the United States. Others chose to protest in a variety of ways, like the members of the National Education Workers' Coordinating Committee (CNTE), which was organized in 1979 by teachers dissatisfied with the government-leaning leadership of the official union and reductions in their salaries. Still others decided to participate in elections, challenging and then defeating the PRI in influential municipal elections, especially in the capitals of the northern Mexican states of Durango and Chihuahua, and in the border city of Ciudad Juárez in 1983. From then on, dissident social groups were increasingly active, occupying streets and plazas, blocking highways and toll booths, taking over government offices, boycotting television stations, and holding sit-ins, marches, and hunger strikes. This kind of protest had existed before, but it now occurred more often and involved not only impoverished workers and peasants, but also business and urban and rural middle classes.

The earthquakes of September 19 and 20, 1985, shook much of central and western Mexico. In Mexico City the dead numbered in the thousands. The government's response was feeble and slow in coming. Neighbors, however, made a massive effort to help each other. The contrast between the government's failings and society's strength did not go unnoticed. It seemed that the government, saddled with economic woes, was unable to act. It demonstrated the same weakness in addressing the drug problem as narcotrafficking became increasingly common. During the 1980s and 1990s, drug trade expanded due to the growing demand for marijuana, cocaine, and other illegal substances in the United States. This market enabled Colombian producers, Mexican traffickers, and U.S. distributors to strengthen their alliances. Bribing authorities in charge of apprehending criminals, drug-related murders, money laundering, the capture of some kingpins such as Rafael Caro Quintero, and news of confiscated drug shipments attracted public attention. Another aspect was a spike in crime and kidnapping in cities, as well as highway robbery, all similar to what had occurred in the nineteenth century.

Serious economic difficulties led top government officials and some business sectors to question the viability of relying on the import substitution model to drive the economy. This led to a gradual opening to world markets. Mexico's entry into the General Agreement on Tariffs and Trade (GATT) in 1986 confirmed this fundamental change of course in the management of the country's economy. Thanks to U.S. economic prosperity, the *maquila* industry (which imports materials and components and assembles them in Mexico, but exclusively for export) started to boom. The same success was enjoyed by automotive companies that opened new plants in Aguascalientes, Sonora, Chihuahua, and Coahuila. Many factories in Mexico City began to close or relocate. The capital, the crowning symbol of the government's modernization project, began to see its economic wealth shrink.

The 1988 presidential election campaign began under those conditions and in the wake of inflation of almost 160% in 1987. A movement known as the Democratic Current emerged from a division within the PRI and was led by Cuauhtémoc Cárdenas, the son of former President Lázaro Cárdenas, who had been a militant in the official party for years and then governor of Michoacán. This group attracted others, who subsequently founded the National Democratic Front. The PRI candidate turned out to be Carlos Salinas de Gortari, from Mexico City. The PAN chose as its candidate Manuel J. Clouthier of Sinaloa, a member of business groups that had been alienated from the government and the PRI by the nationalization of the banking system.

The July 2 election of 1988 is remembered above all for the shocking "system failure" of computerized vote counting. The breakdown aroused opposition parties' suspicion and anger, which did not prevent the electoral authorities, led by the Minister of the Interior, from declaring the PRI candidate Carlos Salinas de Gortari the winner. Pro-PAN and pro-Cárdenas voters protested furiously. They maintained that the official-party candidate had been defeated, prompting resort to a cybernetic sleight of hand to cover up the loss. But little by little, largely because the defeated candidates Clouthier and Cárdenas were never able to agree on a common strategy, the protests against electoral fraud subsided, and Salinas took office. Although the PRI got its way, the 1988 election had major repercussions. The new administration was inaugurated with very little legitimacy. To strengthen his position, President Salinas decided to strike an effective blow via the media: in January 1989 police and army units captured the powerful leader of the oil workers' union, Joaquín Hernández Galicia, nicknamed "La Quina." Another result was the recognition in 1989 of the first election of an opposition candidate (PAN member Ernesto Ruffo) to a governorship, in this case in the State of Baja California. Yet another was the establishment, also in 1989, of the Party of the Democratic Revolution (*Partido de la Revolución Democrática*, PRD), created by former PRI members, communists, and socialists of various political stripes.

The government began to take action in an international context shaken by momentous changes. Between 1989 and 1991, the Berlin Wall, the bloc of European socialist countries, and the Soviet Union ceased to exist. These events reinforced the official positions of the United States and Britain, which advocated less public spending, more open world markets, greater private investment, and new trade rules—policies popularly known as "neoliberalism." In Mexico, an attentive administration obedient to these guidelines promoted a "leaner" State, controlling inflation by reducing spending and selling more government enterprises, such as banks and the Mexican telephone company, *Teléfonos de México* (TELMEX), which had been in government hands since 1972. New stars, such as Carlos Slim, rose in the constellation of business successes. Other significant reforms were introduced, for example Article 27 of the Constitution was amended to put an end to agrarian reform and create the possibility of transferring ownership of *ejido* lands. Another was an amendment of Article 130 of the Constitution, which granted legal recognition to churches and religious freedom to citizens. This reform also opened the way to re-establishing diplomatic relations with the Vatican.

Mexico's foreign debt, which had weighed so heavily on public finances since 1981, was renegotiated between 1989 and 1990. The renegotiation had a positive effect on the macroeconomic accounts of foremost government concern, such as a substantial decrease in the public deficit and inflation, although it did not manage to prevent a decline in economic activity. Neither wages nor employment showed improvement. Budget cuts in public health and education made life for broad sectors of the population increasingly precarious. In rural areas, agriculture among peasants and even small businessmen suffered the consequences of a government policy aimed at sustaining only the few who could export their products. The emergence of the *El Barzón* movement (literally, the yoke used on oxen) in 1993, whose members owed money to the banks and many of whom were farmers, reflected the malaise among middle-income levels of society. Nevertheless, government spokespersons continued to repeat that Mexico was just one step away from the First World. They said that all that was lacking was one final push, that "push" being the signing of the North American Free Trade Agreement (NAFTA) with the United States and Canada.

Indeed, reducing state intervention in the economy and fostering the free flow of goods among nations was another component of the country's new economic development model, which was justified by claiming that it was an intelligent way of adapting to economic globalization. Consistent with Mexico's adherence to GATT in 1986, the Salinas administration began talks to achieve a trade agreement with the United States and Canada. This confirmed the government's decision to abandon the import substitution model, which was replaced by the opening of trade and a focus on exports to sustain national development. Such a change implied greater economic integration with the United States, which was already apparent in the labor market, the expansion of the *maquila* industry, increased exports, and multi-million-dollar deposits by Mexicans in U.S. banks. Thereafter, the fate of Mexico's economy would depend more and more on the economy of its neighbor. NAFTA was approved in 1993 and came into effect on January 1, 1994. Everything seemed to be going along smoothly, but that year had surprises in store.

The first was the rebellion of the Zapatista National Liberation Army in Chiapas on the first day of 1994. Indigenous Mexicans belonging to that organization declared war on the Mexican Army and on the president, its commander-in-chief. They took several towns, the most important being San Cristóbal de las Casas. Huge protest demonstrations in Mexico City and elsewhere demanded an end to hostilities. The uprising lasted only 11 days, but its impact was extraordinary. A step away from becoming part of the First World, voices rose up insisting on satisfaction of a combination of social demands (health and education services) and political changes that would strengthen the rights of indigenous peoples. It was not that Chiapas was the nation's only area where poor Indians lived, but there poverty was combined with activities of radical urban militant groups—such as *Subcommander* Marcos and Catholic partisans of Liberation Theology—in the midst of rifts caused by the rapid expansion of livestock and agrarian land distribution, as well as the remarkable success of Protestantism. The rebellion completely refuted the Salinas administration's optimism.

The second one was the assassination in March of Luis Donaldo Colosio of Sonora, the PRI candidate for the presidency. The fissures in the ruling party were becoming apparent, and it seemed to be dragging society to the brink of disaster. Perhaps because of the widespread fear prompted by divisions at the highest levels of government, the new PRI candidate from the capital, Ernesto Zedillo, easily won the presidential election in July 1994. The crime of political assassination occurred again in September, and the victim this time was a high-level PRI official, José Francisco Ruiz Massieu.

The third surprise of 1994—this one in the economy—took place a little before Christmas. A sudden devaluation of the peso by almost 100% rattled Mexico's economy, which contracted more than 6% in 1995. Unemployment rose, wages fell even lower vis-à-vis the cost of living, and interest rates spiked upward. Many borrowers—who had perhaps adopted Salinas' optimism—found themselves unable to pay debts (some in dollars) incurred for the purchase of machinery, materials, homes, and cars, causing problems for the banks. The Mexican middle class, which arose in the warmth of the post-war economic boom, experienced its worst times. With financial help from the United States, President Zedillo's administration survived the storm and the economy managed to recover for the large part the following year due, among other things, to a rise in oil prices. But all of this took an enormous toll: the government made a commitment to assume bank liabilities (bad loans), some of highly doubtful legality, through the Banking Fund for the Protection of Savings, better known as FOBAPROA. The official justification was that it was protecting depositors' savings, which were at risk in case of bank failures. That decision created a new burden on the already fragile public treasury, to the tune of US$60 billion plus interest.

The balance for 1995 aggravated the difficulties experienced in the 1980s, the so-called "lost decade" of Latin American development. By then, millions of Mexicans had been born and had grown up during continuing crises. Furthermore, in the 1990s a drought complicated matters in agriculture, which was already reeling from the withdrawal of government support in the previous decade and competition from cheap foreign products that enjoyed government subsidies in their countries of origin. Migration to the United States grew as never before. In 1997, nearly nine million Mexicans, most of them at the height of their productive years, were living in the United States. These migrants became the source of foreign exchange of an unexpected magnitude: about US$6 billion in 1997, a little more than the income from tourism. These remittances increased to more than US$13 billion in 2003, second only to oil exports, but more than foreign investment and income from tourism. Four states in the center of the country—Michoacán, Jalisco, Guanajuato, and México—received the greatest amounts.

Toward the end of the twentieth century, three quarters of the population lived in cities, while the rest was scattered throughout a surprisingly large number of small rural localities. Women, who were giving birth to fewer children (the average dropped from 6.1 in 1974 to 2.5 in 1999), had joined the work force en masse. Illiteracy dropped from 45% in 1960 to 9.5% in 2000. Protestants organized in many different denominations were increasingly numerous, particularly in the Southeast. The number of divorces and that of households headed by women rose. On another front, public opinion, more numerous means of communication, competition among them, and independence with respect to government positions facilitated public participation in a variety of issues, including defense of human rights and the rights of women, as well as those of "the disappeared" (victims of government kidnapping), indigenous peoples, those infected by AIDS, and homosexuals. The proliferation of nongovernmental organizations was yet another characteristic of this civic activism. The hundreds of undocumented people dying each year in an effort to reach the United States or the more than 300 young women murdered in Ciudad Juárez, Chihuahua since 1990 received wide coverage in newspapers and the electronic media.

We must stress that as Mexico experienced great economic difficulties, a strong movement was afoot to transform the political system and promote more democratic practices, at least in the electoral process. The 1996 constitutional amendments that granted complete autonomy to the Federal Electoral Institute (*Instituto Federal Electoral*, IFE) were one sign of this. For the first time since 1946, the federal government did not control elections, the management of which was placed in the hands of citizens without party affiliation. The IFE reflected the fact that the old political arrangement based on the PRI as the ruling party and its connection to the presidency was threadbare. It also illustrated the clear decision to work out a new accommodation based on the demands of an ever more active citizenry. This desire also was apparent in the reforms that required election of the head of government of the Federal District, previously an appointed position under the old-style presidentialism. The opposition won more and more municipal elections, as well as state legislative and gubernatorial elections. Outstanding among them was the success of PRD candidate Cuauhtémoc Cárdenas, who became the first elected chief executive of the Federal District government in 1997. That year, the PRI also lost its majority in the Chamber of Deputies for the first time.

In the year 2000, with a population of 97.5 million, almost five times more than in 1930, Mexico was the eleventh most populous country in the world. Some data indicated improvements in the social sphere: life expectancy rose to 75 years, when in 1930 it was only 36. Drops in the birth rate and child mortality meant this was an aging society. On the downside, since 1984 social inequality had increased, favoring the richest social stratum. In contrast, according to government figures a little more than half the population could be considered poor, while some academics put the ratio at almost two-thirds. Geographically, there was great contrast between wealthy areas like the Federal District, the West, and the North, and poor ones, including the ever more impoverished areas of the South (states of Guerrero, Oaxaca, and Chiapas).

The 2000 presidential election took place under conditions characterized by insecurity apparently linked to institutional corruption, with scandals of bank fraud and white-collar crime, in an economy growing only very slowly, and with unrelenting unemployment rates and wages whose purchasing power had dropped 73% since 1976. The PRI candidate for president, Francisco Labastida of Sinaloa, competed with Cárdenas and the PAN candidate Vicente Fox, former governor of Guanajuato.

On the night of July 2, 2000, to the astonishment of the Mexican people and the rest of the world, the Federal Electoral Institute and outgoing president announced that Fox had been elected. People's hopes were pinned on this charismatic figure who had abandoned the business world to enter politics. Fox attracted the votes of diverse groups. Clearly, the majority of Mexican citizens wanted a change of political regime, but it was also obvious that they did not have complete confidence in Fox. This was demonstrated by the fact that the PAN was far from having a majority in Congress. Nevertheless, the opposition candidate's victory upset the political arrangement that had emerged out of the crisis caused by Obregón's assassination in 1928 because it put an end to the era of single-party rule and the PRI's subordination to the presidency. Fortunately for all, other components of this arrangement—such as the submission of the armed forces to the president—remained intact. Thus, the nation entered a new century with a fundamental change, although it was limited to the political sphere. The hope was that this change would bring about substantial improvement in living conditions for the majority of Mexicans. A society increasingly involved in public issues, growing, with an ever more vocal citizenry would see to it that this would happen.

During the seven decades discussed here, Mexico underwent a period of political and social stability. The extreme importance of this aspect of the twentieth century in Mexico should not be underestimated, particularly when compared to the turbulence of the nineteenth century. It was also a stage of history that contained periods of economic development which facilitated the remarkable growth of cities and the urban middle class. These features do not, however, cancel out the high cost of impoverishing or maintaining in poverty the majority of the rural and urban population and of repressing dissenters and those who opposed the government. Persistent social inequality seemed to recede between 1960 and 1980, but then started to make a comeback. World economic cycles (the Great Depression, the postwar boom, and the crisis beginning in 1973) marked an inescapable pattern for Mexican society. The reorientation of the economy toward the world market and the United States, as well as the abandonment of the model of the "interventionist State" in the mid-1980s, contributed to the crisis of the nation's political system that dated back to 1929. While at the beginning of the 1930s Mexico suffered the depths of a world economic depression and severe internal instability, in the year 2000 it peacefully reorganized its political system, again in the context of economic difficulties that were perhaps not as serious as those of 1929, but more prolonged. One of the clearest gains Mexican society made in this period was precisely to enhance the strength of its position toward the end of the century, which accounts for the political change of the year 2000. At the same time, it is evident that this stronger and more active society still has a long way to go to achieve broader, deeper changes.

GLOSSARY

ALCABALA. A toll or tax on merchandise transported along some roads; pueblo and church goods were exempt from this tax.

ALCALDE DE BARRIO. Justice of the peace established for each *cuartel* set up by Viceroy Matías de Gálvez.

ALCALDES MAYORES (also called CORREGIDORES). Spanish local governors and judges. They also gradually replaced the *encomenderos* as the liaison with the pueblos and took charge of collecting tribute.

ALTÉPETL. In Post-Classic and early colonial Mexico, a sovereign or autonomous principality or lordship (including population and land). It was also known as *pueblo de indios* or merely *pueblo* in colonial times.

AMPARO (Writs of…). Appeal for legal protection in the case of violations by government officials of individual guarantees.

ARBITRIOS (and ARBITRISTAS). Different principles of governance geared to preventing or mitigating the end of Spain's imperial hegemony. Also: during the colonial period, taxes or the resulting public funds set aside for public works and events; these funds belonged to pueblos, villages, and urban settlements; persons advocating such principles.

ASIENTO. Britain's exclusive right to import African slaves to the Americas to sell them there.

ATLANTES. Great figures of warriors sculpted in the round.

AUDIENCIA. Royal tribunal or court of justice with governing powers. In the absence of a viceroy, it was the supreme government in New Spain.

BASES ORGÁNICAS. Organic laws in the late colonial period.

BRACEROS. Mexican laborers admitted to the U.S. under immigration treaties for chiefly seasonal contract labor in agriculture or industry.

BÚHO-LANZADARDOS. Spearthrower Owl. In ancient Mexico, a ruler from Teotihuacán installed by Siyaj Kak in Tikal.

CABECERA. Head village or seat of government in each *pueblo de indios* or municipality.

CABILDO. A town council or body of local government in the Castilian tradition; this word can also refer to the building that houses municipal government.

CACIQUE. The hereditary lord or prince of an *altépetl* or *pueblo de indios*. This term was used later to refer to a local political boss who controls a given area.

CAJA DE COMUNIDAD. The local public treasury in the *pueblos de indios* of colonial Mexico; the money was used to pay tribute or for community works.

CALPULTIN (singular CALPULLI). In pre-Hispanic times, neighborhoods created on the basis of former clans; members (called *calpuleque* or sometimes *mayeque*) were related and recognized common ancestors, but at the same time, once established in a city and subject to its laws, the *calpulli* functioned as an administrative unit for purposes of tax collection and participation in war and religious observance.

CAMPESINO. A native of a Latin American rural area who may be a subsistence farmer, a farm laborer, and/or a small businessperson. In this book, "peasant" is used to facilitate understanding of the term among non-Spanish-speaking readers, with no derogatory connotations intended.

CARRANCEOS. Used to refer to serious abuses committed against groups and individuals under President Venustiano Carranza.

CASTAS [*CASTES*]. A variety of racial combinations considered a separate group of a lower class than either Mestizos or Creoles. *Castas* were mixtures of Spanish, Creole, Indian, Black, Mulatto, and Mestizo. In sociological terms, this was a perception-based system of racial and social differentiation in seventeenth-century Mexico.

CAUDILLO. A military dictator or strongman; type of Latin American political leader that arose with the nineteenth-century wars of independence.

CAUSAS. The tasks consisting of collecting taxes, administering justice, organizing militias, and managing the cities and pueblos within the jurisdiction headed by an *intendente*.

CHAC-MOOL. Pre-Columbian Mesoamerican anthropomorphic stone altar that depicts a human figure in an awkward position of reclining with the head up and turned to one side, holding a tray over the stomach (believed to have been used for offerings of incense and of human hearts from human sacrifices).

CHARROS. As used in Chapter 7, sympathetic union leaders. More widely: A *charro* is a skilled Mexican horseman dressed in an elaborate, traditional costume.

CHINAMPA. Human-made small agricultural plot anchored in the bottom of a lake or pond. A *chinampa*, of pre-Hispanic origin, is made by piling soil dredged from the bottom of a body of water onto a mat of twigs and planting thereon.

CIENTÍFICOS. Literally "scientists" or "those scientifically oriented," these were a circle of professional advisors to Porfirio Díaz.

COCHINILLA. Cochineal, an insect used to produce a red dye.

COMPADRE. Close friend. Strictly speaking, godfather of one's child.

CONSULADO [*CONSULATE*]. A guild of merchants that controlled trade in a given area.

CONTRATAS. Special agreements for provision of supplies and services for the army during the period in which Mexico slowly became a republic.

CORTES. In Spain, States General, that is, an assembly of representatives of the nobility, the clergy, and the people.

COSTUMBRISTAS. Works of art, especially novels, that depict regional customs and manners.

CREOLE. This word has different meanings in different contexts. In New Spain, Creoles were the American-born descendants of European-born Spaniards; some were people with varying proportions of mixed blood.

CRISTEROS (and the CRISTERO WAR). Local defensive militias led by residents with little or no military experience who defended their religious beliefs and the Catholic Church against the government. The Cristero War lasted from the end of 1926 to mid-1929, where it devastated the countryside in several central and western states: Jalisco, Colima, Michoacán, Guanajuato, Querétaro, Aguascalientes, and Zacatecas.

CUARTELES. Wards of Mexico City created by Viceroy Matías de Gálvez.

CUERPOS DE REPÚBLICA. Literally, "Republican bodies," meaning local corporate governments or municipal councils of the pueblos. They were composed of Indian mayors and councillors with roles fairly similar to those of their Spanish counterparts.

CUERPOS RURALES [*RURAL MILITIAS*]. This was the name used during Madero's administration (the early phase of the Revolution) for groups of rural soldiers that the government wanted to disarm. Not to be confused with *rurales*, rural police representing the government.

CUICACALLI. House of song, where evening dance practice was conducted in ancient Mexico.

DIPUTACIONES PROVINCIALES. Provincial councils; there were six in New Spain.

DOCTRINAS (and DOCTRINEROS). Units (and friars responsible for or working in them) engaged in evangelization and ecclesiastic administration established by mendicant religious orders (Franciscans, Dominicans, and Augustinians) in each of the conquered lordships or *pueblos de indios* during and after the Conquest.

EJIDOS. Collectively owned lands. After the Revolution, by means of presidential resolutions, a group of peasants in a given location would receive land, water, and forest resources that could not be sold or mortgaged, but could be inherited. The *ejidos* had their own local authorities, and this created rifts among and on occasion weakened municipal authorities.

EL BARZÓN. Literally, the yoke used on oxen. This was the name of a movement that emerged in 1993, whose members owed money to the banks and many of whom were farmers, and which reflected the malaise among middle-income levels of society.

ENCOMIENDA (and ENCOMENDERO). A formal cession by the Spanish Crown of a *pueblo de indios* to an individual conquistador, who became the *encomendero* or overseer of that political entity. Using the *encomienda* system allowed pre-Hispanic lordships or principalities to remain the same as they had been before the Conquest, with equivalent powers to govern and collect tribute. The *encomendero* would receive a substantial part of that tribute and was responsible for staying on the alert militarily and for ensuring there were no reversals of the Spanish victories and alliances.

ENGANCHE. An initial sum that hacienda owners gave workers at their place of origin that they had to repay, which put them into debt from the start.

FLOTAS. Fleets or convoys which had exclusive rights to trade between Spain and its possessions in the Americas.

GOBERNACIONES. Provincial governments.

GUAJE. Bottle gourd.

INTENDENCIA (and INTENDENTE). An administrative office and jurisdiction; each covered a region and was set up in the late colonial era (eighteenth century) to administer justice, oversee tax collection, and promote agriculture, economic growth, and defense. The *intendente* was the official in charge of an *intendencia*, who had assistants known as *subdelegados* or subdelegates.

JEFE MÁXIMO. Supreme chief, a name ascribed to General Calles, referring to the Mexican Revolution.

JUICIOS DE RESIDENCIA. Public performance assessments through which all of the Spanish Crown's representatives, including the viceroys, were subject to public review and possibly censure at the end of their terms of office.

JUNTAS. In the colonial period, regional councils that formed in Spain when Napoleon took over the monarchy; this term can now refer to any committee or even to a meeting. Various *juntas* are discussed or referred to in Chapter 4.

LIBRANZAS. Letters of credit.

MACEHUALTIN (singular MACEHUALLI). The common people living in pre-Hispanic and colonial Mexico. They were agriculturists, fishermen, artisans, and other workers who all paid tribute to the nobility and lived austerely. Their status was acquired at birth.

MAQUILA. Industry that imports materials and components and assembles them in Mexico, but exclusively for export.

MATLAZÁHUATL. In general, an epidemic; this term was used in 1736 to refer specifically to a typhus epidemic.

MAYORDOMOS. Substitutes for absentee hacienda owners. Also, in other contexts, persons who accept a full year of religious and administrative duty in a village taking care of its saints, administrative matters, and schedule of festivities and celebrations.

MESTIZAJE. Crossbreeding, miscegenation or mixture; also interracial marriage.

MESTIZOS. People of mixed race, primarily European (as Spanish and Portuguese) and Amerindian.

METATE. A stone with a concave upper surface used as the lower millstone for grinding grains, usually corn, with a club-like pestle.

MONTEPÍOS. Funds that civil servants and military officers set aside for their widows.

MOTECZUMA. The Mexica emperor heading the Triple Alliance of Indian kingdoms at the time of the Conquest. Also spelled Montezuma in English.

NAVÍOS DE REGISTRO. Crown-registered ships.

OBRAJES. Workshops dedicated to the production of textiles, especially woolens; they employed an average of about 50 workers each.

OFICIAL MAYOR. Senior official of a ministry.

OIDORES. High court judges of an *audiencia*.

PAISANO. Person from the same state of the country.

PIPIÁN. A sauce made of ground pumpkin seeds, spices, and chili peppers.

PIPILTIN (singular PILLI). Nobles in pre-Hispanic and early colonial Mexico, whose status was acquired at birth. They were engaged in tasks related to government, the administration of justice, and the organization of war and religion.

POBLADORES. Spanish immigrants—as opposed to the conquistadors, royal government officials, and clergymen—who began arriving in New Spain as of about 1522 or 1523 with the idea of establishing permanent settlements.

PRESIDIO. A military outpost or garrison.

PRINCIPALES. A Spanish word used to refer to the *pipiltin*; noblemen or people of distinguished lineage in the colonial period.

PRONUNCIAMIENTO. Military declaration and uprising. For a discussion of this phenomenon, see Chapter 4.

PUEBLOS (also known as PUEBLOS DE INDIOS). *Altépetl*, or native autonomous municipalities, that might include one or several villages, one of them designated as the *cabecera* or head town.

PULQUE. A milk-colored, somewhat viscous alcoholic beverage made from the fermented sap of various maguey plants.

PUTUNES. Powerful groups of merchants with Mayan affiliation.

RANCHEROS (and RANCHOS). Free settlers who were also small proprietors (that is, not obliged to pay tribute and not part of either a pueblo or hacienda). They originally lived in *ranchos* or small informal villages. Some found a place as tenant farmers on haciendas. In certain cases, aware of the legal advantages of formalizing their settlements, the *rancheros* incorporated their settlements as pueblos.

REAL PATRONATO. Royal Patronage; privileges that popes granted to the Spanish monarchs.

REPARTIMIENTO. Literally, parceling out or sharing; in colonial Mexico, a system of obligatory (although paid) labor imposed on the male inhabitants of the *pueblos de indios*.

REPARTIMIENTO DE MERCANCÍAS. In late colonial Mexico, compulsory consumption of goods, which amounted to the *alcaldes mayores* serving as intermediaries for members of the Mexico City merchant guild. The *alcaldes mayores* sold imported or colonial goods at high prices to the Indians in exchange for local products, which they purchased at low prices.

RETABLO. Altarpiece; a votive offering, in the form of a religious picture portraying Christian saints, painted on a panel, and hung in a church or chapel.

RURALES. Members of the Mexican Rural Guard (rural mounted police).

SEPTENTRIÓN. Literally, "the North"; a term used in colonial times to refer to what is now the northern part of Mexico and the Southwest of the United States.

SITUADOS. Subsidies to fund building of fortifications and finance defensive armies located in the Caribbean or other places outside of New Spain's territories.

TALUD Y TABLERO. Slope and panel construction characteristic of Teotihuacán.

TAMEME. Market porter.

TELPOCHCALLI. A sort of school which the *capulli's* male children were obliged to attend to receive military training (whose meaning in Nahuatl is "youth house").

TLATOANI. The king or ruler of a city in Post-Classic and early colonial Mexico. A Nahuatl word for the head of an *altépetl*; a lord or ruler of a large city. The Spanish later translated this as cacique.

TZOMPANTLI. A kind of gigantic abacus made of skewers of human skulls.

UNIÓN DE ARMAS. A financial scheme that required the Spanish Empire's wealthiest corporations to contribute large sums of money to aid the Crown.

VALES REALES. Royal bonds or promissory notes the King of Spain had signed which circulated almost like currency there during the colonial period.

VALIDO. In Spain, a position equivalent to prime minister.

VIRREY. Viceroy (literally, a vice-king). Most of the *virreyes* were members of the Castilian high nobility.

VISITA. During the colonial period, an official tour of inspection ordered by the king.

AUTHORS*

Pablo Escalante-Gonzalbo

Ph.D. in History, Faculty of Philosophy and Letters, National Autonomous University of Mexico (UNAM). Professor at that faculty since 1986; as of 1990, researcher at the Institute of Aesthetic Research (UNAM). His main lines of investigation are: sixteenth-century art; iconography and style of pre-Hispanic art; and history of daily life and social history of Nahua groups and others in the Central Mexican Plateau prior to the Conquest and in the sixteenth century. Some of his major publications are: *La idea de nuestro patrimonio histórico y cultural* [Mexico's historical and cultural heritage] (co-coordinator; Mexican National Council for Culture and the Arts, Publications Department, 2011); *Los códices mesoamericanos antes y después de la conquista española: Historia de un lenguaje pictográfico* [Mesoamerican codices, history of a pictographic language] (Fondo de Cultura Económica, 2010); and *El arte prehispánico* [pre-Hispanic art] (Mexican National Council for Culture and the Arts, Publications Department, 2000). He has authored chapters for the compact histories of education and daily life in Mexico published in 2010 by El Colegio de México. Member of the National System of Researchers.

Bernardo García-Martínez

Professor at the Center for Historical Studies, El Colegio de México. He has focused his research work on historical geography and the history

---

* After titles of publications in Spanish, we provide in brackets a brief explanation of the topic(s) covered in each. This is not meant to indicate that a full English translation of these works is available.

of institutions, especially the colonial period, as well as certain issues in the twentieth century. Author, among others, of the following books: *Los pueblos de la sierra: El poder y el espacio entre los indios del norte de Puebla hasta 1700* [on the corporate organization of the Indians of northern Puebla up to 1700] (El Colegio de México, 1987) and *El Marquesado del Valle: Tres siglos de régimen señorial en Nueva España* [on the seignorial administration of parts of New Spain] (El Colegio de México, 1969). He has written numerous works for the general public, including an original synthetic study, *Historia de México* (Everest, 1985), and two chapters of the *Nueva historia general de México* [New General History of Mexico] (El Colegio de México, 2010). He has to his credit articles that have been published in academic journals such as *Historia Mexicana* and often makes contributions to *Arqueología Mexicana*. He is currently preparing a detailed analysis of the corporate organization of the *pueblos de indios* in colonial Mexico and municipalities in the national period, and also a dictionary of colonial political terminology. He is a member of the National System of Researchers and Mexican Academy of History. His most recent book, *Las regiones de México: Breviario geográfico e histórico* [an overview of the geography and history of Mexico's regions] (El Colegio de México, 2008) received the "Antonio García Cubas Prize" to the best higher education textbook of 2008.

Luis Jáuregui

Since 2005, he has been the Director General of the José María Luis Mora Institute (Mexico City). He holds a Ph.D. in History (El Colegio de México). Author of many essays and books on the economic and fiscal history of eighteenth- and nineteenth-century Latin America, such as: *La Real Hacienda de Nueva España. Su administración en la época de los intendentes: 1786-1821* [administration of the Royal Treasury in New Spain] (UNAM, 1999) and *Las contingencias de una larga recuperación. La economía mexicana, 1821-1867* [the long recovery of the Mexican economy] (co-author; UNAM, 2003). He has also coordinated works on fiscal matters, such as: *Hacienda y política. Las finanzas públicas y los grupos de poder en la Primera República Federal Mexicana* [public finances and power groups in the first Mexican Federal Republic] (co-editor; Instituto Mora, 1998); *Penuria sin fin. La historia de los impuestos en México, siglos XVIII al XX* [history of taxes in Mexico, eighteenth to twentieth centuries] (co-coordinator; Instituto Mora, 2005); and *Finanzas y política en el mundo iberoamericano: Del antiguo régimen a las naciones independientes, 1754-1850* [finance and policy in Ibero-America] (co-coordinator; UNAM, 2001). He has taught at different higher learning institutions in Mexico. President of the Mexican Economic History Association and member of the National System of Researchers.

Josefina Zoraida Vázquez
Ph.D. in History. She studied at the National Autonomous University of Mexico (UNAM), Central University of Madrid, and Harvard. Researcher at El Colegio de México since 1960, she is Professor Emerita there and in the National System of Researchers. Her work has specialized in eighteenth- and nineteenth-century Mexican social, political, and diplomatic history, and also the history of the United States. She has taught at the UNAM, Ibero-American University, Texas-Austin, University of California-Berkeley, Duke, and Goethe Universität Frankfurt. Member of the Science Advisory Board of the Office of the Mexican President, Mexican Academy of History, and American Historical Association. She has authored over twenty books and two hundred articles and book chapters, including: *Nacionalismo y educación en México* [nationalism and education in Mexico] (El Colegio de México, 1970); *Tratados de México: Soberanía y territorio, 1821-1910* [sovereignty and territory in Mexican treaties] (co-author; Mexican Ministry of Foreign Affairs, 2000); *El establecimiento del federalismo en México, 1821-1827* [establishment of federalism in Mexico] (co-coordinator; El Colegio de México, 2003); *Dos décadas de desilusiones: En busca de una fórmula adecuada de gobierno, 1832-1854* [searching for a proper form of government] (El Colegio de México, 2009); *Décadas de inestabilidad y amenazas: México, 1821-1848* [decades of instability and threats] (El Colegio de México, 2010); and *Práctica y fracaso del primer federalismo mexicano (1824-1835)* [first period of federalism in Mexico] (co-

coordinator; El Colegio de México, 2012). She has received the "Andrés Bello" Award (OAS, 1991), the Mexican National Award for Sciences and Arts (1999), and the 2008 Medal of the Government of the Federal District, among others.

Elisa Speckman-Guerra
Ph.D. in History (El Colegio de México). Researcher at the Institute for Historical Research of the National Autonomous University of Mexico (UNAM) and member of the National System of Researchers, Mexican Academy of Penal Sciences, and Mexican Academy of Sciences. She specializes in the sociocultural history of nineteenth- and twentieth-century Mexico City, particularly the history of law, juridical culture, and justice. Author of: *Crimen y castigo: Legislación penal, interpretaciones de la criminalidad y administración de justicia, Ciudad de México, 1872-1910* [penal law, criminality, and justice, Mexico City] (El Colegio de México, 2002) and has coordinated several works, such as: *Modernidad, tradición y alteridad: La Ciudad de México en el cambio de siglo (XIX-XX)* [Mexico City at the turn of the twentieth century] (co-editor; UNAM, 2001); *El mundo del derecho: Aproximaciones a la cultura jurídica novo-hispana y mexicana, siglos XIX y XX* [justice and legal culture in New Spain and Mexico] (co-coordinator; UNAM, 2009); *Los miedos en la historia* [fears in history] (co-coordinator; El Colegio de México, 2009); and *De normas y transgresiones: Enfermedad y crimen en América Latina, 1850-1950* [sickness and crime in Latin America] (co-editor; UNAM, 2005). She has received awards from the Mexican Academy of Sciences and the Mexican Committee of Historical Sciences.

Javier Garciadiego
Ph.D. in Mexican History from El Colegio de México and Latin American History from the University of Chicago. He specializes in the Mexican Revolution, in particular its political and cultural aspects. Most of his teaching career has been at El Colegio de México. Visiting professor and lecturer in many universities throughout the world. Since 1984, he has been a member of the National System of Researchers, as of 2008,

the Mexican Academy of History and, since 2013, the Mexican Academy of the Spanish Language. Author and/or co-coordinator of: *Así fue la Revolución Mexicana* [Mexican Revolution] (general academic coordinator; Mexican Ministry of Public Education/Mexican Senate, 8 vols., 1985-1986); *Rudos contra científicos. La Universidad Nacional durante la Revolución Mexicana* [the National University of Mexico during the Mexican Revolution] (El Colegio de México/UNAM, 1996); *Porfiristas eminentes* [eminent supporters of Porfirio Díaz] (Breve Fondo Editorial, 1996); *Alfonso Reyes* (Planeta DeAgostini, 2002); *La Revolución Mexicana. Crónicas, documentos, planes y testimonios* [chronicles and documents of the Mexican Revolution] (UNAM, 2003); *Introducción histórica a la Revolución Mexicana* [historical introduction to the Mexican Revolution] (El Colegio de México/Mexican Ministry of Public Education, 2006); *Cultura y política en el México posrevolucionario* [culture and politics in Mexico after the Revolution] (National Institute of Historical Studies on the Mexican Revolutions [INEHRM], 2006); *Revolución y exilio en la historia de México. Del amor de un historiador a su patria adoptiva: Homenaje a Friedrich Katz* [tribute to Friedrich Katz, an Austrian-born anthropologist and historian who specialized in the Mexican Revolution] (co-compiler; El Colegio de México/Ediciones Era/The University of Chicago, 2010); *Textos de la Revolución Mexicana* [texts from the Mexican Revolution] (Fundación Biblioteca Ayacucho, 2010); and *Ensayos de historia sociopolítica de la Revolución Mexicana* [socio-political history of the Mexican Revolution] (El Colegio de México, 2011). In 1994, he received the "Salvador Azuela" Award from the INEHRM and again in 2010, in recognition of his contributions to his profession. Honorary doctorates from the universities of Athens and General San Martín (Argentina). Since 2005, he has held the position of President of El Colegio de México.

Luis Aboites-Aguilar

Professor-researcher at the Center for Historical Studies, El Colegio de México. Ph.D. in History from that center. Member of the National System of Researchers. His research and publications concentrate on three major themes: the uses of water in Mexico, twentieth-century Mexico's fiscal history, and the history of the northern part of the country. He teaches courses on the political history of twentieth-century Mexico and the history of water uses in the country during the nineteenth and twentieth centuries. He is presently conducting research on cotton growing in Mexico (1930-1970). Author of the following books, among others: *La irrigación revolucionaria: Historia del sistema nacional de riego del río Conchos, Chihuahua, 1927-1938* [national irrigation system] (Center for Research and Higher Studies in Social Anthropology [CIESAS], 1988); *Cuentas del reparto agrario norteño, 1920-1940* [agricultural land distribution in northern Mexico] (CIESAS, 1991); *Norte precario: Poblamiento y colonización en México, 1760-1940* [colonization in northern Mexico] (El Colegio de México, 1995); *El agua de la nación: Una historia política de México, 1888-1946* [water as a national property] (CIESAS, 1998); *Excepciones y privilegios: Modernización tributaria y centralización en México, 1922-1972* [modernization and centralization of the Mexican tax system] (El Colegio de México, 2003); *La decadencia del agua de la nación: Estudios sobre desigualdad social y cambio político en México (segunda mitad del siglo XX)* [water, social inequality, and political change in the second half of the twentieth century in Mexico] (El Colegio de México, 2009); and *Chihuahua: Historia breve* [brief history of the State of Chihuahua] (Mexican Ministry of Public Education/El Colegio de México/History of the Americas Trust Fund/Fondo de Cultura Económica, 2010).

NAME AND PLACE INDEX

323

A New Compact History of Mexico
se terminó de imprimir en septiembre de 2013 en los talleres de
Editores e Impresores Profesionales, EDIMPRO, S.A. de C.V.,
Tiziano 144, Col. Alfonso XIII,
01460 México, D.F.
Portada: Pablo Reyna
Composición tipográfica y formación a cargo de
Socorro Gutiérrez, en Redacta, S.A. de C.V.
Bajo la coordinación de la Dirección de Publicaciones
de El Colegio de México.